# A Comprehensive Guide to AI and Expert Systems

# A Comprehensive Guide to AI and Expert Systems

**Robert I. Levine**

*Senior Research Engineer, Sperry Corporation*

**Diane E. Drang**

*Director of Educational Services, Jewish Board Family & Children's Services*

**Barry Edelson**

*Editor and author*

**McGraw-Hill Book Company**

New York  St. Louis  San Francisco  Auckland  Bogotá
Hamburg  Johannesburg  London  Madrid
Mexico  Montreal  New Delhi  Panama
Paris  São Paulo  Singapore
Sydney  Tokyo  Toronto

**Library of Congress Cataloging-in-Publication Data**

Levine, Robert I.
  A comprehensive guide to AI and expert systems.

  Bibliography: p.
  Includes index.
  1. Artificial intelligence.   2. Expert systems
(Computer science)   3. Microcomputers.   I. Drang,
Diane.   II. Edelson, Barry.   III. Title.
Q335.L47   1986              005.3              85-23750
ISBN 0-07-037470-8

234567890     DOC/DOC     8932109876

ISBN 0-07-037470-8

The editors for this book were Stephen Guty and Nancy Young,
the designer was Naomi Auerbach, and the production supervisor
was Thomas J. Kowalczyk. It was set in Century Schoolbook
by Achorn Graphics.

Printed and bound by R. R. Donnelley & Sons Company.

# Contents

# Preface

Over the next few years, artificial intelligence programming techniques will invade every area of computer technology; it has already started. Artificial intelligence systems are showing up everywhere from the computer engineering industry to big business to the military. The professional opportunities for people who are knowledgeable about artificial intelligence are virtually unlimited. And given the speed with which technological innovations reach the marketplace these days, it won't be long before everyone who's ever touched a computer keyboard will need to know about artificial intelligence. This is nothing short of a revolution in computer programming, and you're going to want to know about it *now*.

This book introduces and explains the concepts of artificial intelligence and expert systems in a language that everyone can understand. You don't need any mathematical expertise, and even if your knowledge of computers is small, you will still learn a great deal about this vital new area of computer engineering. By the time you finish reading this book, you will not only have grasped the fundamentals of these new ideas, but you will be on your way to designing and implementing your own expert systems.

Up to now, most people thought that personal and home computers have memories that are too small and speeds that are too slow to make use of artificial intelligence programming. This book destroys that myth. All the programming you will see in these pages can be implemented on a first-generation personal and home computer. Short programs, written in BASIC, are provided in each of the chapters that contain concepts. These programs are easy to use and understand. They are written in fundamental BASIC, which also allows them to be transported to any personal and home computers.

This book provides you with a simple uncomplicated view of the field of artificial intelligence and expert systems. It has been carefully planned so that each chapter is self-contained. This technique allows you to learn concepts without having to refer to previous chapters. The combination of this technique, a simple approach, and examples that will appeal to a wide range of people could make this book required reading for anyone trying to understand the basics of artificial intelligence. The book is designed to be used by advanced high school students, college students, corporate presidents who want to understand artificial intelligence, and curious noncomputer people. All of the book's information was extracted from popular texts in the field, expanded, and then greatly simplified. There are many illustrations and more than 50 examples. These are designed to make the subject matter very easy to understand.

Chapter 1 provides the reader with an overview of the concept of intelligence and how this concept can be identified.

Chapter 2 shows how this concept can be transferred to a computer to create artificial intelligence.

Chapter 3 discusses the concept of expert systems and its relationship to artificial intelligence.

Chapter 4 provides a brief and simple overview of natural language processing.

Chapter 5 discusses forward chaining, providing an extensive set of examples and a forward chaining tool written in BASIC. The tool can be used in a limited way to experiment with the concepts; it can also be easily modified into a more powerful structure.

Chapter 6 discusses backward chaining in a way that is similar to Chapter 5. A backward chaining tool is also provided in this chapter.

Chapter 7 discusses bayesian probability and fuzzy conditions as they apply to expert systems. A programming example illustrating how the concepts can be applied to a rule-based system is provided.

Chapter 8 provides a discussion of the design of a truncated expert system for personal finance. This topic applies to anyone who has money dealings.

Chapter 9 provides a discussion of the design of a truncated expert system for optimizing a sales effort with a customer. This topic applies to all corporations and people since everyone is always selling something.

Chapter 10 discusses the design of an expert system that diagnoses learning problems. This is of interest to schools, corporations analyzing employee capabilities, concerned parents, and individuals.

Chapter 11 discusses object-oriented programming as it applies to expert systems. A set of examples which clearly illustrate some of the concepts is provided. An object-oriented system is written in BASIC to allow you to experiment with the concepts.

Chapter 12 discusses an engineering application using object-oriented programming. A worked-out example is provided.

Chapter 13 provides an expert system example that issues flood warnings using object-oriented programming.

Chapters 14, 15, and 16 discuss semantic nets, certainty factors, and automated learning. A program in BASIC is provided for each of these topics.

Chapter 17 discusses how PROLOG can be used as a tool for answering questions about a knowledge base. Examples illustrating the concepts are provided.

Chapter 18 discusses some basic concepts in LISP and provides you with some understanding of the language.

Also included is a bibliography that provides you with a list of books and articles, which can be used to augment this book, and a short description of the pertinent topics contained in each.

If you're a student, a programmer, a home computer novice, a professional using a personal computer in your business, a person already involved in artificial intelligence, or just curious about it, this book is for you.

# Acknowledgments

We would like to acknowledge Professor Robert Hong of Grumman Corporation and Polytechnic Institute of New York for his thought-provoking seminars in artificial intelligence. Grateful acknowledgment goes to Betty Haufrecht for her unique, holistic approach to the field of learning problems. Her creative insight helped launch a new idea—the use of computers in artificial intelligence.

# A Comprehensive Guide to AI and Expert Systems

# Human and Machine Intelligence

*Section 1 introduces artificial intelligence and expert systems, acquainting us with how they work. Artificial intelligence is simply the transfer of intelligence to machines. Expert systems deal with a small area of expertise that can be converted from human to artificial intelligence.*

*We will take a close look at these concepts, using some common everyday experiences as examples. This will allow us to dissect the pieces of artificial intelligence and see how we can make them work for us. The process is simple, so let's get started.*

# An Overview of Intelligence

## What Is Artificial Intelligence?

Artificial intelligence (AI) is simply a way of making a computer think intelligently. This is accomplished by studying how people think when they are trying to make decisions and solve problems, breaking those thought processes down into basic steps, and designing a computer program that solves problems using those same steps. AI thereby provides a simple, structured approach to designing complex decision-making programs.

## What Is Programming Like without Artificial Intelligence?

A standard computer program can only provide answers to problems for which it is specifically programmed. If a standard program needs to be modified in order to accommodate new information, the entire program may have to be scanned until the optimum space is found to insert the modification. This is not only time consuming, but other parts of the program may be adversely affected in the process and errors may result.

Artificial intelligence, as its name implies, really does enable a computer to think. By simplifying the way programs are put together, AI imitates the basic human learning process by which new information is absorbed and made available for future reference. The human mind can incorporate new knowledge without changing the way the mind works or disturbing all the other facts that are already stored in the brain. An AI program works in very much the same way. It will become apparent as you read this book that changes made to AI programs are far simpler to implement than those made to standard programs.

## How Does Artificial Intelligence Make Programming Better?

AI techniques allow the construction of a program in which each piece of the program represents a highly independent and identifiable step toward the solution of a problem or set of problems. Let's consider this carefully. Each piece of the program is like a piece of information in a person's mind. If that information is disputed, the mind can automatically adjust its thinking to accommodate a new set of facts. One doesn't have to go about reconsidering every piece of information one has ever learned, only those few pieces that are relevant to the particular change.

A standard program can do everything an artificial intelligence program can do, but it cannot be programmed as easily or as quickly. In both types of programs, all pieces are interdependent in the way they carry out their designed function. But an AI program possesses a notable characteristic which is equivalent to a vital characteristic of human intelligence. Each minute piece can be modified without affecting the structure of the entire program. This flexibility provides greater programming efficiency and understandability—in a word, intelligence.

## How Does Human Intelligence Work?

Since AI is a science rooted in human thought processes, an examination of how people think is essential. Of course, no one knows exactly how the mind works. Human intelligence is a complex function that scientists have only begun to understand, but enough is known for us to make certain assumptions about how we think and to apply those assumptions in designing AI programs.

## Goals

All thinking helps us accomplish something. When the alarm clock rings in the morning, a thought process must be employed to guide your hand to the button to turn it off. It isn't an automatic reaction; a specific response was sought to solve a particular problem. The final results to which all our thought processes are directed are called "goals."

Once you have reached the goal of turning off the alarm, your mind is immediately confronted with other goals to be reached, such as getting to the bathroom, brushing your teeth, getting dressed, making and eating breakfast, going to the bus stop, and so on. These are all goals which, when accomplished, lead you to the ultimate goal of getting to work and getting there on time. None of the thoughts guiding you to this final result are random or arbitrary. They have been pressed into service because every step of the way you had a specific goal in mind. When engaged in the most simple physical task or the most complex mental activity, the mind is sharply focused on a goal. Without goals, we have no reason to think. Examples of various types of goals are listed below:

1. Mapping the shortest route between New York and Boston
2. Deciding on the best type of wine to drink with certain fish
3. Learning to tie my shoes
4. Deciding how to determine if my child understands the concepts of arithmetic

When designing an AI system, the goal of the system must always be kept in mind. Remember, we don't do things because we think, we think because there are things we have to do.

Now that we understand where our minds are going when they're at work, let's consider just how we arrive at the multitude of goals we must reach every day.

## Facts and Rules

We all know that the human mind possesses a vast store of knowledge relating to a countless array of objects and ideas. Survival depends on our ability to apply this knowledge to any situation that arises and to continuously learn from new experiences so that we will be able to respond to similar situations in the future. What is generally considered to be "intelligence" can be broken down into a collection of facts and a means of utilizing these facts to reach goals. This is done, in part, by formulating sets of rules relating to all the facts stored in the brain. An example of the type of facts and related rules we use every day follows:

Fact/rule set 1
  Fact 1:  A burning stove is hot.
  Rule 1:  If I put my hand on a burning stove, THEN it will hurt.

Fact/rule set 2

   Fact 2: During rush hour, streets are crowded with cars.
   Rule 2: IF I try to cross a major highway on foot during rush hour, THEN I
      may get hit by a car.

Fact/rule set 3

   Fact 3a: Quiet dark streets are dangerous.
   Fact 3b: Old people usually don't commit violent crimes.
   Fact 3c: Police protect people from crime.
   Rule 3a: IF I am on a quiet dark street and I see an old person, THEN I
      should not particularly worry about my safety.
   Rule 3b: IF I am on a quiet dark street and see a police officer, THEN I
      should feel secure.

Fact/rule set 4

   Fact 4: When two digits whose sum is greater than nine are added, a carry-
      ing procedure is called for.
   Rule 4: IF I have to add a column of digits and the sum is greater than nine,
      THEN I must refer to fact 4 to know how to carry out the addition.

Notice that in the example just given all the rules are expressed in an IF-THEN, or conditional, relationship. That is, IF a certain condition exists, THEN an action or other response will result. Some facts are obviously more complicated than others, and some rules relate to more than one fact. In general, human beings have the capacity to relate very complex sets of rules and facts in the attempt to reach some very complicated goals.

## Pruning

When the human mind sets out to solve even the simplest problem, it has a vast store of information on which to draw in determining the proper course of action. Let's go back to the example we used earlier. You step out of your house on your way to work, and you walk to the street corner. As you wait to cross the street, your brain is bombarded with all kinds of data. The speed and volume of the traffic, the distance to the other curb, the traffic signals at the intersection—all these factors must be considered before you make a move. In addition, an enormous number of sensory impressions that are totally irrelevant to the problem of crossing the street are also being processed at the same time—weather conditions, the color and models of the passing cars, the type and height of the trees on the edge of the curb, the appearance of all the nearby buildings. You are also undoubtedly thinking about where you are going and how quickly you want to get there, whom you might see when you arrive, and so on.

As you can see, if you had to deal with this multitude of directly related, indirectly related, and totally unrelated facts before you stepped off the curb, you might very well stand there for years. If we do indeed have so many facts and rules to process all the time, how does the mind extract the right set of rules quickly to fit each particular situation? When you want to cross the street, how does the mind know to apply, among others, fact/rule set 2, which pertains to traffic, and not fact/rule set 4, which pertains to arithmetic?

There exists a more sophisticated system which guides the selection of a proper response to a specific situation. This process is known as "pruning." As its name suggests, pruning eliminates pathways of thought that are not relevant to the immediate objective of reaching a goal. Just as one might cut off the lower branches of a tree to help its overall growth, so the pruning mechanism in our brains cuts us off from any facts and rules that won't lead us to the goal. When the mind is confronted with a situation, the pruning mechanism guides the thought processes by focusing only on those rules that are pertinent to solving the immediate problem.

An overview of how pruning helps the brain to distinguish one set of rules from another is shown in Figure 1-1. In this case pruning helps us decide whether to take path A or path B. It does this with an IF-THEN test of a condition. If the condition is A, it takes path A; if B, it takes path B.

Pruning can be likened to the task of an office manager who delegates tasks according to a set of priorities. The secretary, the word processor, the clerk, and everyone else on the staff have their assigned jobs to perform. But when everyone is called upon to help complete a particular project quickly, someone must decide not merely what everyone has to do, but when they must do it. Without such decisions being made, some personnel might sit idle, waiting for others to com-

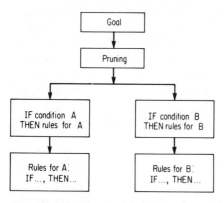

Figure 1-1 Pruning in action.

plete related tasks, while some might waste precious time performing tasks that can wait until later. A lot of work may get done, but all that good energy is wasted if, in the end result, the goal of putting the project together properly isn't met.

Without pruning, our brains would be crippled in much the same way the office would without the manager. We would have to process every rule in our brains for every single problem we had to solve. Everything we need to know to make decisions may be present in our brains all the time—like the capable members of the staff who are all doing what they're supposed to be doing—but unless the right information is pulled out at just the right time, all our knowledge is wasted. Pruning provides a vital order to our thoughts, without which life would not merely be slowed down, as in the office, but would be virtually impossible.

### Inference Mechanism

When we reach a goal, we are not only solving an immediate problem but are also acquiring new knowledge at the same time. Consider the following information:

1. Jim's parents are John and Mary.
2. Jane's parents are John and Mary.

The goal is to determine the relationship between John and Jane. Pruning zeroes in on a rule safely tucked away in the brain that instantly ends the mystery: IF a male person and a female person have the same parents, THEN they are brother and sister.

We reach our goal by inferring the answer to the question of Jim and Jane's relationship from the rule we had previously learned. And in the process of reaching the goal, a new fact is derived: Jim and Jane are brother and sister. The portion of the intelligence that helped us arrive at this new fact is called the "inference mechanism." It is central to our ability to learn from experience because it enables us to generate new facts from existing ones by applying already acquired knowledge to new situations. We will see in the next chapter that the inference mechanism also aids in the detection of errors in our thinking and allows us to modify and improve the rules we use in reaching the goals.

### Summary

Since the concepts described in this chapter will be applied in the following chapters to artificial intelligence systems, we should briefly review what we've discussed so far.

1. A specific goal sets our thought process in motion.

2. A vast collection of facts and their related rules wait to be called upon to help reach the goal.

3. Pruning helps us carry out a quick efficient search for only those rules that pertain to the immediate goal.

4. The inference mechanism completes the process by drawing inferences from the rules called upon by the pruning mechanism and by generating new facts that instantly become a part of our storehouse of knowledge.

# Developing an Artificial Intelligence System

All the elements that comprise the human decision-making process—goals, facts, rules, inference mechanism, and pruning—must be collected in a computer program for it to be properly described as possessing artificial intelligence. All the AI system designs we will discuss in this book have the same basic configuration. Figure 2-1 illustrates the components of a rule-based AI system.

This program structure, which is based on the separate identification of its various components, is the single most important factor in making AI programming superior to ordinary programming. Modifications can be made to one or more of the parts of the design without upsetting the structure of the entire system. This design concept is also revolutionary in another fundamental way. Because we've identified the elements that comprise human thought processes, we can transfer the way we think about any problem into the AI program. If we can determine what our minds do at a given stage of any decision-making process, we can easily find in this program design a section that corresponds to an equivalent aspect of human intelligence.

## Defining Goals

Since reaching goals is the aim of any AI system, the first step in designing such a system is to define a set of goals. You must know what sort of problem you want to solve and be able to describe the problem in concrete terms before you can go about creating a program to solve it.

Let's go back to the goal of getting to work, which we talked about in Chapter 1. We will assume that your beautifully designed human intelligence system has guided you safely and quickly across the street. Now you are waiting at the bus stop, and you have only a moment or two to consider which of two buses that pick up passengers on this corner is the best one for you to take this morning. Only a half a block away is the bus that makes all the local stops, and it's approaching fast. Do you want to board the local bus or wait for the express bus? This decision—which bus will be better—is the goal.

There are any number of essential facts to be weighed before the decision can be made, all based on prior experience in traveling on the buses to work. For instance, how long will it be before the express bus arrives? On which bus will I be more likely to get a seat? Certain rules are called into play as well, thanks to pruning, such as "IF I have to wait more than 10 minutes for the express bus, THEN it will take longer for me to get to work than if I'd taken the local bus." Rules are at work all the time, even those within the pruning mechanism which oversee all thought processes by locating the specific rules needed to make the decision at hand. Facts and rules related to the tasks that await you when you arrive at work have no bearing at all on the goal of getting there. Similarly, in an AI program, all facts and rules are irrelevant except those that aid in reaching the stated goal.

Let's now focus on another goal, which is one of the goals we will discuss extensively in Section 3 when we design actual AI programs. The goal is to determine if a child has learning problems in arithmetic. This may seem like a radical departure from the example we have just been using, but that is precisely why we've chosen it: to make it perfectly clear that our basic thought processes are the same when we try to solve similar problems and that the same fundamental AI system design can be utilized to reach a vast range of goals, however diverse

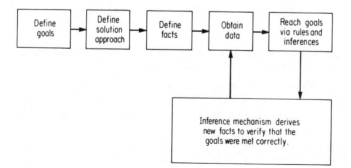

Figure 2-1   Components of a rule-based AI system.

they may appear. Our new goal can be broken down into different areas of arithmetic and can be expressed in several different ways:

Does PERSON have a learning problem in ADDITION?

Does PERSON have a learning problem in SUBTRACTION?

Does PERSON have a learning problem in MULTIPLICATION?

Does PERSON have a learning problem in DIVISION?

The object PERSON is known as a variable because it does not represent a specific individual but *any* individual. We have made PERSON a variable so that we can use the same goals in evaluating many different people, just as we might have made bus a variable in our previous example so that we might be able to consider the route of any bus. The way to represent the variable with an actual person is to substitute a person's name for that variable. The way to represent a variable with a person in a computer is by the following BASIC statement:

```
INPUT"ENTER NAME OF PERSON BEING EVALUATED" ;PERSON
```

When this BASIC input statement is executed by the computer, the following will appear on the screen:

```
ENTER NAME OF PERSON BEING EVALUATED ?
```

You would then enter the name of the person—let's say, Andrew Jones—in response to the computer's question. Whenever the variable PERSON is now referred to anywhere in the facts, rules, or goals, the name Andrew Jones will be substituted for it. When a variable has been assigned a specific value, it is referred to as "instantiated." We can now say that our goal is to find out if the individual Andrew Jones has a learning problem in any or all areas of arithmetic.

## Defining Facts

Facts are an essential ingredient in an AI system. Without them, there would be no way to reach the goals. To reach the goal of deciding which bus to take, some supporting facts specific to that situation were needed. Obviously, as every predicament has its own particular scenario, every goal has its own facts. Let's concentrate on just one of the arithmetic goals to see how the use of facts is implemented:

Does PERSON have a learning problem in subtraction?

Subtraction is a function that requires certain mathematical skills. These skills are the facts that support the goal, some of which follow. In order to subtract, a person must be able to

1. Subtract two numbers without borrowing (2)
2. Subtract two numbers with single column borrowing (1)
3. Subtract two numbers with multiple column borrowing (1)

The numbers in parentheses at the end of the facts represent their relative importance to one another in our evaluation of the individual's learning problem. These numbers are similar to ones we are given on school tests. Some test questions are worth more than others. Each of the facts defines a required skill for mastering subtraction, and the inability to perform any one of these skills indicates a problem in this area. The higher the number assigned to each fact, the more important that fact is in contributing to a learning problem in subtraction. We will see shortly how placing these numerical values on facts is used in reaching goals.

## Obtaining Data

Once the facts that we will use to reach the goal have been defined, we must acquire data that is needed to instantiate the variables. That is, we've established what people in general must know to do subtraction, but now we need to find out how much our subject, Andrew Jones, knows. To do this, the facts must first be turned into questions; the answers we receive are the data we can use as we move toward our goal. The list below shows what questions should be asked to obtain data about the facts listed under subtraction.

Can PERSON subtract two numbers without borrowing?

Can PERSON subtract two numbers with single column borrowing?

Can PERSON subtract two numbers with multiple column borrowing?

Just as we replace the variable PERSON with Andrew Jones, we replace the facts, as represented by these questions, with responses. The instantiated facts become the data. In simple terms, the yes and no answers we will receive are the data that we are assigning to the facts. This data is then placed in a database so that it can be analyzed in our evaluation of Andrew Jones' possible learning problem. We need a

computer program that will ask these questions and accumulate the
necessary data. An example follows:

```
 5  REM the variable PERSON will contain the name of the

 7  REM person being evaluated

10  INPUT"Enter name of person being evaluated";PERSON

15  REM S1$ will contain a yes or no answer to the following

20  PRINT"Can" ;PERSON; "subtract two numbers without borrowing"

25  INPUT S1$

30  REM S2$ will contain a yes or no answer to the following

35  PRINT"Can" ;PERSON; "subtract two numbers with single
    column borrowing"

40  INPUT S2$

45  REM S3$ will contain a yes or no answer to the following

50  PRINT"Can" ;PERSON; "subtract two numbers with multiple
    column borrowing"

55  INPUT S3$
```

When this program is run, a dialogue will appear on the personal
computer screen that will ask questions that will provide the relevant
data concerning an individual's learning problem in subtraction. This
dialogue follows. The computer output is in capital letters and the
answers that might be given are in lower case.

```
ENTER NAME OF PERSON BEING EVALUATED ? andrew jones

CAN ANDREW JONES SUBTRACT TWO NUMBERS WITHOUT BORROWING ? yes

CAN ANDREW JONES SUBTRACT TWO NUMBERS WITH SINGLE COLUMN
BORROWING ? no

CAN ANDREW JONES SUBTRACT TWO NUMBERS WITH MULTIPLE COLUMN
BORROWING ? no
```

Each of the instantiated variables now becomes part of the database,
as shown in Figure 2-2.

What we've done so far is quite simple. We defined some facts necessary to understanding subtraction, we designed a computer program
that would ask the relevant questions pertaining to these facts, and
then we stored the answers so they can be analyzed. This is the equivalent to what your brain does automatically when trying to decide between the local and express buses. That is, you "ask" yourself all the

relevant questions concerning these two buses based on the facts you already know about them and about buses in general. The answers to the questions that are derived from the facts help you make your final decision. The facts and rules, which we will soon discuss, are stored in an area of the computer known as the "knowledge base."

When you are facing the bus dilemma, not all considerations are equal. You may not care as much about getting a seat, for example, as you do about getting to work on time, or vice versa. Colloquially, we say that we "weigh" these considerations in coming to a conclusion, and that is why the numbers in parentheses are referred to as "weighting factors." Some aspects of getting to work are not as important as others, just as some requirements for doing subtraction are more crucial than others in diagnosing a learning problem.

A no answer to any of the questions in Figure 2-2 indicates that Andrew has a problem with the subtraction skill represented by the fact; a yes answer indicates that Andrew possesses that skill. By obtaining the sum of all the weighting factors associated with the no answers, we can get an indication of the severity of Andrew's problem in subtraction, as follows:

$$
\begin{array}{ll}
\text{S1\$ (2) yes} & 0 \\
\text{S2\$ (1) no} & 1 \\
\text{S3\$ (1) no} & 1 \\
\text{Sum weighting factor} & = \ 2
\end{array}
$$

The total number representing the degree of Andrew's learning problem is called simply the "sum weighting factor." As we have said, this number can be used to determine whether Andrew has a problem in subtraction and just how severe that problem is. Sum weighting factors are simply means of quantifying for the computer program a wide range of possibilities. The maximum sum weighting factor in this example—which would indicate a serious problem in doing subtraction—would be obtained if all the answers were no. Here, that number is 4. The equivalent worst-case scenario in our bus example might be that you decided to wait for the express bus and ended up getting to work an hour late and had to stand all the way. You might very well

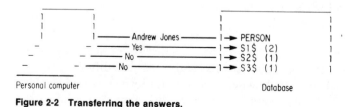

Figure 2-2   Transferring the answers.

want to consider the very worst that could happen as a consequence of your decision.

## Rules and Inferences

As we saw in Chapter 1, we need rules in order to apply the facts we know to situations that arise. The rules in our AI system must be designed to help us evaluate the data so that we can reach the goal of finding out if a person has a learning problem in arithmetic. We have singled out subtraction, so let us establish a rule related to the subtraction goal and call it the "subtraction rule." It reads like this:

> IF the sum weighting factor for subtraction is greater than 1, THEN PERSON has a learning problem in subtraction.

Since the sum weighting factor for Andrew Jones is 2, we can use the subtraction rule to infer that Andrew does indeed have a problem in subtraction. The rule has provided a practical application of the data we've accumulated. The value 1 in the rule is called a "threshold" of decision level.

We promised that AI makes programming easier and more flexible, and now you can begin to see how. Instead of establishing the subtraction rule, we could have employed a set of facts which would have covered all the possible ways the sum weighting factor could be greater than 1. The facts we would need to cover all possible contingencies and their weighting factors follow. A learning problem in subtraction exists when

1. (S1$ = no) and (S2$ = yes) and (S3$ = yes)
   sum weighting factor = 2
2. (S1$ = no) and (S2$ = yes) and (S3$ = no)
   sum weighting factor = 3
3. (S1$ = no) and (S2$ = no) and (S3$ = yes)
   sum weighting factor = 3
4. (S1$ = no) and (S2$ = no) and (S3$ = no)
   sum weighting factor = 4
5. (S1$ = yes) and (S2$ = no) and (S3$ = no)
   sum weighting factor = 2

Notice that the sum weighting factor for each set of facts is greater than 1. What we have in this list are really just five different sets of facts. The subtraction rule, however, covers *all* these facts and renders the programming of these facts unnecessary. It is obviously a lot easier to program a single all-encompassing rule than several specialized facts that are much more limited in their application. Without rules, you would still be standing on the corner waiting to cross the street, assaulted by an army of facts and associated data but with no means of processing them. You wouldn't have to worry about the bus because you'd never even make it to the bus stop!

So far the design of our program has included

1. Defining goals
2. Defining facts to support the goals
3. Obtaining data that corresponds to the facts and is specific to a given situation or subject
4. Evaluating the data via rules and inferences

The process of reaching goals in this way is known as "forward chaining," that is, using the data to arrive at a conclusion. It enables us to proceed in a logical fashion from one step to another as outlined in Figure 2-1.

## Verification through the Inference Mechanism

Let's take another example to illustrate how inferences are verified. Suppose a murder has been committed: A person is found locked in an apartment, shot three times. The medical examiner rules out the possibility of suicide because of the angle of the wounds (pruning in action), and the police immediately go to work. The first thing they consider is who else besides the victim had a key to the apartment. They question the landlord and several neighbors, who say the murdered person had a friend who frequently came to use the apartment. Further investigation reveals that the couple had recently been quarreling.

The police now have a suspect. They are able to infer from their interviews that the victim's friend is probably the murderer (forward chaining), using the data from the interviews to arrive at the conclusion, but they need some concrete evidence to nail down the case. Their best chance of nabbing the suspect is to find the murder weapon. They obtain a search warrant for the friend's apartment and look through the belongings, but to no avail. Finally, a detective finds a gun in a garbage can in a nearby alley. A fingerprint check verifies that the gun indeed was handled by the friend, and a ballistics test establishes that it is the murder weapon. Case solved. By obtaining a new piece of data and seeing if it was consistent with their original conclusion, the police verified the goal of identifying the murderer. The process of using a conclusion to look for supporting data is known as "backward chaining." In this case, the conclusion is the suspect and the data is the weapon.

In an AI program, the goal is also verified by a similar process. Were we correct when we concluded earlier that Andrew Jones has a learning problem in subtraction? The goal has been reached, but to determine if it was reached correctly we must approach the problem again with new data and new rules. A rule that might verify if an individual has a learning problem in subtraction might be

> IF a person achieves a score on a standard arithmetic test in subtraction that is below grade level, THEN the person will achieve a weighting factor in subtraction that is greater than 1 (that is, the person has a problem in subtraction).

All we must do to confirm that we have reached our goal of identifying a learning problem in subtraction is to verify that the score achieved on a standardized subtraction test is below grade level. This BASIC program does just that:

```
 5  REM grade level on subtraction test

10  INPUT"Enter grade level on subtraction test";GT

15  REM student's grade level

20  INPUT"Enter student's grade level";GS

25  G=GS-GT

30  IF G>0 THEN VER=1
```

Taking new data derived by the inference mechanism, which assumes the conclusion is correct, and matching it against the original data for verification is another example of backward chaining. As its name implies, backward chaining moves in the opposite direction from forward chaining. Rather than moving toward a goal by defining facts and obtaining data, backward chaining begins after the goal has initially been reached. An overview of forward and backward chaining as they figure in our original AI program design model is illustrated in Figure 2-3.

If it is determined that Andrew Jones has a problem with subtraction, the inference mechanism will check to see if he also received deficient test scores in subtraction. If he did, it is assumed that the goal was reached correctly. If his test scores are not deficient, there is insufficient data to support reaching the goal, and some new steps must be taken to reverify the goal. That is, we must resolve the conflict that Andrew Jones is deficient in certain subtraction skills, yet he received a passing score on a standardized subtraction test.

### Pruning

In the brain, the pruning mechanism guides the search for additional rules to verify a goal until all possible avenues have been exhausted. Since the brain possesses an enormous store of information, there may be many rules that apply to reaching or verifying a single goal, some or all of which may be called upon in any given instant.

Pruning enables the computer to skip or process any portion of the knowledge base according to its relevance to a particular goal. If Andrew Jones scored extremely well on a standardized arithmetic test, the pruning mechanism would skip over the portion of the knowledge base that evaluates data concerning arithmetic skills. On the other hand, if Andrew scored poorly on such a test, the pruning mechanism would guide the program to process that section. This eliminates processing paths that won't help in reaching our goal.

Remember that in Chapter 1 we discussed how pruning can be expressed as a set of rules. The pruning mechanism makes use of its own special rules in order to make decisions. A pruning rule that pertains to the subtraction example would be

> IF the subtraction test score exceeds the student's grade by 2 years or more, THEN skip the portion of the program that inputs subtraction data and evaluates it.

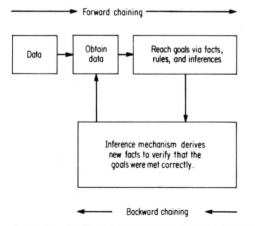

**Figure 2-3  Configuration and operation of an AI program.**

This rule can be implemented in BASIC as follows:

```
110  INPUT"Subtraction test score" ;SS

115  INPUT"Student grade level" ;GL

120  REM if subtraction test score is 2 years or more

121  REM above student's grade, skip subtraction

122  REM learning problem evaluation section

125  G=SS-(GL+2)

130  IF G>=0 THEN GOTO 140

135  GOSUB 1500

140  REM next learning problem

145  . . .
       .
       .
       .

1500  REM subtraction learning problem evaluation section
```

Pruning simply overrides unnecessary and irrelevant considerations in both the brain and in artificial intelligence systems. A pruning rule for our getting-to-work example might be

> IF it's raining very hard, THEN ignore all information regarding the local and express buses and take the first bus that comes along.

Just how we provide the computer with sufficient information to create an artificial intelligence program is discussed in the next chapter.

# 3

# Defining Expert Systems

We saw in the previous chapter how goals can be reached in an artificial intelligence system via facts, rules, an inference mechanism, and pruning. Specific areas of interest for which we can design an AI system, such as diagnosing learning problems or riding buses, are called "domains." If you're now thinking that you can create AI programs to cover every domain imaginable, you're going to run into some serious problems. In the first place, the facts and rules needed to reach all goals in all domains are virtually infinite. It will be a very long time, if ever, before we can record the vast amount of knowledge required to accomplish such a task. Furthermore, there is no computer yet in existence that can store or process anything even approaching that much information. What we need to do is confine ourselves to those areas that contain just enough information that can be shaped into a computer program.

Even though we must be realistic about the present limits of this new technology, we have just seen in Chapter 2 that there certainly are practical applications for artificial intelligence programs. Working AI systems can be developed for small domains, some examples of which are illustrated in Figure 3-1.

For practical reasons, we must choose to work in domains that contain a manageable amount of information. An artificial intelligence system created to solve problems in a particular domain is called an "expert system." All the knowledge in the expert system is provided by people who are experts in that domain. Remember the weighting factors we assigned to the subtraction skills in Chapter 2? Those numbers were not arrived at arbitrarily; they represent knowledge that comes from research in a field of study. All expert systems are based on up-to-date expert information for a given domain.

## Heuristic Rules

Suppose a group of experts is called upon to solve this problem: There is an oil spill in a river, and any one of several factories situated along the river's edge might be the source of the spill. The goal is to determine exactly where oil is coming from so that it can be stopped.

An expert system for solving this type of problem will first of all contain a mechanism for performing calculations. For example, the rate at which oil disperses in water, the direction and velocity of the river's currents, and other such factors can be employed to approximate the location of the spill. Once this information is gathered and a determination of the spill site is made, let's say to within an accuracy of 1 mile, a special set of rules is used to zero in on the precise factory location, as shown in the listing of rule H1 and rule H2 that follows. These rules are called "heuristic rules," and they differ from rules we discussed in the previous chapters in one fundamental way: Heuristic rules are not formulated as a result of ordinary, accepted knowledge but are rules that only an expert would know.

Rule H1:
   IF there is one factory along the river within 1 mile upstream from the spill's calculated location, THEN assume it is that factory that caused the spill.
Rule H2:
   IF there is more than one factory within 1 mile upstream from the spill's calculated location, THEN assume as a first choice that it is the factory that uses the most oil in its operations.

We saw in Chapters 1 and 2 how the pruning mechanism makes our thought processes more efficient by reducing the number of avenues of thought we must consider before getting down to the business of satisfying a goal. In an expert system, a pruning mechanism which utilizes heuristic rules is called the "heuristic search mechanism." The heuristic search mechanism can be represented in much the same way as the pruning mechanism in Chapter 1, as shown in Figure 3-2.

How to fix an          How to cook          How to swim
electrical problem      Chinese food
in a car

Figure 3-1   Some manageable domains.

Once the heuristic search mechanism has focused attention on the factory most likely to be causing the spill, the expert system can then apply another set of rules to verify that factory X is the source. For example, certain vulnerable spots in the factory's oil pipeline system would probably be considered first. Here is a heuristic rule that might be useful in this situation.

> IF the oil pipeline pressure in factory location 1 is less than the surrounding water pressure of the river, THEN examine pipeline location 32.

Only a person experienced with these problems in that factory would know that rule. It is a rule-of-thumb, or a heuristic rule.

## Blackboard

It is often the case that a problem may be too complex for one expert system to solve by itself. In our oil slick problem, for example, one expert system was able to find the location of the spill, but if we wanted to contain the spill, another kind of expertise would be needed. The expert system called upon to do the containing would need to have certain information that was included in the expert system that found the spill location. Then the second expert system would bring its specific calculation and heuristic search mechanism to bear upon the problem and might ultimately recommend that a certain chemical is best suited to neutralize oil of that particular grade under these particular circumstances. The communication of information between expert systems is done by a mechanism called a "blackboard." The blackboard is a location within the computer's memory in which information that is stored within an expert system is "posted" so any other expert system can refer to it if it needs the information contained there to reach its goals.

The blackboard is a structure that contains information that can be viewed by cooperating expert systems. What these systems do with

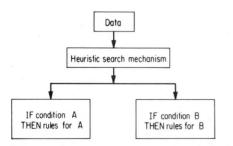

Figure 3-2   How pruning works in an expert system.

this information depends on the application. Have you ever come into a classroom and seen a message on the blackboard saying that the class has been changed to another room? This message may have been written by the school secretary who was informed that the teacher would be absent for the day; therefore, the need arose to combine similar classes under one teacher. The secretary was alertly watching for this situation and reacted accordingly. The concept of the blackboard for posting, modifying, and *watching for changes* is very important for cooperating systems.

## You Can Do It

To create an expert system, a team consisting of an expert and a knowledge engineer gathers the facts, rules, and heuristic rules for a domain and organizes them into an AI program. You're probably now thinking, "But I'm not a knowledge engineer; how does all this apply to me?" The understanding you have gained about AI in the first two chapters has already begun to make you one. If you know how to program a computer in this way, you'll be well on your way before you get to the end of this book. If you know how to fix cars, cook Chinese food, or swim, you can be the knowledge engineer who designs an expert system in any of these or comparable domains.

Section 2 will outline some methods for implementing expert systems that can be done on a personal computer. Section 3 will detail the design of some popular topics into expert systems. You will be able to use some of these designs as paradigms for creating other expert systems.

Chapter

# Natural Language Processing

Communication between people and computers is an area in which a tremendous amount of research is now being done. The ultimate goal—still some distance away—is to enable the user to "speak" to the computer entirely in a human language such as English and have the computer speak back in that language. A true artificial intelligence must be able to do this. It is hoped that someday, by simply having a conversation, people will be able to explain what task they want performed and the computer will respond in kind.

This may sound like a simple matter, but that's because you've been speaking and hearing human language since you were a small child and you take most of its complex characteristics entirely for granted. If you've worked with BASIC or any other computer language, you know how accurately you must write a program to get the computer to do exactly what you want. Computers are only as smart as the people make them; since they can't "think" for themselves, we have to give them very specific instructions for every minute function they perform. Human beings come into the world "programmed" to learn language; half the job is already done. To make a computer understand language, we not only have to break language down into its basic elements and enter this data into the computer, but we have to design computers and computer programs that can accept this information in the first place.

Creating this kind of communication system between people and computers is called "natural language processing." The purpose of this chapter is to give you some understanding of this vital and exciting aspect of artificial intelligence.

Let's see just how tough this task really is. If you had an artificial intelligence robot that could fix things, you might give it one of the following commands:

1. Fix the car by the house with the flat tire.
2. Fix the car by the house with the red curtains.

Even though sentence 1 is grammatically incorrect, any person can make sense out of it—we all know that a house cannot have a flat tire. We may recognize the error, but more important, we instantly correct it in our minds; that is, it is obviously the car that has the flat tire and not the house. The robot would have to know more than just the meaning of the words and their relationship to one another, or it might very well attempt to find a house with a flat tire on it somewhere. Since both sentences have the identical structure, the robot must not only possess a knowledge of grammar but must also be able to associate descriptions and objects. It is important to keep in mind that *our* rules of language only make sense to *us*; the robot needs its own special rules to understand what we are talking about.

An artificial intelligence, like the robot, must also be able to analyze sentences in relation to other sentences. Take these two sentences, for example:

1. John drank milk.
2. He then put on his coat.

The "He" in sentence 2 naturally refers to "John" in sentence 1. Without sentence 1, sentence 2 would have little meaning. All human languages are referred to as "context sensitive." That is, sentence 2 needed, or was sensitive to, sentence 1 in order to be fully interpreted. A language whose sentence interpretation can be accomplished without knowledge of other sentences is called "context free," that is, free of what took place before or after.

The process employed in getting a computer to understand sentences is made up of programs which together comprise the "natural language analyzer." The three basic functions of language analysis are

1. Lexical analysis (analyzing words)
2. Syntactical analysis (analyzing the placement of words in a sentence, including rules of grammar)
3. Semantic analysis (analyzing the meaning of a sentence by itself and in relation to other sentences)

## Lexical Analysis

Dividing sentences into words and punctuation marks (written) or pauses (spoken) is called "lexical analysis." The words themselves can be further divided into roots, prefixes, and suffixes. For example, a very simple word such as "going" can be subdivided as

going  (word)

go    (root)

ing   (suffix)

The word "understand" consists of

under  (prefix)

stand  (root)

A lexicon or dictionary defines words, but to get the computer to understand them in context is a considerably more difficult task.

## Syntax Analysis

Breaking a sentence down into its component parts is a vital step in getting the computer to understand language. We must be able to translate the rules of grammar and syntax into a form that the computer can handle.

A sentence (S) is generally composed of a noun phrase (NP) and a verb phrase (VP) which can be represented as

S → NP, VP

A noun phrase can usually be further broken down into a determiner (such as an article, conjunction, pronoun, etc.) and a noun, represented as

NP → DET, N

A verb phrase can also be broken down further into a verb followed by another noun phrase, as

VP → V, NP

A noun phrase, however, can also be just a simple noun:

NP → N

A common way of breaking down a sentence is by creating a parse tree, which is a diagrammatic representation of the syntactical structure of a sentence. The sentence

  A plane flew home

could have the structure shown in Figure 4-1. The words of the sentence are identified and each word is classified by type. The word "A" is a determiner (DET), "plane" is a noun (N), "flew" is a verb (V), and "home" is a noun (N).

## Semantic Analysis

Once the sentence is broken down, it undergoes semantic analysis, the process by which the computer attempts to make meaning out of it. In an artificial intelligence system, we would apply a set of rules to establish the meaning in a way that the computer can use. Let's take the previous sentence as an example:

  DET    N      V      N
   A    plane  flew   home.

The semantic analyzer might have the following set of rules in its knowledge base for interpreting the sentence:

Rule 1:
  IF a determiner is the first part of a sentence and is followed by a noun, THEN the noun is known as the subject.
Rule 2:
  IF a verb follows a subject, THEN the verb tells us what the subject did.
Rule 3:
  IF a noun follows a subject and a verb in that order, THEN the verb is an object.

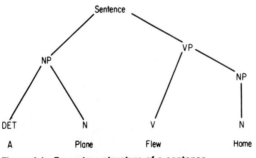

Figure 4-1   Parse tree structure of a sentence.

**Figure 4-2    Natural language processor.**

Rule 4:

IF a sentence has the form subject, verb, object, THEN we know what the subject did (verb) in relation to the object.

To make this more comprehensible, let's put this to a practical application. Suppose an artificial intelligence system had to perform the following task: Find out what the plane did and what its objective was. The task caused the sentence "A plane flew home" to trigger rule 1 which identified the plane as the subject. Rule 2 then told us the plane flew. Rules 3 and 4 identified "home" as the objective. This example illustrates how a natural language processor using its knowledge base of lexical, syntactical, and semantic rules processes or "understands" a sentence.

A natural language processor can be used at the front of another artificial intelligence system, allowing data to be passed on verbally, as in Figure 4-2.

Essentially, natural language processing can free the computer user from the limitation of the complexities of computer languages. Once the programs that will enable the computer to understand us and "talk" to us in plain English have been perfected, we will have taken a major step toward achieving a genuinely "intelligent" computer.

# Inference Mechanisms: Tools for Machine Thinking

*In Section 2 we will build a more comprehensive understanding of how to plan and use an expert system. We will provide the tools for you to construct your own expert system. By explaining how the tools work, we will put you in a position to design your own.*

# 5

# Forward Chaining

Now we are ready to design an actual expert system tool. Remember, a tool is used to help make a task easier. The tool we will create is used for solving a particular type of problem. There are many ways to solve a problem; some methods are better than other methods for solving certain types of problems. The tool we need must be applicable to the kinds of problems found in the expert domain being considered, or it won't be much help in solving problems within that domain. A saw can't help you fix a car, and a wrench can't help you cut down a tree.

Let's consider this problem: What would you do if you were driving and the temperature in your engine started rising? Of course, you'd get nervous. Most of us have encountered this problem when stuck in heavy traffic on a hot day. Let's restate this problem in a more general way. We have a condition (overheating) and we want to know what the result or consequence of this condition will be (Will the car stall?). Stop a minute and consider what happened. We first stated that a condition occurred, which was the overheating of the engine. Then we thought about all the rules we knew that were related to that condition. Some of these rules are

Rule 1
  IF the car overheats, THEN the car will stall.
Rule 2
  IF the car stalls, THEN it will cost me money, AND I will be late getting home.

How do you arrive at the conclusion that this situation will cost money and cause you to be late? Keep in mind, as we describe the course of events, these two words: forward and chaining. The condition that triggered a chain of events is the car overheating. This caused the first part of rule 1, the condition, or IF part, to be called upon. Rule 1 being true caused the THEN part of the rule to be invoked, which is that the car will stall. The chaining continues: The IF part of rule 2 is triggered by the car actually stalling or because rule 1 is invoked. Your conclusion that a stall will cost money and make you late getting home can result from the stall itself or the observation of an overheating engine.

Why do we use the word "forward" in describing this problem? When a condition such as overheating takes place, something is affected by it (the THEN part, or conclusion). Since the condition *comes before* the conclusion, and we begin with conditions, we are going forward. Thereby we use the term forward chaining.

Now let's define what we mean by a forward chaining tool. The tool helps us find answers to questions by applying forward chaining principles to a knowledge base. In other words, the tool will ask you for conditions—engine overheating—and the name of the appropriate knowledge base—automobile mechanical problems—. Once you have supplied these answers to the tool's questions, the tool will refer to the information stored in the knowledge base and apply the forward chaining techniques we've just discussed. It will provide you with the conclusions or results you need, such as "the car will stall" or "a stall will cost you money, and you will be late getting home."

In order to explain the design of the tool in the simplest way, we will first lead you through the process you might use to solve a problem if no computer was available. This part of making the tool is known as developing an "algorithm," which is a logical step-by-step organization of the problem and all its aspects.

Since we know that computers do the same things people do, only faster, the second step is to transform this organized scheme of the problem into the tool itself—a computer program. This chapter will explain both steps clearly.

The BASIC version of the expert tool is simple and is written in fundamental BASIC so that it can be entered and run on almost any personal computer, including yours. You will be able to construct a knowledge base that covers a field of interest to you, and you can try it out by yourself. The design is also open-ended, so you can expand it in the future to make the tool more powerful for solving even more difficult and complex problems.

Sound simple? It is. In this chapter we'll diagram a problem carefully and then make an expert system tool out of it. If you follow our explanations carefully and then parallel them with a domain of interest to you, you will be on your way to being a knowledge engineer.

## Example Using Forward Chaining

Here is a simple set of rules that might be part of a stock market expert system.

    10  IF INTEREST RATES = FALL
        THEN STOCK MARKET = RISE

    20  IF INTEREST RATES = RISE
        THEN STOCK MARKET = FALL

    30  IF DOLLAR EXCHANGE RATE = FALL
        THEN INTEREST RATES = RISE

    40  IF DOLLAR EXCHANGE RATE = RISE
        THEN INTEREST RATES = FALL

Using these rules, we ambitiously set up a stock market consulting company. Our first customer comes to us and tells us that the dollar exchange rate is declining (falling) against the money values of the major industrial nations. What should he do in the stock market? Obviously, the goal is to do well in the stock market, but whether or not our customer will make a profit will be decided by as yet undetermined conditions. Remember that forward chaining systems make predictions by considering conditions defined in clauses of the IF part of the rule and come to conclusions that are defined in the THEN part. In this case, the condition is

DOLLAR EXCHANGE RATE = FALL

Scanning our rules, we find that rule 30 contained DOLLAR EXCHANGE RATE in its IF clause. That is

    30  IF DOLLAR EXCHANGE RATE = FALL
        THEN INTEREST RATES = RISE

From it we can conclude that interest rates will rise. Scanning the rest of the IF-THEN rules for DOLLAR EXCHANGE RATE, we find it again in rule 40. But the IF clause

    40  IF DOLLAR EXCHANGE RATE = RISE

does not match the known condition of falling exchange rates. So rule 40 is not true. We are not yet finished since rule 30 introduced a new condition:

INTEREST RATES = RISE

We must now scan the rules to see if this condition leads to other conclusions, and we see that rule 10

    10   IF INTEREST RATES = FALL
         THEN STOCK MARKET = RISE

is not true but that rule 20 is:

    20   IF INTEREST RATES = RISE
         THEN STOCK MARKET = FALL

The chain continues by the introduction of a new condition:

    STOCK MARKET = FALL

Therefore, we are still not finished. We must check all the rules for this new condition. Scanning all the IF clauses, we see that none contains STOCK MARKET. We can go no further, and therefore the session is over. We hand our customer a report as follows:

> When the dollar exchange rate is falling, interest rates will rise and the stock market will fall.

The report, in reality, may need more complex rules, but the forward chaining system, like any system, acts only upon what is in the knowledge base.

From this example, we can describe the workings of a typical forward chaining system:

1. The system is presented with one or more conditions.
2. For each condition the system searches the rules in the knowledge base for those rules that correspond to the condition in the IF part.
3. Each rule can in turn *generate new conditions* from the conclusions of the invoked THEN part. These new conditions are added to the ones already existing.
4. Any conditions that have been added to the system are processed. If there are any such conditions, the system goes back to step 2 and searches the rules in the knowledge base again. If there are no more new conditions, this session ends.

## The Knowledge Base

In this example you, as the expert, enter rules directly into the knowledge base and use these rules to direct your stock market decisions. But first you must create a variable name table, as shown in Figure

5-1, to make it easier to deal with long, clumsy variable names and to help you write the rules.

Using the variable name table you can write the following stock market rules:

10  IF INTEREST = FALL
    THEN STOCK = RISE

20  IF INTEREST = RISE
    THEN STOCK = FALL

30  IF DOLLAR = FALL
    THEN INTEREST = RISE

40  IF DOLLAR = RISE
    THEN INTEREST = FALL

50  IF FEDINT = FALL AND FEDMON = ADD
    THEN INTEREST = FALL  .

A word of caution: These rules are not a complete list of rules needed to do a proper stock market analysis but merely show the general principles involved. We must always remember that an expert system is only as good or as bad as the experts who formulate the rules. Keeping that in mind, let's continue to examine how the system uses the rules to arrive at answers.

## Processing the Knowledge Base

Now that we have established the knowledge base using the variable name table, we are ready to begin processing that information using forward chaining principles. Our expert technique requires the construction of a number of useful tables that will aid in answering questions and making decisions about the problem we are trying to solve. These tables, or data structures, therefore serve an indispensable pur-

| Variable name | Meaning |
|---|---|
| INTEREST | Interest rate direction |
| DOLLAR | Dollar exchange rate |
| FEDINT | Federal reserve interest rate goals |
| FEDMON | Federal reserve money circulation goals (i.e., add or remove reserves from the banking system) |
| STOCK | Stock market direction |

Figure 5-1   Variable name table.

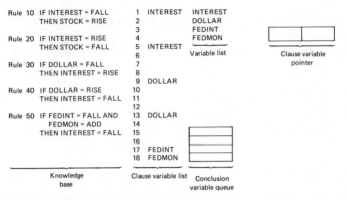

Figure 5-2   The knowledge base of the stock market expert system
and its related data structure.

pose as they are derived directly from the knowledge base. A full
description of each data structure will be provided in this chapter. The
knowledge base with all its derived data structures is shown in Figure
5-2.

The first data structure we will use is the clause variable list. This
simple list, as shown in Figure 5-3, lets us know which variables in our
problem are associated with the IF parts of specific IF-THEN statements. The numbers 1 through 18 shown to the left of the variable
names represent the array location in the data structure that the variable names are placed in. There are four array locations reserved for
each rule. If a rule does not utilize all of these locations, they are left
blank.

```
Rule 10  IF INTEREST = FALL        1   INTEREST
         THEN STOCK = RISE         2
                                   3
Rule 20  IF INTEREST = RISE        4
         THEN STOCK = FALL         5   INTEREST
                                   6
Rule 30  IF DOLLAR = FALL          7
         THEN INTEREST = RISE      8
                                   9   DOLLAR
Rule 40  IF DOLLAR = RISE         10
         THEN INTEREST = FALL     11
                                  12
Rule 50  IF FEDINT = FALL AND     13   DOLLAR
            FEDMON = ADD          14
         THEN INTEREST = FALL     15
                                  16
                                  17   FEDINT
                                  18   FEDMON
```

|            Knowledge     |     **Clause Variable list**     |
|             base         |                                  |

Figure 5-3   Clause variable list.

As an example of how the clause variable list is used, suppose we want to understand the effects of the dollar exchange rate falling, that is

DOLLAR = FALL

Rules 30 and 40 both contain clauses with DOLLAR as the variable. In order to always remember that DOLLAR is the variable in which we are interested, we will place this variable in a data structure we call the conclusion variable queue, shown in Figure 5-4.

Before continuing let us explain what a queue is and why we need one. People waiting on a supermarket checkout line are on a queue in which first come are first served. Shoppers enter a queue at the back of a line and are served when they reach the front. After being served, each person exits the queue. Why then must the conclusion variable queue be a queue? Let's use the variable DOLLAR as an example. We try to see if any statement containing DOLLAR meets the condition of DOLLAR = FALL. If it does, the THEN part of the statement is invoked and a new condition variable—INTEREST—is instantiated. In our case this would occur in rule 30:

   30   IF DOLLAR = FALL
          THEN INTEREST = RISE

We would now have to see what the effect would be of interest rising after we finished processing all the rules containing DOLLAR. To remember that we are now dealing with a new variable, INTEREST, we place it on the conclusion variable queue after DOLLAR, as shown in Figure 5-5.

After we are through processing all the IF-THEN rules with IF parts

Rule 10  IF INTEREST = FALL
          THEN STOCK = RISE

Rule 20  IF INTEREST = RISE
          THEN STOCK = FALL

Rule 30  IF **DOLLAR** = FALL
          THEN INTEREST = RISE

Rule 40  IF **DOLLAR** = RISE
          THEN INTEREST FALL

Rule 50  IF FEDINT = FALL AND
          FEDMON = ADD
          THEN INTEREST = FALL

| DOLLAR |
| --- |
|  |
|  |
|  |

Knowledge
base

Conclusion
variable queue

**Figure 5-4**  Conclusion variable queue.

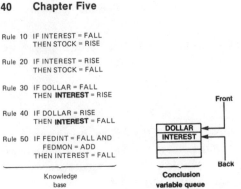

Figure 5-5   Conclusion variable queue.

containing DOLLAR, we remove it from our queue as shown in Figure 5-6. We are finished with checking the effects of a falling dollar, and now we want to see only the effects of rising interest rates. Since INTEREST has moved to the front of the queue, we will process it in the same way we processed DOLLAR. When there is nothing left on the queue, we have ended our forward chaining and are ready to provide the answers.

Let us examine the last two data structures needed for implementing forward chaining. These are the variable list and the clause variable pointer. The variable list tells us if a variable has been instantiated yet. Initially, before any questions are asked, the variable list will show that none of the variables have been instantiated, as shown in Figure 5-7. In our example so far, with DOLLAR and INTEREST instantiated, the variable list would look different, as shown in Figure 5-8.

The clause variable pointer keeps track of the clause within the rule we are examining and is made up of the rule number and the clause number. We need this pointer in our forward chaining tool to keep

Rule 10   IF INTEREST = FALL
          THEN STOCK = RISE

Rule 20   IF INTEREST = RISE
          THEN STOCK = FALL

Rule 30   IF DOLLAR = FALL
          THEN **INTEREST** = RISE

Rule 40   IF DOLLAR = RISE
          THEN **INTEREST** = FALL

Rule 50   IF FEDINT = FALL AND
          FEDMON = ADD
          THEN INTEREST = FALL

Knowledge                      Conclusion
base                           variable queue

Figure 5-6   Conclusion variable queue.

```
Rule 10  IF INTEREST = FALL
         THEN STOCK = RISE

Rule 20  IF INTEREST = RISE
         THEN STOCK = FALL

Rule 30  IF DOLLAR = FALL
         THEN INTEREST = RISE

Rule 40  IF DOLLAR = RISE
         THEN INTEREST = FALL

Rule 50  IF FEDINT = FALL AND
            FEDMON = ADD
         THEN INTEREST = FALL
```

Knowledge
base

|          |    | Value |
|----------|----|-------|
| INTEREST | NI |       |
| DOLLAR   | NI |       |
| FEDINT   | NI |       |
| FEDMON   | NI |       |

Variable list

**Figure 5-7   Variable list.**

track of where we are. That is, to know which rule and which clause within the rule we are now processing. Remember, the processing of each clause is a function of the variable in the front of the conclusion variable queue. For example, assume we have the variable DOLLAR in the front of the conclusion variable queue, that is, we want to see the consequence of the change in the dollar. The first rule in which DOLLAR appears as a condition (the IF part) is rule 30. We therefore want to process rule 30 to see if we can invoke a consequence of the dollar changing. The clause variable pointer will initially point to rule 30, as shown in Figure 5-9.

In short, the clause variable pointer actually points to an entry in the clause variable list. That entry contains the condition variable (DOLLAR, in this case) that we are interested in processing at the moment and that is at the front of the conclusion variable queue.

Let's take a moment to review these four data structures we have designed before we put them all together in a working example. All along we've said that artificial intelligence works because it imitates the way people actually think when they solve problems. Seen in this

```
Rule 10  IF INTEREST = FALL
         THEN STOCK = RISE

Rule 20  IF INTEREST = RISE
         THEN STOCK = FALL

Rule 30  IF DOLLAR = FALL
         THEN INTEREST = RISE

Rule 40  IF DOLLAR = RISE
         THEN INTEREST = FALL

Rule 50  IF FEDINT = FALL AND
            FEDMON = ADD
         THEN INTEREST = FALL
```

Knowledge
base

|          |    | Value |
|----------|----|-------|
| INTEREST | I  | RISE  |
| DOLLAR   | I  | FALL  |
| FEDINT   | NI |       |
| FEDMON   | NI |       |

Variable list

**Figure 5-8   Variable list.**

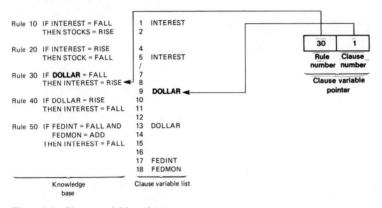

Figure 5-9  Clause variable pointer.

context, the structures we've just been working with do not simply comprise an abstract problem-solving method; they relate specifically to human thought processes. How?

When you set out to solve a problem in which you need to predict the consequences of various conditions, you first ponder all the variable conditions that could affect the end result (variable list). Then, you instantiate (establish conditions for) any of the variables for which you possess information (e.g., DOLLAR = FALL). Next, you consider all the rules you know that might help predict the outcome of the situation and see if any of the conditions you've come up with are consistent with any of the rules you know (clause variable list). The way you would "process" that information would be to put all the variable conditions in some kind of order (conclusion variable queue) and somehow focus on them, one at a time, to see how they might lead you to a possible conclusion (clause variable pointer).

In your mind, of course, all this happens automatically, very quickly, and in not so linear a manner. Most of the time, we aren't even aware that we are processing information and coming to conclusions about circumstances we encounter. As soon as you see the needle hovering at the high point of the temperature gauge of your car, you say "Oh, no!" because you've immediately come to the conclusion that the car might stall. The human brain works very fast because the neurons work together simultaneously. In parallel, when dealing with a highly complex problem containing many, many variables, a computer can work just as fast if the problem is organized into data structures like the ones we've discussed, and if algorithms are used in our expert tool to simulate the forward chaining inference process. If we are successful in designing the data structures and the expert tool, another person who sees the conclusions will judge that they make sense.

## Forward Chaining Example

As an example, let's use the stock market knowledge base and pose the following question to the forward chaining tool:

> What is the effect of the Federal Reserve adding reserves to the banking system? That is: FEDMON = ADD

The forward chaining tool in the computer will read the stock market knowledge base from a peripheral storage device such as a disk and will conduct the lists, pointers, and queues, which we have already discussed, as shown in Figure 5-10. The conclusion variable queue will of course contain the initial condition variable, FEDMON, whose value is known. The tool searches the clause variable list for the first instance of FEDMON and finds that this occurs in rule 50. The clause variable pointer is therefore initially set to rule number 50, clause number 1. From the clause variable list we see that we have to instantiate two clause variables, FEDINT and FEDMON. We already know that FEDMON was instantiated to ADD as the original condition. Since FEDINT is not instantiated, the tool asks the user of the expert system the following question:

> Does the Federal Reserve want interest rates to rise or fall?

Let's say the user responds with "fall." This causes FEDINT to acquire the value FALL and be instantiated in the variable list. The clause number of the clause variable pointer is then incremented from 1 to 2. Since FEDMON, the second clause of rule 50, is already instantiated and there is no more rule 50 clauses, we can execute the entire IF part.

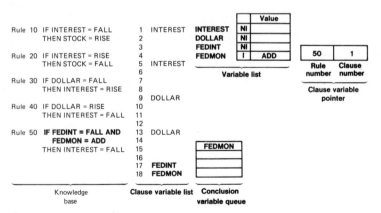

Figure 5-10  Forward chaining system.

| Rule 10 | IF INTEREST = FALL<br>THEN STOCK = RISE | 1<br>2<br>3 | INTEREST |
|---------|------------------------------------------|-------------|----------|
| Rule 20 | IF INTEREST = RISE<br>THEN STOCK = FALL | 4<br>5<br>6 | INTEREST |
| Rule 30 | IF DOLLAR = FALL<br>THEN INTEREST = RISE | 7<br>8<br>9 | DOLLAR |
| Rule 40 | IF DOLLAR = RISE<br>THEN INTEREST = FALL | 10<br>11<br>12 | |
| Rule 50 | IF FEDINT = FALL AND<br>**FEDMON** = ADD<br>THEN **INTEREST** = FALL | 13<br>14<br>15<br>16<br>17<br>18 | DOLLAR |

Conclusion variable queue:
FEDMON
INTEREST

17 FEDINT
18 **FEDMON**

Knowledge base          Clause variable list          Conclusion variable queue

**Figure 5-11    Conclusion variable queue.**

Both conditions of the FEDINT = FALL and FEDMON = ADD are true. Therefore, the THEN part of the rule 50 is invoked, resulting in

INTEREST = FALL

Since INTEREST may represent a new condition, it is placed on the conclusion variable queue, which now looks like Figure 5-11, and the variable list is modified to look like Figure 5-12.

The remainder of the rules in the variable list are scanned for FED-MON. Since there are no more rules with FEDMON, it is removed from the conclusion variable queue. INTEREST now moves to the front. We search the clause variable list for INTEREST and find it in rule 10. The way our forward chaining system looks now is shown in Figure 5-13.

| Rule 10 | IF **INTEREST** = FALL<br>THEN **STOCK** = RISE |
|---------|-------------------------------------------------|
| Rule 20 | IF **INTEREST** = RISE<br>THEN **STOCK** = FALL |
| Rule 30 | IF **DOLLAR** = FALL<br>THEN INTEREST = RISE |
| Rule 40 | IF **DOLLAR** = RISE<br>THEN INTEREST = FALL |
| Rule 50 | IF **FEDINT** = FALL AND<br>**FEDMON** = ADD<br>THEN INTEREST = FALL |

Knowledge base

| | | Value |
|----------|-----|-------|
| INTEREST | I | FALL |
| DOLLAR | NI | |
| FEDINT | I | FALL |
| FEDMON | I | ADD |

Variable list

**Figure 5-12    Variable list.**

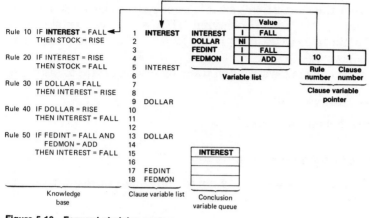

**Figure 5-13  Forward chaining system.**

You will note that both rules 10 and 20 contain INTEREST as conditions:

10  IF INTEREST = FALL
    THEN STOCK = RISE

20  IF INTEREST = RISE
    THEN STOCK = FALL

Since INTEREST is instantiated to FALL, the IF part of rule 10 is true. This causes the THEN part to be invoked, which instantiates STOCK to RISE. This will in turn result in STOCK being placed on the conclusion variable queue as shown in Figure 5-14. Rule 20 is not true because it contains the condition INTEREST = RISE while INTEREST has already been instantiated to FALL. INTEREST will then be

Rule 10  IF **INTEREST** = FALL
         THEN **STOCK** = RISE

Rule 20  IF **INTEREST** = RISE
         THEN **STOCK** = FALL

Rule 30  IF DOLLAR = FALL
         THEN INTEREST = RISE

Rule 40  IF DOLLAR = RISE
         THEN INTEREST = FALL

Rule 50  IF FEDINT = FALL AND
         FEDMON = ADD
         THEN INTEREST = FALL

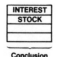

Knowledge          Conclusion
base               variable queue

**Figure 5-14  Conclusion variable queue.**

removed from the conclusion variable queue since there are no more rules containing INTEREST, leaving STOCK in front as shown in Figure 5-15. Since STOCK is not in the IF part of any rule, the session ends. The answers to "What is the effect of the Federal Reserve adding reserves to the banking system and wanting interest rates to fall?" are

1. Interest rates will fall.

2. The stock market will rise.

### Concepts for Design Implementation

Let us review the steps we have taken to implement the forward chaining structure:

1. The condition is identified.

2. The condition variable is placed on the conclusion variable queue and its value is marked on the variable list.

3. The clause variable list is searched for the variable whose name is the same as the one in the front of the queue. If found, the rule number and a 1 are placed into the clause variable pointer. If not found, go to step 6.

4. Each variable in the IF clause of the rule that is not already instantiated is now instantiated. The variables are in the clause variable list. If all the clauses are true, the THEN part is invoked.

5. The instantiated THEN part of the variable is placed in the *back* of the conclusion variable queue.

6. When there are no more IF statements containing the variable that is at the *front* of the conclusion variable queue, that variable is removed.

```
Rule 10  IF INTEREST = FALL
         THEN STOCK = RISE

Rule 20  IF INTEREST = RISE
         THEN STOCK = FALL

Rule 30  IF DOLLAR = FALL
         THEN INTEREST = RISE

Rule 40  IF DOLLAR = RISE
         THEN INTEREST = RISE

Rule 50  IF FEDINT = FALL AND
            FEDMON = ADD
         THEN INTEREST = FALL
```

STOCK

Knowledge
base

Conclusion
variable queue

Figure 5-15  Conclusion variable queue.

7. If there are no more variables on the conclusion variable queue, end the session. If there are more variables, go to step 3.

We can use the above concepts to design, in BASIC, a simple forward chaining expert tool.

## Programming Applications

In this part of the chapter is a forward chaining tool for you to apply to your knowledge base (see Listing 5-1). This tool will allow you to insert a set of rules into statement locations 1500 through 1610 of the program, type RUN, and obtain answers about your knowledge base.

### Program Explanation

As an example to acquaint you with the way the program is used, we have inserted the rules governing the stock market and interest rates. This is the same example used to explain the forward chaining concepts. For example, the rule

    IF interest rates fall
    THEN stock market will rise

is covered by statement numbers 1500 through 1510. The rule

    IF dollar is falling
    THEN interest rates will rise

is covered by statement numbers 1540 through 1550.
Each variable in the variable list is specified in statement number 367. These are the condition variables that start a forward chaining operation. The clause variable list is constructed in statements 407 and 408.
The system responses have been abbreviated. For example:

    ST = FALL means the stock market will fall.
    IN = RISE means interest rates will rise.

### Program Listing

Listing 5-1 is followed by a sequence of sample RUNS.

**Listing 5-1 Forward chaining.**

```
1 REM******************** FORWARD CHAINING ***********************************
2 REM*****************************************************************************
10 REM INSTALL YOUR IF CLAUSES IN SEQUENCE AT LOCATIONS 1500,1520,..,1540
20 REM FORMAT EXAMPLE 1500 IF (A1=2) AND (A2=6) OR (A3$="YES") THEN S=1
22 REM              1502 RETURN
30 REM              1520 IF (J$="NO") THEN S=1
32 REM              1522 RETURN
40 REM   THE THEN PART OF THE ABOVE CONSTRUCTION ALWAYS CONTAINS, THEN S=1
50 REM INSTALL YOUR THEN CLAUSES IN SEQUENCE IN STATEMENTS 1510,1530,..,1550
200 REM ************ INITIALIZATION SECTION *************
210 REM VARIABLE LIST (V$), INSTANTIATED LIST (IN)
230 REM  CLAUSE VARIABLE LIST (CV$) AND CONDITION VARIABLE QUEUE
240 DIM Q$(10),V$(10),CV$(40),IN(10)
255 FP=1: BP=1: REM FRONT (FP) AND BACK (BP) CONDITION VARIABLE QUEUE POINTERS
260 FOR I=1 TO 10
270 Q$(I)="": V$(I)="": IN(I)=0: SS(I)=0: CS(I)=0
280 NEXT I
340 REM ENTER VARIABLES WHICH ARE IN THE IF PART, 1 AT A TIME IN THE
350 REM EXACT ORDER THAT THEY OCCUR. UP TO 3 VARIABLES PER IF STATEMENT.
360 REM DO NOT DUPLICATE ANY VARIABLES NAMES. ANY NAME IS USED ONLY ONCE
365 REM IF NO MORE VARIABLES LEFT, JUST HIT RETURN KEY.
367 V$(1)="DO":V$(2)="FT":V$(3)="FM":V$(4)="IN":V$(5)="ST"
368 PRINT"*** VARIABLE LIST ***"
370 FOR I=1 TO 10
380 PRINT"ENTER VARIABLE ";I;
385 PRINT V$(I)
395 NEXT I
396 INPUT"HIT RETURN TO CONTINUE";I
400 REM ENTER VARIABLES AS THEY APPEAR IN THE IF CLAUSES. A MAXIMUM OF 3
405 REM VARIABLES PER IF STATEMENT. IF NO MORE VARIABLES HIT RETURN KEY
407 CV$(1)="IN":CV$(5)="IN":CV$(9)="DO":CV$(13)="DO"
408 CV$(17)="FT":CV$(18)="FM"
409 PRINT"*** CLAUSE-VARIABLE LIST ***"
410 FOR I=1 TO 8:PRINT"** CLAUSE ";I
420 FOR J=1 TO 4:PRINT"VARIABLE ";J;
423 K=4*(I-1)+J
424 PRINT CV$(K)
430 NEXT J
432 IF I=4 THEN INPUT"HIT RETURN TO CONTINUE";Z
435 NEXT I
450 REM *************** INFERENCE SECTION ***********************************
465 INPUT"ENTER CONDITION VARIABLE ";C$
470 REM PLACE CONDITION VARIABLE (C$) ON CONDITION VARIABLE QUEUE (Q$)
475 Q$(BP)=C$: BP=BP+1: REM MOVE BACKPOINTER (BP) BACK
480 REM SET THE CONDITION VARIABLE POINTER CONSISTING OF THE
482 REM  STATEMENT NUMBER (SN) AND THE CLAUSE NUMBER (CN)
485 SN=1: CN=1
490 REM FIND THE NEXT STATEMENT NUMBER CONTAINING THE CONDITION VARIABLE
492 REM  WHICH IS IN FRONT OF THE QUEUE [Q$(FP)]. THIS STATEMENT NUMBER
494 REM  IS LOCATED IN THE CLAUSE VARIABLE LIST (CV$)
495 F=1:REM START AT BEGINNING
496 GOSUB 3000: CN=1 :REM POINT TO FIRST CLAUSE OF STATEMENT
500 IF SN=0 THEN GOTO 700: REM NO MORE STATEMENTS
505 I=4 * (SN-1)+CN :REM LOCATE THE CLAUSE
510 V$=CV$(I): REM CLAUSE VARIABLE
560 REM ARE THERE ANY MORE CLAUSES FOR THIS STATEMENT?
565 IF V$="" THEN GOTO 580 :REM NO MORE CLAUSES PROCESS IF-THEN STATEMENT
570 GOSUB 2400: REM CHECK INSTANTIATION OF THIS CLAUSE
575 CN=CN+1 : GOTO 505 : REM CHECK NEXT CLAUSE
580 REM NO MORE CLAUSES CHECK IF PART OF STATEMENT
585 S=0: ON SN GOSUB 1500,1520,1540,1560,1580,1600
590 REM SEE IF THE THEN PART SHOULD BE INVOKED I.E. S=1
600 IF S=1 THEN GOTO 630 :REM INVOKE THEN PART
605 REM SEARCH FOR NEXT STATEMENT IN CLAUSE VARIABLE LIST
610 F=SN+1 :GOTO 496
630 REM IF PART TRUE INVOKE THE THEN PART
635 ON SN GOSUB 1510,1530,1550,1570,1590,1610
650 F=SN+1: GOTO 496: REM NO MORE STATEMENTS
700 REM NO MORE CLAUSES IN THE CLAUSE VARIABLE LIST (CV$) CONTAINING
705 REM THE VARIABLE IN FRONT OF THE QUEUE [Q$(FP)]
710 REM THEN REMOVE FRONT VARIABLE [Q$(FP)] AND REPLACE IT BY THE NEXT
715 REM VARIABLE [Q(FP+1)]. IF NO MORE VARIABLES ARE AT THE FRONT OF THE QUEUE
720 REM ONE STOP.
725 FP=FP+1: REM NEXT QUEUE VARIABLE
730 IF FP>=BP THEN STOP: REM ** END NO MORE CONCLUSION VARIABLES ON QUEUE.
735 GOTO 495 :REM CHECK OUT THIS CONDITION VARIABLE
1490 REM ********** IF-THEN STATEMENT STARTING AT 1500 ******************
1492 REM SAMPLE IF-THEN STATEMENTS FROM THE POSITION KNOWLEDGE BASE
1494 REM  ONLY THE FIRST TWO LETTERS OF EACH VARIABLE IS USED TO MAKE
```

```
1496 REM   THE EXAMPLE COMPATIBLE WITH SOME VERSIONS OF BASIC. FOR EXAMPLE
1498 REM DOLLLAR WAS SHORTENED TO DO, STOCK TO ST,FEDINT TO FT,FEDMON TO FN
1499 REM ** STATEMENT 1
1500 IF IN$="FALL" THEN S=1
1502 RETURN
1505 REM PUT VARIABLE ON THE CONCLUSION VARIABLE QUEUE
1510 ST$="RISE":PRINT "ST=RISE":V$="ST":GOSUB 3100: RETURN
1519 REM ** STATEMENT 2
1520 IF IN$="RISE" THEN S=1
1522 RETURN
1530 ST$="FALL":PRINT "ST=FALL":V$="ST":GOSUB 3100: RETURN
1539 REM ** STATEMENT 3
1540 IF DO$="FALL" THEN S=1
1542 RETURN
1545 REM PUT VARIABLE ON THE CONCLUSION VARIABLE QUEUE
1550 IN$="RISE":PRINT "IN=RISE":V$="IN":GOSUB 3100: RETURN
1559 REM ** STATEMENT 4
1560 IF DO$="RISE" THEN S=1
1562 RETURN
1565 REM PUT VARIABLE ON THE CONCLUSION VARIABLE QUEUE
1570 IN$="FALL":PRINT "IN=FALL":V$="IN":GOSUB 3100: RETURN
1579 REM ** STATEMENT 5
1580 IF (FT$="FALL") AND (FM$="ADD") THEN S=1
1582 RETURN
1585 REM PUT VARIABLE ON THE CONCLUSION VARIABLE QUEUE
1590 IN$="FALL":PRINT "IN=FALL":V$="IN":GOSUB 3100: RETURN
1599 REM ** STATEMENT 6
1600 IF (QU$="YES") AND (GR>=3.5) THEN S=1
1602 RETURN
1610 PO$="YES":PRINT"PO=YES" :RETURN
1611 REM ****** END OF POSITION KNOWLEDGE BASE ***********
1690 REM ********** INPUT STATEMENTS STARTING AT 1700 *********************
1699 REM **** INPUT STATEMENTS FOR SAMPLE POSITION KNOWLEDGE BASE
1700 INPUT"RISE OR FALL FOR DO-";DO$ :RETURN
1705 INPUT"RISE OR FALL FOR FT-";FT$ :RETURN
1710 INPUT"ADD OR SUBTRACT FOR FM-";FM$ :RETURN
1715 INPUT"RISE OR FALL FOR IN-";IN$ :RETURN
1720 INPUT"RISE OR FALL FOR ST-";ST$ :RETURN
1750 REM ****** END OF INPUT STATEMENTS FOR THE POSITION KNOWLEDGE BASE **
1999 REM ******************** SUBROUTINE SECTION ***************************
2400 REM ROUTINE TO INSTANTIATE A VARIABLE (V$) IF IT ISN'T ALREADY. THE
2402 REM  INSTANTIATE INDICATION (IN) IS A 0 IF NOT, A 1 IF IT IS. THE
2404 REM  VARIABLE LIST (VL$) CONTAINS THE VARIABLE (V$)
2420 FOR I=1 TO 10: REM FIND VARIABLE IN THE LIST
2430 IF V$=V$(I) THEN GOTO 2445: REM FOUND VARIABLE IN LIST
2440 NEXT I
2445 IF IN(I)=1 THEN RETURN: REM ALREADY INSTANTIATED
2450 IF IN(I)=1 THEN RETURN: REM ALREADY INSTANTIATED
2460 REM THE DESIGNER OF THIS KNOWLEDGE BASE PLACES THE INPUT STATEMENTS
2462 REM  TO INSTANTIATE THE VARIABLES STARTING AT LOCATION 1700
2464 REM FORMAT IS INPUT STATEMENT FOLLOWED BY A RETURN STATEMENT
2465 IN(I)=1:REM MARK INSTANTIATED
2470 ON I GOSUB 1700,1705,1710,1715,1720
2480 RETURN
3000 REM SEARCH CLAUSE VARIABLE LIST FOR A VARIABLE (CV$) EQUAL TO THE ONE
3005 REM  IN FRONT OF THE CONCLUSION QUEUE (Q$). RETURN THE STATEMENT NUMBER
3010 REM  (SN) IF THERE IS NO MATCH I.E. SN=0. THE FIRST STATEMENT NUMBER
3015 REM  FOR THE SEARCH IS F.
3025 FOR SN= F TO 10
3030 FOR CN= 1 TO 4
3035 K=(SN-1)*4+CN
3040 IF CV$(K)=Q$(FP) THEN RETURN
3045 NEXT CN
3050 NEXT SN
3055 SN=0: RETURN
3100 REM ROUTINE TO INSTANTIATE VARIABLE (V$) AND THEN PLACE IT ON THE
3105 REM  BACK OF THE QUEUE Q$(BP) IF IT IS NOT ALREADY THERE.
3110 REM FIND VARIABLE IN THE VARIABLE LIST [V$(10)]
3115 FOR I=1 TO 10
3117 IF V$=V$(I) THEN GOTO 3125
3120 NEXT I
3125 IN(I)=1:REM INSTANTIATE IT
3130 REM DETERMINE IF (V$) IS OR ALREADY HAS BEEN ON THE QUEUE (Q$)
3135 FOR I=1 TO 10: IF V$=Q$(I) THEN RETURN
3140 NEXT I
3155 REM VARIABLE HAS NOT BEEN ON THE QUEUE STORE IT IN BACK OF THE QUEUE
3160 Q$(BP)=V$:BP=BP+1
3170 FOR I=1 TO 10
3176 NEXT I
3180 RETURN
```

## Sample Runs

When we enter RUN, the following happens:

```
RUN
*** VARIABLE LIST ***
ENTER VARIABLE   1 DO
ENTER VARIABLE   2 FT
ENTER VARIABLE   3 FM
ENTER VARIABLE   4 IN
ENTER VARIABLE   5 ST
ENTER VARIABLE   6
ENTER VARIABLE   7
ENTER VARIABLE   8
ENTER VARIABLE   9
ENTER VARIABLE  10
HIT RETURN TO CONTINUE?
*** CLAUSE-VARIABLE LIST ***
** CLAUSE   1
VARIABLE   1 IN
VARIABLE   2
VARIABLE   3
VARIABLE   4
** CLAUSE   2
VARIABLE   1 IN
VARIABLE   2
VARIABLE   3
VARIABLE   4
** CLAUSE   3
VARIABLE   1 DO
VARIABLE   2
VARIABLE   3
VARIABLE   4
** CLAUSE   4
VARIABLE   1 DO
VARIABLE   2
VARIABLE   3
VARIABLE   4
HIT RETURN TO CONTINUE?
** CLAUSE   5
VARIABLE   1 FT
VARIABLE   2 FM
VARIABLE   3
VARIABLE   4
** CLAUSE   6
VARIABLE   1
VARIABLE   2
VARIABLE   3
VARIABLE   4
** CLAUSE   7
VARIABLE   1
VARIABLE   2
VARIABLE   3
VARIABLE   4
** CLAUSE   8
VARIABLE   1
VARIABLE   2
VARIABLE   3
VARIABLE   4
```

The preceding sample run appears with each of the following system-user interactions:

```
ENTER CONDITION VARIABLE ? DO
RISE OR FALL FOR DO-? RISE
IN=FALL
ST=RISE
Break in 730
Ok

ENTER CONDITION VARIABLE ? DO
RISE OR FALL FOR DO-? FALL
IN=RISE
ST=RISE
Break in 730
Ok

ENTER CONDITION VARIABLE ? IN
RISE OR FALL FOR IN-? FALL
ST=RISE
Break in 730
Ok

ENTER CONDITION VARIABLE ? FM
RISE OR FALL FOR FT-? RISE
ADD OR SUBTRACT FOR FM-? ADD
Break in 730
Ok
```

There are no conclusions for the above conditions since we can't satisfy any rule, i.e.,

```
IF      FT  = FALL
        FM  = ADD
THEN   IN  = FALL
```

```
ENTER CONDITION VARIABLE ? FM
RISE OR FALL FOR FT-? FALL
ADD OR SUBTRACT FOR FM-? ADD
IN=FALL
ST=RISE
Break in 730
Ok
```

## Forward Chaining Worksheet

The following worksheet is an aid to simplifying the process of placing a new knowledge base into the program to replace the one that is there now. It is included to allow you to validate the concepts of the relationship between the knowledge base and expert system data structures. As a future exercise, you can develop an input "compiler" which reads a knowledge base and makes transfers to the data structures automatically. You should do this only after understanding the concepts fully.

This worksheet will help you create and transfer the variables (variable 11, variable 12, etc.) and values (value 11, value 12, etc.) of your knowledge base into the program (it allows for *three* condition variables per rule). First create the rules for the IF-THEN statements below. Then transfer them onto the worksheets that follow.

IF _____ = _____ AND
Variable 11      Value 11

_____ = _____ AND
Variable 12      Value 12

_____ = _____
Variable 13      Value 13

THEN _____ = _____
Variable 14      Value 14

IF _____ = _____ AND
Variable 21      Value 21

_____ = _____ AND
Variable 22      Value 22

_____ = _____
Variable 23      Value 23

THEN _____ = _____
Variable 24      Value 24

IF _____ = _____ AND
Variable 31      Value 31

_____ = _____ AND
Variable 32      Value 32

_____ = _____
Variable 33      Value 33

THEN _____ = _____
Variable 34      Value 34

IF _____ = _____ AND
Variable 41      Value 41

_____ = _____ AND
Variable 42      Value 42

_____ = _____
Variable 43      Value 43

THEN _____ = _____
Variable 44      Value 44

IF   _____ = _____   AND
            Variable 51            Value 51

     _____ = _____   AND
            Variable 52            Value 52

     _____ = _____
            Variable 53            Value 53

THEN   _____ = _____
            Variable 54            Value 54

This worksheet inserts variables into the clause variable list (statements 407 and 408).

CV$(1)  = _____
           Variable 11

CV$(2)  = _____
           Variable 12

CV$(3)  = _____
           Variable 13

CV$(5)  = _____
           Variable 21

CV$(6)  = _____
           Variable 22

CV$(7)  = _____
           Variable 23

CV$(9)  = _____
           Variable 31

CV$(10) = _____
           Variable 32

CV$(11) = _____
           Variable 33

CV$(13) = _____
           Variable 41

CV$(14) = _____
           Variable 42

CV\$(15) = _____
<br>Variable 43

CV\$(17) = _____
<br>Variable 51

CV\$(18) = _____
<br>Variable 52

CV\$(19) = _____
<br>Variable 53

Use this worksheet to insert variables into the variable list (statement 367). Do not insert a variable name more than once.

V\$(1) = _____
<br>Variable _____

V\$(2) = _____
<br>Variable _____

V\$(3) = _____
<br>Variable _____

V\$(4) = _____
<br>Variable _____

V\$(5) = _____
<br>Variable _____

This one if for insertion of the IF-THEN rules (see statements 1490–1611). The IF portions are listed first, followed by the THEN clause.

**IF Rules**

1500   IF _____\$ = "_____"   AND
<br>        Variable 11              Value 11

_____\$ = "_____"   AND
<br>Variable 12              Value 12

_____\$ = "_____"   THEN S = 1
<br>Variable 13              Value 13

1520  IF  _____$ = "_____"    AND
          Variable 21                    Value 21

          _____$ = "_____"    AND
          Variable 22                    Value 22

          _____$ = "_____"    THEN S = 1
          Variable 23                    Value 23

1540  IF  _____$ = "_____"    AND
          Variable 31                    Value 31

          _____$ = "_____"    AND
          Variable 32                    Value 32

          _____$ = "_____"    THEN S = 1
          Variable 33                    Value 33

1560  IF  _____$ = "_____"    AND
          Variable 41                    Value 41

          _____$ = "_____"    AND
          Variable 42                    Value 42

          _____$ = "_____"    THEN S = 1
          Variable 43                    Value 43

1580  IF  _____$ = "_____"    AND
          Variable 51                    Value 51

          _____$ = "_____"    AND
          Variable 52                    Value 52

          _____$ = "_____"    THEN S = 1
          Variable 53                    Value 53

**THEN Rules**

1510  _____$ = "_____"
      Variable 14                    Value 14

      :PRINT "_____ = _____" :RETURN
             Variable 14                    Value 14

1530  _____$ = "_____"
      Variable 24                    Value 24

      :PRINT "_____ = _____" :RETURN
             Variable 24                    Value 24

1550 _____$ = "_____"
       Variable 34              Value 34

   :PRINT "_____ = _____" :RETURN
            Variable 34            Value 34

1570 _____$ = "_____"
       Variable 44              Value 44

   :PRINT "_____ ▬ _____" :RETURN
            Variable 44            Value 44

1590 _____$ = "_____"
       Variable 54              Value 54

   :PRINT "_____ = _____" :RETURN
            Variable 54            Value 54

Chapter

# Backward Chaining

Suppose your car will not start. Is it because the battery is weak? Does the car need a tune-up? Or is the starter broken? We can state the problem in a more general way: We have a result or consequence (the car will not start) and want to determine the conditions causing the problem. In other words, we have a symptom (car doesn't start) and we want to discover what is wrong. Notice how this problem differs from the one we described in the previous chapter on forward chaining—in that car example, the car was overheating, and we didn't know what the outcome would be. The goal was to predict the possible result of the overheating. Here, the result has already happened, and the goal is to find out why.

We need rules to solve this problem as well. Some rules that might pertain to this situation are

Rule 1:
  IF the car is not tuned AND the battery is weak,
  THEN not enough current will reach the starter.
Rule 2:
  IF not enough current reaches the starter,
  THEN the car will not start.

How would you arrive at the conditions that have resulted in the car failing to start? There are two key words to keep in mind as we describe the situation: backward and chaining. The car did not start, triggering a chain of reasoning that led you backward in time from this car sequence to the set of conditions that caused it. Remember, a condition occurs earlier in time than its consequence; therefore, backward chaining works by searching for conclusions, instantiating causes, and seeing if these causes link to earlier conclusions. For example, rule 2 contains the conclusion clause "THEN the car will not start," so that rule, because we found out our car failed to start, is invoked first. Remember, backward chaining starts with the consequence (THEN part). The reason for the car not starting is a condition for rule 2, "IF not enough current reaches the starter." The chain of reasoning continues with the question, why is there not enough current? This question is addressed in rule 1 which identifies the conditions that prevent current from reaching the starter. These conditions are "IF the car is not tuned" and "the battery is weak." If these conditions are true, we have discovered the reason why the car did not start. If these conditions are false, we would need to find and invoke other pertinent rules and follow another chain in search of the cause.

If the conditions causing the problem are not contained in any other rules that pertain to the problem, you—the car owner—or a mechanic must provide additional information that will lead to the solution. To put it plainly, if the conditions suggested by the system are not true, the system needs to know if there are additional consequences (or symptoms) which, if they exist, will shed light on the problem.

You can now see that the word "chaining" signifies the linking of a set of rules. In our example, chaining began in rule 2 and ended in rule 1. What about the word backward? The car has to be untuned and the battery has to be weak before the car fails to start. Since we already know the car won't start—the consequence of these conditions—we try to find out why, that is, we try to pinpoint the conditions. Working from what occurred *last* to what occurred *first* is working backward.

Our backward chaining tool will help us solve diagnostic problems in which the conclusion is known and the causes are sought. We will construct a knowledge base and, using backward chaining principles, we will process the information in the knowledge base by answering questions put to us by the expert tool. And just as the forward chaining tool provided the conclusions or consequences to the condtiions presented, the backward chaining tool will find the conditions that led to the already known conclusions, consequences, or symptoms.

Backward chaining is just a bit trickier than forward chaining, but once again you will step through the design of an algorithm and the writing of the actual program for the tool.

## A Procedure for Designing the Knowledge Base: The Decision Tree

The first thing to do is to state the problem that the expert system tool should solve. Let's consider an example suited to a backward chaining tool; it's one we will use as our central example throughout this chapter.

You are the personnel director for a large engineering firm, and an applicant, résumé in hand, comes to you for an interview. The applicant's qualifications are before you, as are the requirements of the job and the general standards of the company. Your problem is which position, if any, is this applicant qualified for?

This may not seem like a very complicated problem at first glance, but there are many factors that go into such a decision. Suppose the applicant has little experience in engineering but made an important discovery in his or her field. Or suppose the applicant did not do well in school but has several years of solid work experience. Each applicant is different, and although certain criteria must be met to land a job, there are several different combinations of factors in any applicant's history that may make that person qualified for a particular position.

The reason this problem is appropriate to backward chaining is that the goal is to select among a range of alternatives, in this case possible positions. The answer, in reality, already exists. The individual is sitting in the chair in front of you, perhaps with legs crossed, hands clasped nervously, trying to make a good impression on you. This individual, if qualified, is better suited for one position than another. Your job is to ask the right questions, drawn upon the knowledge you possess, and determine which position is best.

Once the problem has been stated, the next step is to somehow diagram the problem so that all its many aspects are illustrated as simply as possible. One of the most common diagrams used in working out problems of this sort is the decision tree. It is a very useful and effective type of diagram because it enables us to visualize all the factors that must be considered in reaching a decision and to see how one consideration leads to others, which then lead to still others, and so on.

The decision tree is so named because it branches off just like a tree, and at the very end of each branch or system of branches is a conclusion, in this case, should you or should you not offer this applicant a position and if so, which one? Because many problems are complex and difficult to conceptualize (or we wouldn't need expert systems to help solve them) we use the decision tree to illustrate the problem clearly.

Figure 6-1 is a decision tree for our job applicant dilemma. Study it for a few minutes. Notice that the flow diagram consists of circles and rectangles called "nodes"—the numbers in the nodes are for reference. The arrow lines that connect these nodes are known as "arcs" or "branches." The circles which contain questions are "decision nodes." The rectangular shapes contain the goals of the diagram, and they signify conclusions. The arrow lines designate the direction of the diagram. Many of the nodes have branches leaving them, providing pathways to other nodes. The path taken from each node is determined by the response to the condition contained in the node's drawing. For

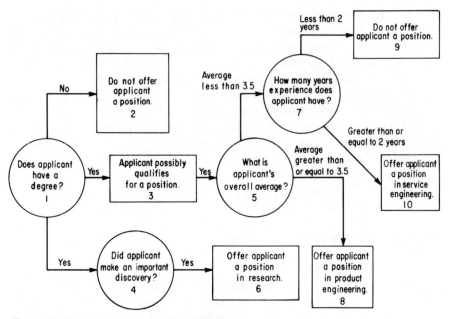

**Figure 6-1    Decision tree for offering job position.**

example, node 5, shown in Figure 6-2, asks a question which has two possible answers and therefore two possible paths depending on what the applicant's school average is. If the average is 3.1, path 1 will be taken since 3.1 is less than 3.5. The applicant's average can be considered a variable and its value the instantiation of that variable. Therefore, each circular node contains a variable, and the paths are conditions placed upon the values of that variable. When we establish rules for this domain, these conditions will become clauses of the IF portion of an IF-THEN rule. The rectangles are conclusions or subconclusions. For example, the rectangular box in Figure 6-3 would be an answer to the problem statement "should we offer applicant a job position?" Our goal would be to provide the answer. Likewise, the rectangular box in Figure 6-4 would be a goal of the problem statement, "Does applicant possibly qualify for a position?" But it could also be a part of a path leading to another conclusion since it has a branch leaving its node. In that case, since the branch is not a condition, that is, it does not depend on anything and we can only emerge from that rectangle along that one branch, it is called a "subconclusion" of another goal. A subconclusion is also a clause in an IF statement. We will see an example of this shortly.

Now that we have carefully and thoroughly diagrammed the prob-

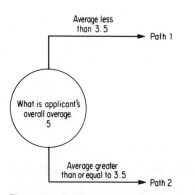

Figure 6-2   Decision node path determination.

Figure 6-3   A conclusion.

lem, we're ready for the next step, creating a knowledge base that is comprised of IF-THEN rules.

## Conversion to IF-THEN Rules

As we discussed in Chapter 2, IF-THEN rules are made up of two parts. The IF part is comprised of conditions called clauses connected to one another with words known as logical operators such as AND, OR, and NOT. The THEN part is evaluated only if the IF part is true. The combination of linked decision nodes (circles) and a conclusion node (rectangle) represents an IF-THEN rule. The IF part contains all the decision nodes in the path leading to a conclusion node; each decision node in the path leading to the conclusion contributes one clause to the IF portion. The conclusion itself forms the THEN portion. Figure 6-5 shows an example.

If we wish to determine if the applicant possibly qualifies for a position, node 3 is the conclusion. The only path leading to this conclusion

Figure 6-4   Another conclusion.

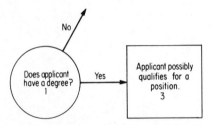

**Figure 6-5    Path of IF-THEN conversion.**

contains decision node 1, "Does applicant have a degree?" the rule that this path generates is

IF applicant has a degree = yes,
THEN applicant possibly qualifies for a position = yes

The clause "applicant has a degree" can have one of two values, namely, yes or no. Therefore, "applicant has a degree" is a variable. In fact, all the nodes contain variables.

Since it is too clumsy to refer to variables with such awkward, long names, we will give each node's variable a short, abbreviated name. Table 6-1 lists all the variable names in the nodes of the diagram in Figure 6-1, along with the variable's full meaning and the numbers of the nodes in which these variables can be found. These abbreviations will simply make creating our rules a little less cumbersome. We can use these simple variable names in the IF-THEN statements.

We are now ready to take a major step, generating all the rules for each of the possible conclusions. This is done according to the following technique.

1. Choose a conclusion (rectangular) node of the decision tree. Record it.

2. Choose a decision node with a connecting branch to the *left* of the node you chose in step 1. Record that node.

**Table 6-1    Variable Name Table**

| Variable name | Meaning | Node(s) |
|---|---|---|
| DEGREE | Does applicant have a degree? | 1 |
| DISCOVERY | Did applicant make an important discovery? | 4 |
| EXPERIENCE | How many years experience does applicant have? | 7 |
| GRADE | What is applicant's overall school average? | 5 |
| POSITION | What position should be offered to applicant? | 2, 6, 8, 9 ,10 |
| QUALIFY | Applicant possibly qualifies for a position. | 3 |

3. Continue doing step 2 until either there are no more nodes to the left or until a conclusion node is reached. If a conclusion (rectangular) node is reached, record it and stop. If there are no more nodes, stop.

4. Each decision node in the path is the variable part of an IF clause. The value associated with the branch is the condition. All connected clauses use the logical AND.

5. The conclusion becomes the THEN part.

### Rule Generating Technique

As an example, consider the path shown in Figure 6-6. Following the steps just outlined, we would make the following listing:

Conclusion node 6

Path 6, 4, 1

Remember, this is a backward chaining technique. We start with the conclusion and move backward through the decision tree.

From this listing and the variable name table we arrive at the following rule:

```
IF DEGREE = YES AND DISCOVERY = YES
THEN POSITION = RESEARCH
```

That is, if the applicant has a degree *and* has made an important discovery, he or she should be offered a position as a researcher.

We are now ready to apply these principles to develop our knowledge base. You can do the same for your domain area, keeping in mind simply that there should be one IF-THEN rule for every unique path to each goal. The IF-THEN rules for Figure 6-1 are written out in Table 6-2. The rule numbers themselves are arbitrary; they simply serve as an easy means of identification.

The six rules cover all the paths leading to every goal of the decision tree of Figure 6-1. Now you can see why the decision tree comes in

**Figure 6-6  A sample path.**

**Table 6-2  IF-THEN Rules**

| Rule | Path |
|---|---|
| 10  IF DEGREE = NO | 1, 2 |
|         THEN POSITION = NO | |
| 20  IF DEGREE = YES | 1,3 |
|         THEN QUALIFY = YES | |
| 30  IF DEGREE = YES AND DISCOVERY = YES | 1, 4, 6 |
|         THEN POSITION = RESEARCH | |
| 40  IF QUALIFY = YES AND AVERAGE < 3.5 AND EXPERIENCE | 3, 5, 7, 10 |
|         >= 2 | |
|         THEN POSITION = SERVICE ENGINEER | |
| 50  IF QUALIFY = YES AND AVERAGE < 3.5 AND EXPERIENCE | 3, 5, 7, 9 |
|         < 2 | |
|         THEN POSITION = NO | |
| 60  IF QUALIFY = YES AND AVERAGE >= 3.5 | 3, 5, 8 |
|         THEN POSITION = PRODUCT ENGINEER | |

handy—it provides a simple and expedient method for establishing the rules that comprise the knowledge base. Without the knowledge base we cannot go forward.

## Processing the Knowledge Base

Now we can implement our expert backward chaining techniques to answer questions based on our knowledge base. Technically, we can say that our knowledge base is used to lead us on a path toward reaching our conclusion. For example, if your path ended at conclusion node 9 of the decision tree, you will "not offer applicant a position." The conclusions contained in the decision (rectangular) nodes are equivalent to the variables contained in the THEN portion of the IF-THEN statements. The decision path we took to reach that conclusion provides an explanation of why we made it. In other words, the THEN portion represents a decision and the succession of IF clauses explains the reasoning.

Our expert technique requires construction of a number of useful tables, or data structures, that will aid in answering questions and making decisions about the problem we want to solve. These data structures are derived directly from the knowledge base, so they serve an indispensable purpose. The knowledge base with all its derived data structures is shown in Figure 6-7. When we have finally arrived at a way of solving this type of problem, we will be able to write a program to do the same thing in the same way.

Let's get on with the task of describing the algorithm and build some of the data structures that will help us along.

| RULE 10 | IF DEGREE = NO | | 1 POSITION | DEGREE | | 1 DEGREE |
|---|---|---|---|---|---|---|
| | THEN POSITION = NO | | 2 QUALIFY | DISCOVERY | | 2 |
| RULE 20 | IF DEGREE = YES | | 3 POSITION | EXPERIENCE | | 3 |
| | THEN QUALIFY = YES | | 4 POSITION | GRADE | | 4 |
| RULE 30 | IF DEGREE = YES AND | | 5 POSITION | | | 5 DEGREE |
| | DISCOVERY = YES | | 6 POSITION | | | 6 |
| | THEN POSITION = RESEARCH | | Conclusion list | Variable list | | 7 |
| RULE 40 | IF QUALIFY = YES AND | | | | | 8 |
| | GRADE < 3.5 AND | | | | | 9 DEGREE |
| | EXPERIENCE > = 2 | | | | | 10 DISCOVERY |
| | THEN POSITION = SERVICE ENGINEER | | | | | 11 |
| RULE 50 | IF QUALIFY = YES AND | | | | | 12 |
| | GRADE<3.5 AND | | | | | 13 QUALIFY |
| | EXPERIENCE <2 | | | | | 14 GRADE |
| | THEN POSITION = NO | | Top of stack | | | 15 EXPERIENCE |
| RULE 60 | IF QUALIFY = YES AND | | | | | 16 |
| | GRADE >= 3.5 | | | | | 17 QUALIFY |
| | THEN POSITION = PRODUCT ENGINEER | | | | | 18 GRADE |
| | | | Rule number  Clause number | | | 19 EXPERIENCE |
| | Knowledge | | | | | 20 |
| | base | | Conclusion stack | | | 21 QUALIFY |
| | | | | | | 22 GRADE |

Clause variable list

**Figure 6-7   The knowledge base and its derived data structures.**

## Conclusion List

The first data structure is the conclusion list which merely lists all the possible conclusions in sequential order. The conclusion list contains three items: first is a rule number, second is the conclusion associated with that rule number, and third is the set of conditions which yield the conclusion. There will be one entry for every IF-THEN rule in our knowledge base. The completed conclusion list for the rules in our knowledge base is shown in Figure 6-8. Let's see how these entries are determined by examining rule 10. The THEN portion of rule 10 contains the variable POSITION; POSITION is therefore the variable associated with the conclusion of rule 10. When the conclusion in the THEN portion of each rule is placed in the same row as its rule number, the conclusion list is complete.

| RULE 10 | IF DEGREE = NO | | **1 POSITION** |
|---|---|---|---|
| | THEN **POSITION** = NO | | **2 QUALIFY** |
| RULE 20 | IF DEGREE = YES | | **3 POSITION** |
| | THEN **QUALIFY** = YES | | **4 POSITION** |
| RULE 30 | IF DEGREE = YES AND | | **5 POSITION** |
| | DISCOVERY = YES | | **6 POSITION** |
| | THEN **POSITION** = RESEARCH | | |
| RULE 40 | IF QUALIFY = YES AND | | **Conclusion list** |
| | GRADE < 3.5 AND | | |
| | EXPERIENCE > = 2 | | |
| | THEN **POSITION** = SERVICE ENGINEER | | |
| RULE 50 | IF QUALIFY = YES AND | | |
| | GRADE < 3.5 AND | | |
| | EXPERIENCE < 2 | | |
| | THEN **POSITION** = NO | | |
| RULE 60 | IF QUALIFY = YES AND | | |
| | GRADE > = 3.5 | | |
| | THEN **POSITION** = PRODUCT ENGINEER | | |

Knowledge
base

**Figure 6-8   Conclusion list taken from THEN portion.**

This structure is used solely to locate a conclusion by its corresponding rule number. If the IF part of the rule is true, we invoke the THEN part, thereby instantiating the conclusion. For example, if we want to know if an applicant should be offered a position, we would scan the conclusion list until we found POSITION. This is found right away in the first entry, that is, rule 10, which is:    .

IF DEGREE = NO
THEN POSITION = NO

If DEGREE is instantiated to NO, we cannot offer the applicant a position. If DEGREE equals YES, we cannot invoke the THEN part because YES differs from the condition for this statement. Therefore we have to scan the list for another rule containing the conclusion POSITION. For now, we are getting a little ahead of overselves; let's describe the other structures we need, and then we will pull them all together.

## Variable List

The next structure we will discuss is the variable list. This structure also contains two items: one is a variable name for each variable contained in the IF part of the knowledge base rules, and the other item tells us whether or not the variable is instantiated. This list is shown in Figure 6-9. A variable only appears *once* in the list no matter how many condition clauses it appears in. It also cannot be a conclusion variable because the values of conclusion variables are determined by rules. The instantiated column is always initially set to not instantiated (NI). It will be changed to instantiated (I) as each variable is set

RULE 10  IF **DEGREE** = NO
              THEN POSITION = NO
RULE 20  IF **DEGREE** = YES
              THEN QUALIFY = YES
RULE 30  IF **DEGREE** = YES AND
              **DISCOVERY** = YES
              THEN POSITION = RESEARCH
RULE 40  IF QUALIFY = YES AND
              **GRADE** < 3.5 AND
              **EXPERIENCE** > = 2
              THEN POSITION = SERVICE ENGINEER
RULE 50  IF QUALIFY = YES AND
              **GRADE** < 3.5 AND
              **EXPERIENCE** < 2
              THEN POSITION = NO
RULE 60  IF QUALIFY = YES AND
              **GRADE** > = 3.5
              THEN POSITION = PRODUCT ENGINEER

Knowledge
base

|  | | Value |
|---|---|---|
| **DEGREE** | NI | |
| **DISCOVERY** | NI | |
| **EXPERIENCE** | NI | |
| **GRADE** | NI | |

Variable list

**Figure 6-9   Variable list.**

to a value, that is, as the applicant's qualifications are considered one by one. Before an IF-THEN statement can be executed, *all* the clause variables in the IF portion must be instantiated. If we are trying to execute an IF statement, we can see if any variable has already been instantiated by checking the variable list. If the variable is marked NI, the variable must first be instantiated. After the applicant has provided an answer and the variable is instantiated, we can set the instantiated value to I in the variable list. We are then in a position to compare the variable's value with the condition part of any clause containing the variable. Take rule 10 as an example:

IF DEGREE = NO
THEN POSITION = NO

Row 1 of the variable list contains DEGREE, which is not yet instantiated (NI). Therefore, the IF clause can't be executed. To instantiate DEGREE, we ask the applicant if he or she has a degree. The value of the answer, yes or no, which is stored in the variable, can then be compared with the condition part of the IF, that is,

IF DEGREE = NO

If DEGREE is instantiated to NO, the THEN part can be executed. In any case, after DEGREE is instantiated, NI is replaced with I in the DEGREE row of the variable list as follows:

| Variable name | Instantiated | Value |
|---|---|---|
| DEGREE | I | NO |

Now whenever the variable DEGREE is encountered in reference to any possible conclusion, it can be treated as having been instantiated in *any* clause of any IF-THEN statement. That is, once the applicant has answered the question, the answer will remain the same from that point on and will be available to other rules.

## Clause Variable List

An IF statement can contain one or more variables. In our system, we allocate room for up to four variables. The variables are connected by logical operators AND, OR, or NOT. In this section we will only consider the AND operator since that is the one used most frequently. For example, rule 30 contains two clauses which are connected by an AND, namely

IF DEGREE = YES AND DISCOVERY = YES

In addition, note that rule 40 contains three clauses, as does rule 50, and so on. The following concept is important:

> If all the clauses in the IF part of a rule are connected by the logical operator AND, all the variables in these clauses must be instantiated before the IF part can be executed.

For example, using rule 30,

    30  IF DEGREE = YES AND DISCOVERY = YES
        THEN POSITION = RESEARCH

you must have a value for both DEGREE and DISCOVERY before you can determine if the THEN part should be executed. You should therefore assemble a list of variables for the IF part of each IF-THEN rule. First, check each variable for instantiation in the variable list. Instantiate those that aren't and then execute the IF-THEN rule. The data structure containing the list of variables for each IF part of IF-THEN rules is called the clause variable list. The clause variable list for the six rules of our knowledge base is shown in Figure 6-10. To simplify the programming of the examples, each rule is allocated room for no more than four IF variables. The numbers, 1 through 22, shown to the left of the variable names represent the array location in the data structure that the variable names are placed in. If a rule does not utilize all of these four locations, they are left blank. Of course this number can always be increased beyond four with additional programming. There is a good reason for allocating the same number of loca-

```
RULE 10  IF DEGREE = NO                          1 DEGREE
         THEN POSITION = NO                       2
RULE 20  IF DEGREE = YES                          3
         THEN QUALIFY = YES                       4
RULE 30  IF DEGREE = YES AND                      5 DEGREE
            DISCOVERY = YES                       6
         THEN POSITION = RESEARCH                 7
RULE 40  IF QUALIFY = YES AND                     8
            GRADE < 3.5 AND                       9 DEGREE
            EXPERIENCE > = 2                      10 DISCOVERY
         THEN POSITION = SERVICE ENGINEER         11
RULE 50  IF QUALIFY = YES AND                     12
            GRADE < 3.5 AND                       13 QUALIFY
            EXPERIENCE < 2                        14 GRADE
         THEN POSITION = NO                       15 EXPERIENCE
RULE 60  IF QUALIFY = YES AND                     16
            GRADE > = 3.5 AND                     17 QUALIFY
         THEN POSITION = PRODUCT ENGINEER         18 GRADE
                                                  19 EXPERIENCE
              Knowledge                           20
                base                              21 QUALIFY
                                                  22 GRADE

                                                  Clause variable list
```

Figure 6-10   Clause variable list.

tions to each rule: The row number at the start of an IF-THEN rule can then be determined by a simple multiplication formula:

4 * (STATEMENT NUMBER / 10 − 1) + 1

For example, rule 50 starts at location 17:

4 * (50 / 10 − 1) + 1 = 17

Let's take a moment to review the three structures we've just designed. As we said in the chapter on forward chaining, these data structures relate specifically to thought processes you might go through when trying to solve a problem. The same is said for backward chaining. First you consider all the possible pathways that would lead to a conclusion (conclusion list). Then, you map out the conditions that constitute those various pathways (variable list and clause variable list). Because variable values often apply to more than one possible conclusion in a given situation, the data structures enable us to manage this information quickly and without repeating the same steps over and over. In other words, if you were considering hiring an applicant and you not only didn't have access to a computer but didn't even have a pencil and a piece of paper, you would probably have to review the same facts several times because they're simply too complicated to keep in one's head at one time. You could do it, of course, but it would just be harder and would take a lot longer.

## Conclusion Stack

The fourth and last structure we will discuss is the conclusion stack. The conclusion stack is the central structure: It ties together all of the other structures we've discussed in the implementation of the backward chaining expert system tool. It is the conclusion stack that tells us which IF-THEN statement contains the conclusion we are trying to reach and which clause in the IF portion is being examined for instantiation.

In order to understand the conclusion stack, let's backtrack a second to the following rule again:

```
40   IF QUALIFY = YES AND      IF clause 1
        GRADE < 3.5      AND      IF clause 2
        EXPERIENCE > = 2        IF clause 3
     THEN POSITION = SERVICE ENGINEERING
```

This rule has three IF clauses, which are numbered 1 to 3, and one THEN clause. In order to evaluate the rule to see if we should invoke the THEN clause, we must examine each IF clause one at a time. If all the IF clauses are true, we can invoke the THEN clause which directs us to offer the applicant a position in service engineering. If any of the IF clauses are false, we must discard this rule. Let's see how we can keep track of the rule by its number and keep track of each clause as it is examined. The conclusion stack data structure will help us do this, as shown in Figure 6-11. We see from this figure that we are examining rule 40 and its clause 1. This tells us that we are examining

QUALIFY = YES

But the value of QUALIFY is determined by rule 20 which is

IF DEGREE = YES      (IF clause 1)
THEN QUALIFY = YES

Therefore we must now examine rule 20 to determine the value of QUALIFY. We place rule 20 on top of the conclusion stack as shown in Figure 6-12. The clause number tells us to look at clause 1 of rule 20 which is

DEGREE = YES

DEGREE will be instantiated to a value of YES or NO by the applicant. Since there are no more IF clauses in rule 20, we can instantiate QUALIFY to YES only if DEGREE = YES. Assume the applicant has a degree (DEGREE = YES); then QUALIFY = YES. Now that we are finished with rule 20, we can remove it from the stack. Since QUALIFY = YES, we are now finished with clause 1 of rule 40 and next must examine clause 2, as shown in Figure 6-13. This interaction of the

Figure 6-11  Conclusion stack.

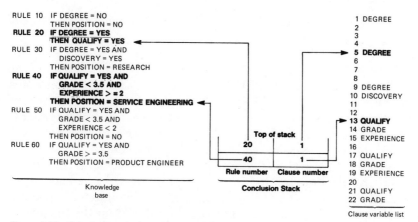

**Figure 6-12** Conclusion stack compares additional rule.

conclusion stack with the knowledge base continues throughout the backward chaining process.

In review, the conclusion stack is the place for keeping track of which rule and which clause within that rule we are trying to verify.

## An Example Using the Knowledge Base

In order to pull all these concepts together, let's examine a typical request to our expert system tool from start to finish. A user will first enter a conclusion that the system can verify. For this example, it is

Should applicant be offered a position?

**Figure 6-13** Conclusion stack advances.

The conclusion variable, taken from the variable name table, is

POSITION

The tool will place on the top of the conclusion stack the number of the next rule that contains POSITION as a conclusion variable. Since this is the first time POSITION has been encountered, we search the conclusion list starting with rule 10. We immediately find POSITION is the conclusion variable of rule 10. Therefore, the conclusion stack will initially contain one item and look like Figure 6-14.

By looking at the clause variable list, we see that the number 1 variable in rule 10 is DEGREE. By scanning the variable list, we see DEGREE is not yet instantiated, that is, it is designated NI. Since DEGREE is also *not* a conclusion variable, it is not on the conclusion list, and the applicant must instantiate it with the following question:

Does applicant have a degree?

The answer—let's say it is yes—causes a change in the variable list as shown in Figure 6-15.

This answer makes rule 10,

10   IF DEGREE = NO
     THEN POSITION = NO

false since DEGREE = YES. We must now remove the false conclusion from the conclusion stack and scan the condition list for the next use of POSITION as a conclusion variable. This is found in rule 30 which is

30   IF DEGREE = YES AND DISCOVERY = YES
     THEN POSITION = RESEARCH

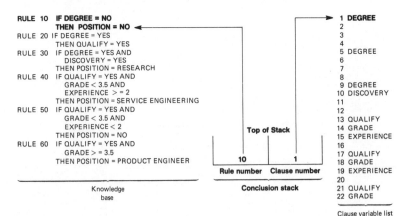

**Figure 6-14    Initial conclusion stack.**

RULE 10   IF **DEGREE** = NO
          THEN POSITION = NO
RULE 20   IF **DEGREE** = YES
          THEN QUALIFY = YES
RULE 30   IF **DEGREE** = YES AND
          **DISCOVERY** = YES
          THEN POSITION = RESEARCH
RULE 40   IF QUALIFY = YES AND
          **GRADE** < 3.5 AND
          **EXPERIENCE** > = 2
          THEN POSITION = SERVICE ENGINEER
RULE 50   IF QUALIFY = YES AND
          **GRADE** < 3.5 AND
          **EXPERIENCE** < 2
          THEN POSITION = NO
RULE 60   IF QUALIFY = YES AND
          **GRADE** > = 3.5
          THEN POSITION = PRODUCT ENGINEER

Knowledge
base

|  |  | Value |
|---|---|---|
| **DEGREE** | I | YES |
| **DISCOVERY** | NI |  |
| **EXPERIENCE** | NI |  |
| **GRADE** | NI |  |

Variable list

**Figure 6-15   Updated variable list.**

We would place rule 30 on top of the conclusion stack as shown in Figure 6-16.

We will now try to instantiate all the condition variables in rule 30, as shown in the clause variable list in Figure 6-17. The clause number of the conclusion stack points to DEGREE in the clause variable list, which we see has already been instantiated (I) in the variable list. Therefore the clause number is incremented to 2, pointing to DISCOVERY in the clause variable list. The updated stack is shown in Figure 6-18.

From the variable list we see DISCOVERY is not instantiated (NI) and is not a conclusion since it is not on the conclusion list. We therefore ask the applicant

Did applicant make an important discovery?

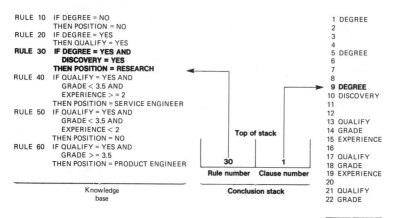

**Figure 6-16   Stack operation.**

```
RULE 10   IF DEGREE = NO                              1 DEGREE
          THEN POSITION = NO                          2
RULE 20   IF DEGREE = YES                             3
          THEN QUALIFY = YES                          4
RULE 30   IF DEGREE = YES AND                         5 DEGREE
          DISCOVERY = RESEARCH                        6
          THEN POSITION = YES                         7
RULE 40   IF QUALIFY = YES AND                        8
          GRADE < 3.5 AND                             9 DEGREE
          EXPERIENCE > = 2                           10 DISCOVERY
          THEN POSITION = SERVICE ENGINEER           11
RULE 50   IF QUALIFY = YES AND                       12
          GRADE < 3.5 AND                            13 QUALIFY
          EXPERIENCE < 2                             14 GRADE
          THEN POSITION = NO                         15 EXPERIENCE
RULE 60   IF QUALIFY = YES AND                       16
          GRADE > = 3.5                              17 QUALIFY
          THEN POSITION = PRODUCT ENGINEER           18 GRADE
                                                     19 EXPERIENCE
                                                     20
                     Knowledge                       21 QUALIFY
                       base                          22 GRADE
```

Clause variable list

**Figure 6-17    Clause variable list snapshot.**

to which, let's say, the answer is no. Since DISCOVERY is now instantiated to NO, we can update the variable list as shown in Figure 6-19.

Now that the first two variables have been instantiated, the clause number of the conclusion stack is updated to 3. Since there is no variable in location 3 of rule 30 in the clause variable list, all of the variables for rule 30 have evidently been instantiated. We are ready to execute the IF-THEN rule,

    30   IF DEGREE = YES AND DISCOVERY = YES
         THEN POSITION = YES

The second clause of rule 30 is false because DISCOVERY has been instantiated to NO. We therefore remove rule 30 from the top of the

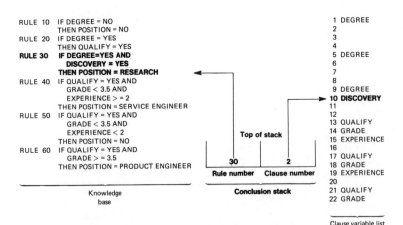

**Figure 6-18    Further updated conclusion stack.**

RULE 10  IF **DEGREE** = NO
THEN POSITION = NO
RULE 20  IF **DEGREE** = YES
THEN QUALIFY = YES
RULE 30  IF **DEGREE** = YES AND
**DISCOVERY** = RESEARCH
THEN POSITION = YES
RULE 40  IF QUALIFY = YES AND
**GRADE** < 3.5 AND
**EXPERIENCE** > = 2
THEN POSITION = SERVICE ENGINEER
RULE 50  IF QUALIFY = YES AND
**GRADE** < 3.5 AND
**EXPERIENCE** < 2
THEN POSITION = NO
RULE 60  IF QUALIFY = YES AND
**GRADE** > = 3.5
THEN POSITION = PRODUCT ENGINEER

Knowledge base

|  |  | Value |
|---|---|---|
| DEGREE | I | YES |
| DISCOVERY | I | NO |
| EXPERIENCE | NI | |
| GRADE | NI | |

Variable list

**Figure 6-19  Variable list.**

conclusion stack. Searching the remainder of the conclusion list, we see that POSITION is also a conclusion variable of rule 40 which is

40  IF QUALIFY = YES AND GRADE < 3.5 AND
EXPERIENCE > = 2
THEN POSITION = SERVICE ENGINEER

We place rule 40 on the conclusion stack as shown in Figure 6-20.

The first clause of rule 40 is QUALIFY. Since QUALIFY has not been instantiated in the variable list and is also in the conclusion list, we find QUALIFY to be a conclusion variable of rule 20. We place a new unit on top of the conclusion stack as shown in Figure 6-21. Rule 20's first and only clause variable is DEGREE. Since DEGREE has

**Figure 6-20  Latest conclusion stack.**

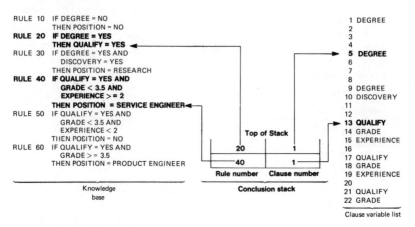

Figure 6-21    Multiunit conclusion stack.

already been instantiated to YES, as shown in the variable list, we can go ahead and execute rule 20

20   IF DEGREE = YES
     THEN QUALIFY = YES

which causes the THEN part to be invoked and QUALIFY to be instantiated to YES. Since QUALIFY is now instantiated, we can remove its unit from the top of the stack and get back to rule 40. The clause number for the unit on top of the stack is incremented to 2 as shown in Figure 6-22.

Since the variable GRADE of rule 40 is not on the conclusion list, it has not yet been instantiated and the applicant is asked

What is your average grade?

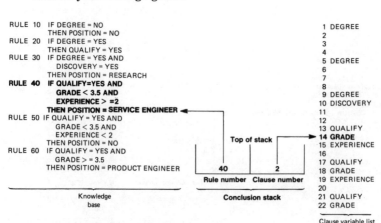

Figure 6-22    Updated conclusion stack.

**Figure 6-23   Example status.**

The applicant answers 3.0, which instantiates GRADE. The clause number is incremented to 3 and the conclusion stack and variable list as they look now are shown in Figure 6-23.

EXPERIENCE, the third clause, has still not been instantiated and is not a conclusion variable. Therefore, the applicant is asked the question

How many years experience do you have?

The reply, 4.5, instantiates EXPERIENCE, causing the variable list to change to an I and the clause number to be incremented to 4. Since there are no more variables in the clause variable list for rule 40, the IF part can now be executed. Since

QUALIFY = YES
GRADE = 3.0
EXPERIENCE $>= 2$

when rule 40's IF clause

IF QUALIFY = YES AND GRADE $< 3.5$ AND EXP $>= 2$

is executed, we find it true, POSITION is instantiated to SERVICE ENGINEERING, because of the THEN part:

THEN POSITION = SERVICE ENGINEERING

This is the moment we have been waiting for. The goal has been reached. We can offer the applicant a position in the service engineering department.

## Concepts for Design Implementation

Let us review the steps we have taken to implement the backward chaining structure:

1. Identify the conclusion.

2. Search the conclusion list for the first instance of the conclusion's name. If found, place the rule on the conclusion stack using the rule number and a (1) to represent the clause number. If not found, notify the user that an answer cannot be found.

3. Instantiate the IF clause (i.e., each condition variable) of the statement.

4. If one of the IF clause variables is not instantiated, as indicated by the variable list, and is not a conclusion variable, that is, not on the conclusion list, ask the user to enter a value.

5. If one of the clauses is a conclusion variable, place the conclusion variable's rule number on the top of the stack and go back to step 3.

6. If the statement on top of the stack cannot be instantiated using the present IF-THEN statement, remove the unit from the top of the stack and search the conclusion list for another instance of that conclusion variable's name.

7. If such a statement is found, go back to step 3.

8. If there are no more conclusions left on the conclusion stack with that name, the rule for the previous conclusion is false. If there is no previous conclusion, then notify the user that an answer cannot be found. If there is a previous conclusion, go back to step 6.

9. If the rule on top of the stack can be instantiated, remove it from the stack. If another conclusion variable is underneath, increment the clause number, and for the remaining clauses go back to step 3. If no other conclusion variable is underneath, we have answered our question. The user can come to a conclusion.

## The Tool Itself

We can use the above concepts to design, in BASIC, our expert system tool. We can insert a set of IF-THEN rules into its knowledge base and use it to answer our questions. So put away your pencil and paper and run the program in Listing 6-1. It will solidify your understanding of all the concepts we have covered.

## Programming Applications

In this part of the chapter we will supply you with a backward chaining tool for you to apply to your knowledge base. This tool will allow you to insert a set of rules into statements 1500 through 1680 of the program, type RUN, and obtain answers from your knowledge base.

### Program Explanation

As an example to acquaint you with the way the program is used, we have inserted the rules for determining if we should give an applicant a position in our company. This is the same example we used to explain the backward chaining concepts. For example, the rule

    IF DEGREE = NO
    THEN POSITION = NO

is covered by statement numbers 1500 through 1510. The rule

    IF (QUALIFY = YES) AND (GRADE < 3.5) AND
    (EXPERIENCE >= 2)
    THEN POSITION = SERVICE ENGINEERING

is covered by statement numbers 1560 through 1570.

Each variable in the variable list (V$) is found in one of the condition clauses (the IF part) but is not a conclusion variable (the THEN part). The variable list is constructed in statement 367. Each of these variables must be instantiated by the backward chaining system. This is done in statements 1700 through 1715. The order in which the variables are placed is determined by the order in statement 367. The conclusion list is constructed in statement 305. The clause variable list is constructed in statements 407 through 409.

### Program Listing

Listing 6-1 is followed by a sequence of sample runs. Note that the system responses have been abbreviated. For example, PO = RE-SEARCH (or SERVICE ENGINEERING or PRODUCT ENGINEERING) means "offer the applicant a position in that department"; PO = NO means "do not offer applicant a position"; QU = YES means "the applicant is qualified but we're not sure as yet for what."

## Listing 6-1  Backward chaining.

```
1 REM ****************** BACKWARD CHAINING *******************
10 REM INSTALL YOUR IF CLAUSES IN SEQUENCE AT LOCATIONS 1500,1520,..,1540
20 REM FORMAT EXAMPLE 1500 IF (A1=2) AND (A2=6) OR (A3$="YES") THEN S=1
22 REM                  1502 RETURN
30 REM                  1520 IF (J$="NO") THEN S=1
32 REM                  1522 RETURN
40 REM  THE THEN PART OF THE ABOVE CONSTRUCTION ALWAYS CONTAINS, THEN S=1
50 REM INSTALL YOUR THEN CLAUSES IN SEQUENCE IN STATEMENTS 1510,1530,..,1550
60 REM FORMAT EXAMPLE 1510 PO="YES"..FOLOWED BY A RETURN STATEMENT
200 REM *********** INITIALIZATION SECTION *************
210 REM CONCLUSION LIST (GL$), VARIABLE LIST (V$), INSTANTIATED LIST (IN)
220 REM CONCLUSION STACK INCLUDES STATEMENT STACK (SS) AND CLAUSE STACK (CS)
230 REM  CLAUSE VARIABLE LIST (CV$) AND STACK POINTER (SP)
240 DIM GL$(10),V$(10),CV$(40),IN(10),SS(10),CS(10)
250 SP=11 :REM STACK SPACE IS 10 WE INITIALLY PLACE SP AT 10+1
260 FOR I=1 TO 10
270 GL$(I)="": V$(I)="": IN(I)=0: SS(I)=0: CS(I)=0
280 NEXT I
290 REM ENTER CONCLUSIONS WHICH ARE THE VARIABLES IN THE THEN PART, 1 AT A TIME
295 REM ENTER THE CONCLUSIONS IN EXACT ORDER STARTING AT THE 1ST IF-THEN.
300 REM AFTER LAST CONCLUSION JUST HIT RETURN KEY FOR REST OF CONCLUSIONS
305 GL$(1)="PO":GL$(2)="QU":GL$(3)="PO":GL$(4)="PO":GL$(5)="PO"
306 GL$(6)="PO"
307 PRINT"*** CONCLUSION LIST ***"
310 FOR I=1 TO 10
320 PRINT"CONCLUSION ";I;
325 PRINT GL$(I)
335 NEXT I
338 INPUT"HIT RETURN TO CONTINUE";Z
340 REM ENTER VARIABLES WHICH ARE IN THE IF PART, 1 AT A TIME IN THE
350 REM EXACT ORDER THAT THEY OCCUR. UP TO 3 VARIABLES PER IF STATEMENT.
360 REM DO NOT DUPLICATE ANY VARIABLES NAMES. ANY NAME IS USED ONLY ONCE
365 REM IF NO MORE VARIABLES LEFT, JUST HIT RETURN KEY.
366 PRINT"*** VARIABLE LIST ***"
367 V$(1)="DE":V$(2)="DI":V$(3)="EX":V$(4)="GR"
370 FOR I=1 TO 10
380 PRINT"VARIABLE ";I;
385 PRINT V$(I)
395 NEXT I
396 INPUT"HIT RETURN TO CONTINUE";I
400 REM ENTER VARIABLES AS THEY APPEAR IN THE IF CLAUSES. A MAXIMUM OF 3
405 REM VARIABLES PER IF STATEMENT. IF NO MORE VARIABLES HIT RETURN KEY
406 PRINT"*** CLAUSE-VARIABLE LIST ***"
407 CV$(1)="DE":CV$(5)="DE":CV$(9)="DE":CV$(10)="DI":CV$(13)="QU"
408 CV$(14)="GR":CV$(15)="EX":CV$(17)="QU":CV$(18)="GR"
409 CV$(19)="EX":CV$(21)="QU":CV$(22)="GR"
410 FOR I=1 TO 8:PRINT"** CLAUSE ";I
420 FOR J=1 TO 4:PRINT"VARIABLE ";J;
423 K=4*(I-1)+J
424 PRINT CV$(K)
430 NEXT J
432 IF I=4 THEN INPUT"HIT RETURN TO CONTINUE";Z
435 NEXT I
500 REM ********************** INFERENCE SECTION ***************************
505 INPUT"** ENTER THE CONCLUSION ";V$
510 REM GET CONCLUSION STATEMENT NUMBER (SN) FROM THE CONCLUSION LIST (GL$)
520 F=1:GOSUB 2200: REM 1ST STATEMENT STARTS SEARCH
525 IF SN=0 THEN STOP: REM NO CONCLUSION OF THAT NAME
530 REM PUSH STATEMENT NUMBER (SN) AND CLAUSE NUMBER=1 ON GOAL STACK WHICH
535 REM  IS COMPOSED OF THE STATEMENT STACK (SS) AND CLAUSE STACK (CS)
540 GOSUB 2000
545 REM CALCULATE CLAUSE LOCATION IN CLAUSE-VARIABLE LIST
550 I=(SS(SP)-1)*4+CS(SP)
555 V$=CV$(I): REM CLAUSE VARIABLE
560 REM IS THIS THE LAST CLAUSE FOR THIS STATEMENT?
565 IF V$="" THEN GOTO 580 :REM LAST CLAUSE PROCESS IF-THEN STATEMENT
567 REM IS THIS CLAUSE VARIABLE A CONCLUSION?
568 F=1:GOSUB 2200:IF SN<>0 THEN GOTO 520 :IT IS A CONCLUSION PUSH IT
570 GOSUB 2400: REM CHECK INSTANTIATION OF THIS CLAUSE
575 CS(SP)=CS(SP)+1 : REM CHECK NEXT CLAUSE
580 REM NO MORE CLAUSES CHECK IF PART OF STATEMENT
582 SN=SS(SP)
585 S=0: ON SN GOSUB 1500,1520,1540,1560,1580,1600
590 REM SEE IF THE THEN PART SHOULD BE INVOKED I.E. S=1
600 IF S=1 THEN GOTO 630 :REM INVOKE THEN PART
605 REM FAILED..SEARCH REST OF STATEMENTS FOR THE SAME CONCLUSION
610 I=SS(SP): V$=GL$(I): REM GET CONCLUSION
615 F=SS(SP)+1 :REM SEARCH FOR CONCLUSION STARTING AT THE NEXT STATEMENT NUMBER
620 GOSUB 2200
```

```
625 SP=SP+1:GOTO 525:REM POP OLD CONCLUSION AND PUT ON NEW ONE
630 REM IF PART TRUE INVOKE THE THEN PART
635 ON SN GOSUB 1510,1530,1550,1570,1590,1610
650 REM POP THE STACK..IF IT REACHED THE INITIAL POINT WE HAD OUR SUCCESS
655 REM   IF NOT JUST KEEP GOING TO VERIFY THE OLD CONCLUSION
660 SP=SP+1:REM POP THE STACK
670 IF SP < 11 THEN GOTO 690 :REM STACK IS NOT EMPTY
680 PRINT"*** SUCCESS": REM FINISHED
685 STOP
690 REM STACK NOT EMPTY GET NEXT CLAUSE THEN CONTINUE
695 CS(SP)=CS(SP)+1
700 GOTO 545
1490 REM ********** IF-THEN STATEMENT STARTING AT 1500 *******************
1492 REM SAMPLE IF-THEN STATEMENTS FROM THE POSITION KNOWLEDGE BASE
1494 REM   ONLY THE FIRST TWO LETTERS OF EACH VARIABLE IS USED TO MAKE
1496 REM   THE EXAMPLE COMPATIBLE WITH SOME VERSIONS OF BASIC. FOR EXAMPLE
1498 REM DEG WAS SHORTENED TO DE AND QUAL TO QU
1499 REM ** STATEMENT 1
1500 IF DE$="NO" THEN S=1
1502 RETURN
1510 PO$="NO":PRINT"PO=NO":RETURN
1519 REM ** STATEMENT 2
1520 IF DE$="YES" THEN S=1
1522 RETURN
1530 QU$="YES":PRINT"QU=YES" :RETURN
1539 REM ** STATEMENT 3
1540 IF (DE$="YES") AND (DI$="YES") THEN S=1
1542 RETURN
1550 PO$="YES":PRINT"PO=RESEARCH" :RETURN
1559 REM ** STATEMENT 4
1560 IF (QU$="YES") AND (GR < 3.5) AND (EX >= 2) THEN S=1
1562 RETURN
1570 PO$="YES":PRINT"PO=SERVICE ENGINEER" :RETURN
1579 REM ** STATEMENT 5
1580 IF (QU$="YES") AND (GR<3.5) AND (EX<2) THEN S=1
1582 RETURN
1590 PO$="NO":PRINT"PO=NO" :RETURN
1599 REM ** STATEMENT 6
1600 IF (QU$="YES") AND (GR>=3.5) THEN S=1
1602 RETURN
1610 PO$="YES":PRINT"PO=PRODUCT ENGINEER" :RETURN
1611 REM ****** END OF POSITION KNOWLEDGE BASE ***********
1690 REM ********** INPUT STATEMENTS STARTING AT 1700 *******************
1699 REM **** INPUT STATEMENTS FOR SAMPLE POSITION KNOWLEDGE BASE
1700 INPUT"INPUT YES OR NO FOR DE-";DE$ :RETURN
1705 INPUT"INPUT YES OR NO FOR DI-";DI$: RETURN
1710 INPUT"INPUT A REAL NUMBER FOR EX-";EX: RETURN
1715 INPUT"INPUT A REAL NUMBER FOR GR-";GR: RETURN
1750 REM ****** END OF INPUT STATEMENTS FOR THE POSITION KNOWLEDGE BASE **
1999 REM ******************** SUBROUTINE SECTION **************************
2000 REM ROUTINE TO PUSH STATEMENT NUMBER (SN) AND A CLAUSE NUMBER OF 1
2002 REM   ONTO THE CONCLUSION STACK WHICH CONSISTS OF THE STATEMENT STACK (SS)
2004 REM   AND THE CLAUSE STACK (CS).....TO PUSH DECREMENT STACK POINTER (SP)
2020 SP=SP-1: SS(SP)=SN: CS(SP)=1
2030 RETURN
2099 REM ***************************************************************
2200 REM ROUTINE TO DETERMINE IF A VARIABLE (V$) IS A MEMBER OF THE CONCLUSION
     LIST
2202 REM   (GL$). IF YES RETURN SN<>0. IF NOT A MEMBER SN=0.
2220 SN=0:REM INITIALLY SET TO NOT A MEMBER
2230 FOR I=F TO 8 :REM MEMBER OF CONCLUSION LIST TO BE SEARCHED IS F
2240 IF V$= GL$(I) THEN GOTO 2270: REM TEST FOR MEMBERSHIP
2250 NEXT I
2260 RETURN: REM NOT A MEMBER
2270 SN=I:REM A MEMBER
2280 RETURN
2299 REM ***************************************************************
2400 REM ROUTINE TO INSTANTIATE A VARIABLE (V$) IF IT ISN'T ALREADY. THE
2402 REM   INSTANTIATE INDICATION (IN) IS A 0 IF NOT, A 1 IF IT IS. THE
2404 REM   VARIABLE LIST (VL$) CONTAINS THE VARIABLE (V$)
2420 FOR I=1 TO 10: REM FIND VARIABLE IN THE LIST
2430 IF V$=V$(I) THEN GOTO 2445: REM FOUND VARIABLE IN LIST
2440 NEXT I
2445 IF IN(I)=1 THEN RETURN: REM ALREADY INSTANTIATED
2450 IF IN(I)=1 THEN RETURN: REM ALREADY INSTANTIATED
2460 REM THE DESIGNER OF THIS KNOWLEDGE BASE PLACES THE INPUT STATEMENTS
2462 REM   TO INSTANTIATE THE VARIABLES STARTING AT LOCATION 1700
2464 REM FORMAT IS INPUT STATEMENT FOLLOWED BY A RETURN STATEMENT
2465 IN(I)=1:REM MARK INSTANTIATED
2470 ON I GOSUB 1700,1705,1710,1715
2480 RETURN
```

## Sample Runs

Let's see how the program works in giving us answers. When we enter RUN, the following happens:

```
RUN
***  CONCLUSION LIST  ***
CONCLUSION  1 PO
CONCLUSION  2 QU
CONCLUSION  3 PO
CONCLUSION  4 PO
CONCLUSION  5 PO
CONCLUSION  6 PO
CONCLUSION  7
CONCLUSION  8
CONCLUSION  9
CONCLUSION  10
HIT RETURN TO CONTINUE?

***  VARIABLE LIST  ***
VARIABLE  1 DE
VARIABLE  2 DI
VARIABLE  3 EX
VARIABLE  4 GR
VARIABLE  5
VARIABLE  6
VARIABLE  7
VARIABLE  8
VARIABLE  9
VARIABLE  10
HIT RETURN TO CONTINUE?

***  CLAUSE-VARIABLE LIST  ***
**  CLAUSE  1
VARIABLE  1 DE
VARIABLE  2
VARIABLE  3
VARIABLE  4
**  CLAUSE  2
VARIABLE  1 DE
VARIABLE  2
VARIABLE  3
VARIABLE  4
**  CLAUSE  3
VARIABLE  1 DE
VARIABLE  2 DI
VARIABLE  3
VARIABLE  4
**  CLAUSE  4
VARIABLE  1 QU
VARIABLE  2 GR
VARIABLE  3 EX
VARIABLE  4
HIT RETURN TO CONTINUE?

**  CLAUSE  5
VARIABLE  1 QU
VARIABLE  2 GR
VARIABLE  3 EX
VARIABLE  4
```

```
**  CLAUSE   6
VARIABLE   1 QU
VARIABLE   2 GR
VARIABLE   3
VARIABLE   4
**  CLAUSE   7
VARIABLE   1
VARIABLE   2
VARIABLE   3
VARIABLE   4
**  CLAUSE   8
VARIABLE   1
VARIABLE   2
VARIABLE   3
VARIABLE   4
```

The preceding printout appears with each of the following runs:

Run 1

```
**  ENTER THE CONCLUSION ? PO
INPUT YES OR NO FOR DE-? NO
PO=NO
***  SUCCESS
Break in 685
Ok
```

Run 2

```
**  ENTER THE CONCLUSION ? PO
INPUT YES OR NO FOR DE-? YES
INPUT YES OR NO FOR DI-? NO
QU=YES
INPUT A REAL NUMBER FOR GR-? 3.0
INPUT A REAL NUMBER FOR EX-? 2.8
PO=SERVICE ENGINEER
***  SUCCESS
Break in 685
Ok
```

Run 3

```
**  ENTER THE CONCLUSION ? PO
INPUT YES OR NO FOR DE-? YES
INPUT YES OR NO FOR DI-? NO
QU=YES
INPUT A REAL NUMBER FOR GR-? 2.0
INPUT A REAL NUMBER FOR EX-? 4.0
PO=SERVICE ENGINEER
***  SUCCESS
Break in 685
Ok
```

Run 4

```
**  ENTER THE CONCLUSION ? QU
INPUT YES OR NO FOR DE-? NO
Break in 525
Ok
```

In this run, there is no rule with QU as a conclusion for the condition DE = NO.

Run 5
```
**  ENTER THE CONCLUSION ? QU
INPUT YES OR NO FOR DE-? YES
QU=YES
***  SUCCESS
Break in 685
Ok
```

## Backward Chaining Worksheet

The following worksheet is an aid to simplifying the process of placing a new knowledge base into the program to replace the one that is there now. This is included to allow the reader to validate the concepts of the relationship between the knowledge base and expert system data structures. As a future exercise, the reader can develop an input compiler which reads a knowledge base and makes transfers to the data structures automatically. The reader should do this only after understanding the concepts fully.

This worksheet will help you create and transfer the variables and values of your knowledge base into the program (it allows for *three* condition variables per rule). First create the rules for the IF-THEN statements below. Then transfer them to the worksheets that follow.

IF _____ = _____   AND
Variable 31                  Value 31

_____ = _____   AND
Variable 32                  Value 32

_____ = _____
Variable 33                  Value 33

THEN _____ = _____
Variable 34                  Value 34

IF _____ = _____   AND
Variable 41                  Value 41

_____ = _____   AND
Variable 42                  Value 42

_____ = _____
Variable 43                  Value 43

THEN _____ = _____
Variable 44                  Value 44

IF _____ = _____   AND
Variable 51                  Value 51

_____ = _____   AND
Variable 52                  Value 52

_____ = _____
Variable 53                  Value 53

THEN _____ = _____
Variable 54                  Value 54

This worksheet inserts variables into the clause variable list (statements 407 through 409).

CV\$(1) = _____
Variable 11

CV\$(2) = _____
Variable 12

CV\$(3) = _____
Variable 13

CV\$(5) = _____
Variable 21

CV$(6)  = _____
Variable 22

CV$(7)  = _____
Variable 23

CV$(9)  = _____
Variable 31

CV$(10) = _____
Variable 32

CV$(11) = _____
Variable 33

CV$(13) = _____
Variable 41

CV$(14) = _____
Variable 42

CV$(15) = _____
Variable 43

CV$(17) = _____
Variable 51

CV$(18) = _____
Variable 52

CV$(19) = _____
Variable 53

Use this worksheet to insert variables into the variable list (statement 367). Do not insert a variable name more than once.

V$(1)  = _____
Variable _____

V$(2)  = _____
Variable _____

V$(3)  = _____
Variable _____

V$(4)  = _____
Variable _____

V$(5)  = _____
Variable _____

Use this worksheet to insert variables into the conclusion list (statements 305 and 306).

GL\$(1) = _____
<br>Variable 14

GL\$(2) = _____
<br>Variable 24

GL\$(3) = _____
<br>Variable 34

GL\$(4) = _____
<br>Variable 44

GL\$(5) = _____
<br>Variable 54

This worksheet is used to insert the IF-THEN rules (see statements 1490 through 1611) into the program.

**IF Rules**

1560  IF _____$ = "_____"  AND
         Variable 41              Value 41

      _____$ = "_____"  AND
         Variable 42              Value 42

      _____$ = "_____"  THEN S = 1
         Variable 43              Value 43

1580  IF _____$ = "_____"  AND
         Variable 51              Value 51

      _____$ = "_____"  AND
         Variable 52              Value 52

      _____$ = "_____"  THEN S = 1
         Variable 53              Value 53

## THEN Portion

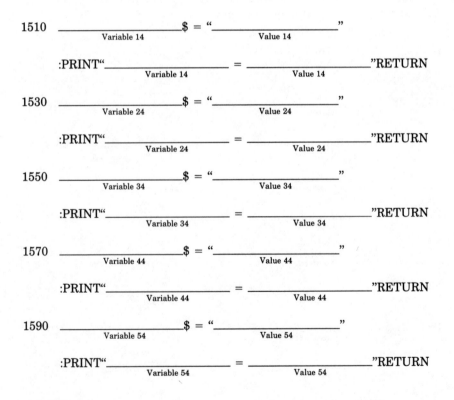

1510  _____$ = "_____"
         Variable 14              Value 14

      :PRINT"_____ = _____"RETURN
              Variable 14              Value 14

1530  _____$ = "_____"
         Variable 24              Value 24

      :PRINT"_____ = _____"RETURN
              Variable 24              Value 24

1550  _____$ = "_____"
         Variable 34              Value 34

      :PRINT"_____ = _____"RETURN
              Variable 34              Value 34

1570  _____$ = "_____"
         Variable 44              Value 44

      :PRINT"_____ = _____"RETURN
              Variable 44              Value 44

1590  _____$ = "_____"
         Variable 54              Value 54

      :PRINT"_____ = _____"RETURN
              Variable 54              Value 54

# Use of Probability and Fuzzy Logic in Expert Systems

When we discussed heuristic rules in Chapter 3, we said they were a special kind of rule that experts use. Many heuristic rules are based upon the likelihood of certain events occurring, a likelihood that only an expert has the knowledge and experience to calculate. In everyday language, we might say that experts make educated guesses about things in their domain.

What this really means is that "something" is known to work in a certain way according to statistical evidence of some kind. The something could be the diagnosis a doctor makes because of the presence of some supporting data. The doctor's educated guess in this case really means that a large percentage of the time, based upon doctors' observations, there is a high probability that the patient has a particular illness. Of course, there is also a probability that the patient does *not* have that illness, and that is why we often seek a second opinion.

Similarly, an oil company may decide to drill for oil based upon certain evidence provided by extensive research that points to an oil deposit. But, the drilling might produce a dry hole.

Probability techniques that are based on predicting that something will happen because of the evidence of something else happening in the past were developed by a man named Bayes. The area of probability that contains these theories is called "conditional probability." Statistical decisions based on Bayes' theories are used extensively in expert systems. We will describe how they are used in a very simple way.

Let's first consider another aspect of probability theory. It is not always possible to describe an event with rules that are absolutely defined. For example, we might say someone has a mild illness when his temperature is more than 99 degrees Fahrenheit but is less than 101 degrees Fahrenheit. A fever that is greater than 101 degrees Fahrenheit gets to be more serious. People cannot always express themselves with exact answers. Can you give me an exact temperature when someone says its mild outside? Probably not. Terms such as tall, hot, and mild are linguistic variables that cannot be defined with single values. The use of these terms in formulating systems is called "fuzzy logic."

This chapter will describe a methodology for incorporating fuzzy concepts into an expert system using bayesian techniques.

## Fundamentals of Probability

Probability is the study of degrees of randomness. We frequently make an educated guess and express a conclusion in terms of probabilities without even realizing we are doing it. How often do you hear someone say something like, "I think it is okay, but I am only 80 percent sure."

Probability may be defined as

$$P = \frac{\text{Total number of ways a specific event can occur}}{\text{Total number of ways any event can occur}}$$

For example, suppose we toss a coin two times. The following is a listing of the total number of ways the two-coin tosses can occur:

| First toss | Second toss |
|------------|-------------|
| 1. Head | Head |
| 2. Head | Tail |
| 3. Tail | Head |
| 4. Tail | Tail |

The probability that a tail would appear in one of the two tosses is

$$P = \frac{\text{Total number of ways a tail can occur in two tosses}}{\text{Total number of different tosses that can occur}} = \frac{3}{4}$$

that is, a tail appears in second, third, and fourth possibilities. As another example, the probability that a tail appears in the first toss of two tosses is $\frac{2}{4}$. The tail appears in the first toss of possibilities 3 and 4. The probability that no tail appears in two tosses in $\frac{1}{4}$. This occurs in the first possibility. As you may have noticed, the denominator of the probability equation always has a number *not* less than the numerator. This is always true because the total number of ways any event can occur is always greater than or equal to, but never less than, the total ways a specific event can occur. Therefore, the probability of something occurring must always be greater than or equal to 0 but less than or equal to 1.

## Bayesian Probability

Bayes developed some of the basic theories of conditional probability. Conditional probability is a type of probability based on the existence of evidence. For example, consider again the two-coin tosses. The probability of having a head followed by a tail occurs only in possibility 2 and is ¼. But the probability of getting a tail in the second toss, already knowing that we received a head in the first toss, is ½. This is so because knowing that a head has already come up creates a new set of possibilities:

| First toss | Second toss |
| --- | --- |
| 1. Head | Head |
| 2. Head | Tail |

We have eliminated all cases with tail occurring in the first toss because we have evidence that a head already occurred. Therefore, there is only one case out of two with a tail in the second toss. This occurs in possibility 2. Hence, the conditional probability of getting a tail in the second toss, knowing we have a head in the first toss, is ½.

We will define conditional probability as the probability of something occurring, which we will designate as $s$, with the evidence that something else has already occurred, which we will designate as $e$. This probability is represented as $P(s|e)$. The probability equation of two things occurring is:

$$P(e \text{ and } s) = P(s|e) * P(e)$$

This is read as follows: the probability of $e$ and $s$ happening, where $e$ happens first, is equal to the probability of $s$ happening if we *know* $e$ has already happened, times the probability of $e$ happening. Let's see how this equation is used with an example. Suppose we have two Is and two Os, as shown, which we can choose at random whenever we need an I or an O.

    I I O O

Using our equation, we will calculate the probability of picking an O first and then an I in two picks. Substituting O and I into our equation, we get

$$P(O \text{ and } I) = P(I|O) * P(O)$$

Since there are two Is and two Os, which make four objects, the probability of picking an O, P(O), is ¾. The probability of picking an I on the assumption that an O was already picked, P(I|O), is ⅔. To see how this works, we would have the following situation on the assumption that one O was already picked and no longer available to us:

I I O

Since there are two Is out of the three remaining items, the probability of choosing an I is ⅔. The probability P(O and I) is

P(I|O) * P(O) = ⅔ * ¾ = ⅓.

Another conditional probability equation that we will make use of in our expert system is

$$P(s) = P(s|e) * P(e) + P(s|\text{NOT } e) * P(\text{NOT } e) \qquad (1)$$

This equation reads as follows: The probability of $s$, $P(s)$, is equal to the conditional probability of $s$ on the assumption $e$ occurred, $P(s|e)$, times the probability of $e$ occurring, $P(e)$, plus the probability of $s$ occurring on the assumption $e$ *does not* occur, $P(s|\text{NOT } e)$, times the probability of $e$ *not* occurring, $P(\text{NOT } e)$. We will refer to this equation as Equation 1 in all of our following examples.

## Example

As an example, in the use of these probability theories let us consider these stock market rules (and assume these are the only rules affecting the stock market).

```
10  IF INTEREST RATES = FALL
    THEN STOCK = RISE

20  IF INTEREST RATES = RISE
    THEN STOCK = FALL

30  IF DOLLAR = FALL
    THEN INTEREST RATES = RISE

40  IF DOLLAR = RISE
    THEN INTEREST RATES = FALL
```

For this example we would like to know the probability of the stock market rising. Of course, we know the situation is more complex, but we want to illustrate a solution approach in a simple way. Our backward chaining system would scan the rules for STOCK = RISE in the THEN part of our rules. This occurs in rule 10. Rule 10 tells us that STOCK = RISE on the condition that INTEREST RATES = FALL.

We can evaluate these conditions using the probability equation, Equation 1, with $s$ being replaced by STOCK = RISE and $e$, by INTEREST = FALL. This gives us Equation 2:

$$P(STOCK = RISE) = P(STOCK = RISE|INTEREST = \quad (2)$$
$$FALL) * P(INTEREST = FALL) + P(STOCK =$$
$$RISE|INTEREST = NOT\ FALL) * P(INTEREST = NOT\ FALL)$$

In order to determine if INTEREST = FALL, we must backward chain to rule 40, which is

40   IF DOLLAR = RISE
       THEN INT = FALL      (We have abbreviated INTEREST RATES
                            to INT.)

This statement translates into the following probability, shown in Equation 3:

$$P(INT = FALL) = P(INT = FALL|DOLLAR = RISE) \quad (3)$$
$$* P(DOLLAR = RISE) + P(INT = FALL|DOLLAR =$$
$$NOT\ RISE) * P(DOLLAR = NOT\ RISE)$$

Since DOLLAR is not in any THEN part, that is, its value can't be determined by a rule, its probability must come directly from the user. Similarly, the conditional probabilities are also not included in the THEN part of the rules and therefore the conditional probabilities also come from the user. Let's assign some numbers to the probabilities to see how things work. We assume the following probabilities based upon our understanding of the problem, which is our educated guess.

$$P(DOLLAR = RISE) = 0.6$$

In fundamental probability theory the sum of the probability of something happening and the probability of it not happening equals 1. We will refer to this as the fundamental probability rule. Therefore a variation of this is

$$P(DOLLAR = NOT\ RISE) = 1 - P(DOLLAR = RISE) = 1 - 0.6$$
$$= 0.4$$

The user estimates each of the conditional probabilities, which are

$$P(INT = FALL|DOLLAR = RISE) = 0.8$$
$$P(INT = FALL|DOLLAR = NOT\ RISE) = 0.1$$

You should note that conditional probabilities based on different evidence conditions do *not* have to add up to 1. The two different evidence conditions above are DOLLAR = RISE and DOLLAR = NOT RISE.

Substituting these values in the conditional probability equation, Equation 3, we get

$$P(INT = FALL) = 0.8 * 0.6 + 0.1 * 0.4 = 0.52 \qquad (3)$$

From the fundamental probability rule, we get

$$P(INT = NOT\ FALL) = 1 - 0.52 = 0.48$$

In order to solve the problem of the P(STOCK = RISE) the user must supply the conditional probabilities, which are

$$P(STOCK = RISE|INT = FALL) = 0.85$$
$$P(STOCK = RISE|INT = NOT\ FALL) = 0.1$$

We can now calculate the probability using Equation 2 for P(STOCK = RISE) which is

$$P(STOCK = RISE) = 0.85 * 0.52 + 0.1 * .48 = 0.49\ or\ 49\%$$

The user can now decide how to invest based on this probability. It is interesting to note that there is less than a 50 percent chance of the stock market rising in this example. This is due directly to the selection of probabilities. If the user increased the conditional probability of the stock market rising when interest rates do not fall, that is, P(STOCK = RISE|INT = NOT FALL), there would be a higher probability of P(STOCK = RISE).

## Fuzzy Concepts

So far we have been talking about terms such as "rise" and "fall." In addition, we have used some of these terms with more than one variable. For example, we used the term "rise" with both the variables STOCK and DOLLAR. When used with STOCK, the word "rise" might mean 10 to 30 points on the Dow Jones average. But the word "rise" when used with DOLLAR might mean that the dollar rises between 20 and 30 Japanese yen. Such a use of the word "rise" is referred to as a "linguistic variable." It is a variable that can not only take on any value in a range of values, but the range might change depending on circumstance. For example, if we use the word "cold," it may have a different range when used in the winter than when used in spring.

Another linguistic variable we used in our rules is the word "fall." Since it is usually too much to ask of a user of an expert system to supply probability values, we will show you how to use linguistic variables to accomplish the same thing. In order to do that we must be a little more specific with our linguistic variables. We must allow the user of our expert system to hedge these variables with prefixes such as low or medium. That is, the user can specify a low rise for the dollar, and we will know exactly what he means. Let's see, with the stock market as an example, how we can determine the probabilities.

## Probability Membership Table

In order to determine if the stock market will rise we encountered two rules and their associated probabilities. These rules are

    10   IF INT = FALL
         THEN STOCK = RISE
    40   IF DOLLAR = RISE
         THEN INT = FALL

with probabilities

P(STOCK = RISE) = P(STOCK = RISE|INT = FALL) * P(INT = FALL) + P(STOCK = RISE|INT = NOT FALL) * P(INT = NOT FALL)

P(INT = FALL) = P(INT = FALL|DOLLAR = RISE) * P(DOLLAR = RISE) + P(INT = FALL|DOLLAR = NOT RISE) * P(DOLLAR = NOT RISE)

In order to solve these equations we will use an expert to construct a table for the user. This table will contain hedge words, that is, words that will be used to define what the user means by, for example, "a medium rise." On the same row as each hedge word we will specify the percentage change represented by the linguistic variable and the probability and conditional probability of that change taking place. Here is the table; an example of how to use it follows.

| | Column 1 | Column 2 | Column 3 |
|---|---|---|---|
| Linguistic variable | Dollar equal rise value in table | P(INT = FALL\| DOLLAR = RISE) | P(DOLLAR = RISE) |
| Low | 1–2% | 0.2 | 0.5 |
| Medium | 3–4% | 0.5 | 0.3 |
| High | Greater than 4% | 0.8 | 0.1 |

For simplicity let's assume that the expert who provides all these values decides that the dollar either rises by the amount shown in column 1 of the table or does not rise at all. There is no in between. The expert, therefore, has to only calculate two types of values. One is related to the dollar rising and has already been recorded in the table.

The other occurs when the dollar does not rise. That is, the expert calculates the conditional probability of interest rates falling when the dollar is not rising and records this value as:

P(INT = FALL|DOLLAR = NOT RISE) = 0.07

The probability of stocks rising if interest rates fall is recorded by the expert as

P(STOCK = RISE|INT = FALL) = 0.2

The probability of stocks rising if interest rates do not fall is recorded by the expert as

P(STOCK = RISE|INT = NOT FALL) = 0.1

These tables and values have to be constructed by an expert. They become part of the knowledge base and may change from time to time. That is, the expert needs to change these tables when the interest rates or dollar probabilities change. The expert making these changes may be another expert system.

When the user of the system asks for the probability of the stock market rising, the expert system will ask the user to respond to the following question:

```
DO YOU WANT TO CALCULATE THE EFFECTS IF THE RISE OF THE
DOLLAR IS

1-LOW

2-MEDIUM

3-HIGH

ENTER ONE NUMBER - ? 2
```

In this case assume that the user responds with 2, which is MEDIUM. From the table, we see this means that the user expects the dollar to rise 3 to 4 percent. The probabilities needed to solve P(INT = FALL) are taken from the table and the values provided by the expert. These are

| Probability | Source |
|---|---|
| P(DOLLAR = RISE) = 0.3 | Row 2, column 3 of table |
| P(DOLLAR = NOT RISE) = 1 − 0.3 = 0.7 | Fundamental rule |
| P(INT = FALL\|DOLLAR = RISE) = 0.5 | Row 2, column 2 of table |
| P(INT = FALL\|DOLLAR = NOT RISE) = 0.07 | Expert |
| P(INT = FALL) = 0.5 * 0.3 + 0.07 * 0.7 = 0.199 | Equation 3 |

Let's now calculate P(STOCK = RISE). We repeat the previous calculation result:

| Probability | Source |
|---|---|
| P(INT = FALL) = 0.199 | Previous calculation |
| P(INT = NOT FALL) = 1 − 0.199 = 0.811 | Fundamental rule |
| P(STOCK = RISE\|INT = FALL) = 0.2 | Expert |
| P(STOCK = RISE\|INT = NOT FALL) = 0.1 | Expert |

We can now calculate the probability of the stock market rising from equation 3.

$$P(STOCK = RISE) = 0.2 * 0.1999 + 0.1 * 0.811 = .121$$

or a probability of 12.1 percent.

By using an expert to construct the table and provide all the values we relieved the user from this chore.

## Summary

Let us review the concepts discussed in this chapter.

1. In order to assess the probability of an event taking place, we calculate that probability according to a specific formula that takes into account the total number of ways a specific event can occur divided by the total number of ways any event can occur. Bayesian probability, which analyzes conditional probability, goes one step further to analyze what will happen based on what has already happened. This can be applied to a backward chaining system in which probability formulas are applied to the rules of a knowledge base.

2. The same terms that are analyzed for their probability of occurrence can be analyzed via fuzzy concepts by analyzing linguistic variables, that is, by analyzing the value of specific words, such as "rise" and "fall" of the stock market, used in a knowledge base to make decisions. Again, the use of formulas is implemented, this time analyzing the variable measures of the terms low, medium, high.

The user must remember that each time a situation is calculated, it is based on the probability values assigned to that situation.

## Programming Applications

Let's examine a program written in BASIC which allows us to apply the bayesian probability concepts we have just discussed.

## Program Explanation

The rules we use in the program are the same two used in the concept description. These are shown in the REM statements 10 through 60. The corresponding probability equations are shown in REM statements 70 and 105. The program simply asks the users to supply the values for the probabilities within the equations and then arrives at the probability of the stock market rising.

## Program Listing

Listing 7-1 is followed by a set of runs.

**Listing 7-1  Bayesian probabilities.**

```
1 REM **************** BAYESIAN PROBABILITIES *****************************
5 REM   IN THIS EXAMPLE THE FOLLOWING TWO RULES ARE USED
10 REM 10 IF INT=FALL
15 REM       THEN STOCK=RISE
20 REM 40 IF DOLLAR=RISE
25 REM       THEN INT=FALL
30 REM   THE BAYESIAN EQUATIONS ARE:
35 REM    FOR RULE 10
40 REM P(STOCK=RISE)=P(STOCK=RISE!INT=FALL)*P(INT=FALL)          (1)
45 REM              +P(STOCK=RISE!INT=NOT FALL)*P(INT=NOT FALL)
50 REM    FOR RULE 40
55 REM P(INT=FALL)=P(INT=FALL!DOLLAR=RISE)*P(DOLLAR=RISE)        (2)
60 REM            +P(INT=FALL!DOLLAR=NOT RISE)*P(DOLLAR=NOT RISE)
65 REM THE FOLLOWING ABREVIATIONS WILL BE USED
70 REM I1=P(INT=FALL)      I2=P(INT=NOT FALL)
75 REM I3=P(INT=FALL!DOLLAR=RISE)   I4=P(INT=FALL!DOLLAR=NOT RISE)
80 REM S1=P(STOCK=RISE)   S2=P(STOCK=RISE!INT=FALL)
85 REM S3=P(STOCK=RISE!INT=NOT FALL)
90 REM D1=P(DOLLAR=RISE)   D2=P(DOLLAR=NOT RISE)
95 REM RE-WRITING THE PROBABILITIES FOR THE RULES WE GET
100 REM S1=S2*I1+S3*I2       (3)
105 REM I1=I3*D1+I4*D2       (4)
110 REM **************** INFERENCE MECHANISM *********************
115 REM FOR THIS EXAMPLE WE WANT TO DETERMINE THE PROBABILITY OF
120 REM   THE "STOCK=RISE". BY BACKWARD CHAINING WE COME TO RULE 10.
125 REM   THE CONDITION PART OF 10 HAS THE VARIABLE "INT". BY
130 REM   CONTINUING BACKWARD CHAINING WE COME TO RULE 40. THE CONDITION
135 REM   PART OF RULE 40 HAS THE VARIABLE "DOLLAR" WHICH IS NOT PART
140 REM   OF ANY OTHER RULE. THEREFORE THE USER INSTANTIATES EACH
145 REM   PROBABILITY VARIABLE IN EQUATION (3)
150 INPUT"WHAT IS THE PROBABILITY OF THE DOLLAR RISING";D1
155 D2=1-D1:REM THE PROBABILITY OF THE DOLLAR NOT RISING
160 PRINT"WHAT IS THE PROBABILITY OF INTEREST RATES FALLING IF THE"
165 INPUT" DOLLAR RISES";I3
170 PRINT"WHAT IS THE PROBABILITY OF INTEREST RATES FALLING IF THE"
175 INPUT" DOLLAR DOES NOT RISE";I4
180 I1=I3*D1+I4*D2
185 PRINT"*** THE PROBABILITY OF INTEREST RATES FALLING IS ";I1
190 INPUT"WHAT IS THE PROBABILITY OF STOCKS RISING IF INTEREST RATES FALL";S2
195 I2=1-I1:REM PROBABILITY OF INTEREST RATES NOT FALLING
200 PRINT"WHAT IS THE PROBABILITY OF STOCKS RISING IF INTEREST RATES"
205 INPUT" DO NOT FALL";S3
210 S1=S2*I1+S3*I2
215 PRINT"*** THE PROBABILITY OF THE STOCK MARKET RISING IS ";S1
220 STOP
```

**Sample Runs**

```
RUN
WHAT IS THE PROBABILITY OF THE DOLLAR RISING? .6
WHAT IS THE PROBABILITY OF INTEREST RATES FALLING IF THE
DOLLAR RISES? .5
WHAT IS THE PROBABILITY OF INTEREST RATES FALLING IF THE
DOLLAR DOES NOT RISE? .5
** THE PROBABILITY OF INTEREST RATES FALLING IS .5
WHAT IS THE PROBABILITY OF STOCKS RISING IF INTEREST RATES FALL? .7
WHAT IS THE PROBABILITY OF STOCKS RISING IF INTEREST RATES
DO NOT FALL? .5
** THE PROBABILITY OF THE STOCK MARKET RISING IS .6
Break in 220
RUN
WHAT IS THE PROBABILITY OF THE DOLLAR RISING? .7
WHAT IS THE PROBABILITY OF INTEREST RATES FALLING IF THE
DOLLAR RISES? .4
WHAT IS THE PROBABILITY OF INTEREST RATES FALLING IF THE
DOLLAR DOES NOT RISE? .5
** THE PROBABILITY OF INTEREST RATES FALLING IS .43
WHAT IS THE PROBABILITY OF STOCKS RISING IF INTEREST RATES FALL? .5
WHAT IS THE PROBABILITY OF STOCKS RISING IF INTEREST RATES
DO NOT FALL? .7
** THE PROBABILITY OF THE STOCK MARKET RISING IS .614
Break in 220
```

We have included in Listing 7-2 the bayesian probability equations.
The program is followed by a sample run.

## Listing 7-2  Bayesian backward chaining.

```
1 REM ****************** BAYESIAN BACKWARD CHAINING *******************
10 REM INSTALL YOUR IF CLAUSES IN SEQUENCE AT LOCATIONS 1500,1520,..,1540
20 REM FORMAT EXAMPLE 1500 IF (A1=2) AND (A2=6) OR (A3$="YES") THEN S=1
22 REM                 1502 RETURN
30 REM                 1520 IF (J$="NO") THEN S=1
32 REM                 1522 RETURN
40 REM  THE THEN PART OF THE ABOVE CONSTRUCTION ALWAYS CONTAINS, THEN S=1
50 REM INSTALL YOUR THEN CLAUSES IN SEQUENCE IN STATEMENTS 1510,1530,..,1550
60 REM FORMAT EXAMPLE 1510 PO="YES"..FOLOWED BY A RETURN STATEMENT
200 REM *********** INITIALIZATION SECTION *************
210 REM CONCLUSION LIST (GL$), VARIABLE LIST (V$), INSTANTIATED LIST (IN)
220 REM CONCLUSION STACK INCLUDES STATEMENT STACK (SS) AND CLAUSE STACK (CS)
230 REM  CLAUSE VARIABLE LIST (CV$) AND STACK POINTER (SP)
240 DIM GL$(10),V$(10),CV$(40),IN(10),SS(10),CS(10)
250 SP=11 :REM STACK SPACE IS 10 WE INITIALLY PLACE SP AT 10+1
260 FOR I=1 TO 10
270 GL$(1)="": V$(1)="": IN(I)=0: SS(I)=0: CS(I)=0
280 NEXT I
290 REM ENTER CONCLUSIONS WHICH ARE THE VARIABLES IN THE THEN PART, 1 AT A TIME
295 REM ENTER THE CONCLUSIONS IN EXACT ORDER STARTING AT THE 1ST IF-THEN.
300 REM AFTER LAST CONCLUSION JUST HIT RETURN KEY FOR REST OF CONCLUSIONS
305 GL$(1)="ST":GL$(2)="ST":GL$(3)="IN":GL$(4)="IN"
307 PRINT"*** CONCLUSION LIST ***"
310 FOR I=1 TO 10
320 PRINT"CONCLUSION ";I;
325 PRINT GL$(I)
335 NEXT I
338 INPUT"HIT RETURN TO CONTINUE";Z
340 REM ENTER VARIABLES WHICH ARE IN THE IF PART, 1 AT A TIME IN THE
350 REM EXACT ORDER THAT THEY OCCUR. UP TO 3 VARIABLES PER IF STATEMENT.
360 REM DO NOT DUPLICATE ANY VARIABLES NAMES. ANY NAME IS USED ONLY ONCE
365 REM IF NO MORE VARIABLES LEFT, JUST HIT RETURN KEY.
366 PRINT"*** VARIABLE LIST ***"
367 V$(1)="DO"
370 FOR I=1 TO 10
380 PRINT"VARIABLE ";I;
385 PRINT V$(I)
395 NEXT I
396 INPUT"HIT RETURN TO CONTINUE";I
400 REM ENTER VARIABLES AS THEY APPEAR IN THE IF CLAUSES. A MAXIMUM OF 3
405 REM VARIABLES PER IF STATEMENT. IF NO MORE VARIABLES HIT RETURN KEY
406 PRINT"*** CLAUSE-VARIABLE LIST ***"
407 CV$(1)="IN":CV$(5)="IN":CV$(9)="DO":CV$(13)="DO"
410 FOR I=1 TO 8:PRINT"** CLAUSE ";I
420 FOR J=1 TO 4:PRINT"VARIABLE ";J;
423 K=4*(I-1)+J
424 PRINT CV$(K)
430 NEXT J
432 IF I=4 THEN INPUT"HIT RETURN TO CONTINUE";Z
435 NEXT I
500 REM ********************** INFERENCE SECTION **************************
505 INPUT"** ENTER THE CONCLUSION ";V$
510 REM GET CONCLUSION STATEMENT NUMBER (SN) FROM THE CONCLUSION LIST (GL$)
520 F=1:GOSUB 2200: REM 1ST STATEMENT STARTS SEARCH
525 IF SN=0 THEN STOP: REM NO CONCLUSION OF THAT NAME
530 REM PUSH STATEMENT NUMBER (SN) AND CLAUSE NUMBER=1 ON GOAL STACK WHICH
535 REM  IS COMPOSED OF THE STATEMENT STACK (SS) AND CLAUSE STACK (CS)
540 GOSUB 2000
545 REM CALCULATE CLAUSE LOCATION IN CLAUSE-VARIABLE LIST
550 I=(SS(SP)-1)*4+CS(SP)
555 V$=CV$(I): REM CLAUSE VARIABLE
560 REM IS THIS THE LAST CLAUSE FOR THIS STATEMENT?
565 IF V$="" THEN GOTO 580 :REM LAST CLAUSE PROCESS IF-THEN STATEMENT
567 REM IS THIS CLAUSE VARIABLE A CONCLUSION?
568 F=1:GOSUB 2200: IF SN<>0 THEN GOTO 520 :IT IS A CONCLUSION PUSH IT
570 GOSUB 2400: REM CHECK INSTANTIATION OF THIS CLAUSE
575 CS(SP)=CS(SP)+1: GOTO 545 : REM CHECK NEXT CLAUSE
580 REM NO MORE CLAUSES CHECK IF PART OF STATEMENT
582 SN=SS(SP)
585 S=0: ON SN GOSUB 1500,1520,1540,1560,1580,1600
590 REM SEE IF THE THEN PART SHOULD BE INVOKED I.E. S=1
600 IF S=1 THEN GOTO 630 :REM INVOKE THEN PART
605 REM FAILED..SEARCH REST OF STATEMENTS FOR THE SAME CONCLUSION
610 I=SS(SP): V$=GL$(I): REM GET CONCLUSION
615 F=SS(SP)+1 :REM SEARCH FOR CONCLUSION STARTING AT THE NEXT STATEMENT NUMBER
620 GOSUB 2200
625 SP=SP+1:GOTO 525:REM POP OLD CONCLUSION AND PUT ON NEW ONE
630 REM IF PART TRUE INVOKE THE THEN PART
635 ON SN GOSUB 1510,1530,1550,1570,1590,1610
650 REM POP THE STACK..IF IT REACHED THE INITIAL POINT WE HAD OUR SUCCESS
655 REM  IF NOT JUST KEEP GOING TO VERIFY THE OLD CONCLUSION
660 SP=SP+1:REM POP THE STACK
670 IF SP < 11 THEN GOTO 690 :REM STACK IS NOT EMPTY
680 PRINT"*** SUCCESS": REM FINISHED
685 STOP
```

```
690 REM STACK NOT EMPTY GET NEXT CLAUSE THEN CONTINUE
695 CS(SP)=CS(SP)+1
700 GOTO 545
1490 REM ********** IF-THEN STATEMENT STARTING AT 1500 *********************
1492 REM SAMPLE IF-THEN STATEMENTS FROM THE POSITION KNOWLEDGE BASE
1494 REM   ONLY THE FIRST TWO LETTERS OF EACH VARIABLE IS USED TO MAKE
1496 REM   THE EXAMPLE COMPATIBLE WITH SOME VERSIONS OF BASIC. FOR EXAMPLE
1498 REM DEG WAS SHORTENED TO DE AND QUAL TO QU
1499 REM ** STATEMENT 1
1500 IF IN$="FALL" THEN S=1
1502 RETURN
1510 I2=1-I1:PRINT"P(INTEREST=NOT FALL)=";I2
1512 INPUT"WHAT IS THE PROBABILITY OF STOCKS RISING IF INTEREST RATES FALL";S4
1514 INPUT"WHAT IS THE PROBABILITY OF STOCKS RISING IF INTEREST RATES DO NOT
      FALL";S5
1516 S1=S4*I1+S5*I2:PRINT"P(STOCK=RISE)=";S1
1518 ST$="RISE":PRINT"ST=RISE":RETURN
1519 REM ** STATEMENT 2
1520 IF IN$="RISE" THEN S=1
1522 RETURN
1530 I2=1-I1:PRINT"P(INTEREST=NOT RISE)=";I2
1532 INPUT"WHAT IS THE PROBABILITY OF STOCKS FALLING IF INTEREST RATES RISE";S4
1534 INPUT"WHAT IS THE PROBABILITY OF STOCKS FALLING IF INTEREST RATES DO NOT
      RISE";S5
1536 S1=S4*I1+S5*I2:PRINT"P(STOCK=FALL)="S1
1538 ST$="FALL":PRINT"ST=FALL" :RETURN
1539 REM ** STATEMENT 3
1540 IF DO$="FALL" THEN S=1
1542 RETURN
1550 INPUT"WHAT IS THE PROBABILITY OF THE VALUE OF THE DOLLAR FALLING";I1
1552 I2=1-I1:PRINT"P(DOLLAR=NOT FALL)=";I2
1554 INPUT"WHAT IS THE PROBABILITY OF INTEREST RATES RISING IF THE DOLLAR
      FALLS";S4
1556 INPUT"WHAT IS THE PROBABILITY OF INTEREST RATES RISING IF THE DOLLAR DOES
      NOT FALL";S5
1558 S1=S4*I1+S5*I2:PRINT"P(INTEREST=RISE)=";S1:I1=S1:IN$="RISE":PRINT"IN=RISE
      :RETURN
1559 REM ** STATEMENT 4
1560 IF DO$="RISE" THEN S=1
1562 RETURN
1570 INPUT"WHAT IS THE PROBABILITY OF THE VALUE OF THE DOLLAR RISING";I1
1572 I2=1-I1:PRINT"P(DOLLAR=NOT RISE)=";I2
1574 INPUT"WHAT IS THE PROBABILITY OF INTEREST RATES FALLING IF THE DOLLAR
      RISES";S4
1576 INPUT"WHAT IS THE PROBABILITY OF INTEREST RATES FALLING IF THE DOLLAR
      DOES NOT RISE";S5
1578 S1=S4*I1+S5*I2:PRINT"P(INTEREST=FALL)=";S1:I1=S1:IN$="FALL":PRINT"IN=FALL"
      :RETURN
1611 REM ****** END OF POSITION KNOWLEDGE BASE ***********
1690 REM ********** INPUT STATEMENTS STARTING AT 1700 *********************
1699 REM **** INPUT STATEMENTS FOR SAMPLE POSITION KNOWLEDGE BASE
1700 INPUT"IS THE DOLLAR EXPECTED TO RISE OR FALL";DO$ :RETURN
1750 REM ****** END OF INPUT STATEMENTS FOR THE POSITION KNOWLEDGE BASE **
1999 REM ******************** SUBROUTINE SECTION **************************
2000 REM ROUTINE TO PUSH STATEMENT NUMBER (SN) AND A CLAUSE NUMBER OF 1
2002 REM   ONTO THE CONCLUSION STACK WHICH CONSISTS OF THE STATEMENT STACK (SS)
2004 REM   AND THE CLAUSE STACK (CS).....TO PUSH DECREMENT STACK POINTER (SP)
2020 SP=SP-1: SS(SP)=SN: CS(SP)=1
2030 RETURN
2099 REM *****************************************************************
2200 REM ROUTINE TO DETERMINE IF A VARIABLE (V$) IS A MEMBER OF THE CONCLUSION
      LIST
2202 REM   (GL$). IF YES RETURN SN<>0. IF NOT A MEMBER SN=0.
2220 SN=0:REM INITIALLY SET TO NOT A MEMBER
2230 FOR I=F TO 8 :REM MEMBER OF CONCLUSION LIST TO BE SEARCHED IS F
2240 IF V$= GL$(I) THEN GOTO 2270: REM TEST FOR MEMBERSHIP
2250 NEXT I
2260 RETURN: REM NOT A MEMBER
2270 SN=I:REM A MEMBER
2280 RETURN
2299 REM *****************************************************************
2400 REM ROUTINE TO INSTANTIATE A VARIABLE (V$) IF IT ISN'T ALREADY. THE
2402 REM   INSTANTIATE INDICATION (IN) IS A 0 IF NOT, A 1 IF IT IS. THE
2404 REM   VARIABLE LIST (VL$) CONTAINS THE VARIABLE (V$)
2420 FOR I=1 TO 10: REM FIND VARIABLE IN THE LIST
2430 IF V$=V$(I) THEN GOTO 2445: REM FOUND VARIABLE IN LIST
2440 NEXT I
2445 IF IN(I)=1 THEN RETURN: REM ALREADY INSTANTIATED
2450 IF IN(I)=1 THEN RETURN: REM ALREADY INSTANTIATED
2460 REM THE DESIGNER OF THIS KNOWLEDGE BASE PLACES THE INPUT STATEMENTS
2462 REM   TO INSTANTIATE THE VARIABLES STARTING AT LOCATION 1700
2464 REM FORMAT IS INPUT STATEMENT FOLLOWED BY A RETURN STATEMENT
2465 IN(I)=1:REM MARK INSTANTIATED
2470 ON I GOSUB 1700,1705,1710,1715
2480 RETURN
```

## Sample Run

```
*** CONCLUSION LIST ***
CONCLUSION  1 ST
CONCLUSION  2 ST
CONCLUSION  3 IN
CONCLUSION  4 IN
CONCLUSION  5
CONCLUSION  6
CONCLUSION  7
CONCLUSION  8
CONCLUSION  9
CONCLUSION  10
HIT RETURN TO CONTINUE?
*** VARIABLE LIST ***
VARIABLE  1 DO
VARIABLE  2
VARIABLE  3
VARIABLE  4
VARIABLE  5
VARIABLE  6
VARIABLE  7
VARIABLE  8
VARIABLE  9
VARIABLE  10
HIT RETURN TO CONTINUE?

*** CLAUSE-VARIABLE LIST ***
** CLAUSE  1
VARIABLE  1 IN
VARIABLE  2
VARIABLE  3
VARIABLE  4
** CLAUSE  2
VARIABLE  1 IN
VARIABLE  2
VARIABLE  3
VARIABLE  4
** CLAUSE  3
VARIABLE  1 DO
VARIABLE  2
VARIABLE  3
VARIABLE  4
** CLAUSE  4
VARIABLE  1 DO
VARIABLE  2
VARIABLE  3
VARIABLE  4
HIT RETURN TO CONTINUE?

** CLAUSE  5
VARIABLE  1
VARIABLE  2
VARIABLE  3
VARIABLE  4
** CLAUSE  6
VARIABLE  1
VARIABLE  2
VARIABLE  3
VARIABLE  4
```

```
** CLAUSE  7
VARIABLE  1
VARIABLE  2
VARIABLE  3
VARIABLE  4
** CLAUSE  8
VARIABLE  1
VARIABLE  2
VARIABLE  3
VARIABLE  4

** ENTER THE CONCLUSION ? ST
IS THE DOLLAR EXPECTED TO RISE OR FALL? RISE
WHAT IS THE PROBABILITY OF THE VALUE OF THE DOLLAR RISING? .6
P(DOLLAR=NOT RISE) = .4
WHAT IS THE PROBABILITY OF INTEREST RATES FALLING IF THE DOLLAR RISES? .5
WHAT IS THE PROBABILITY OF INTEREST RATES FALLING IF THE DOLLAR DOES
NOT RISE? .5
P(INTEREST=FALL) = .5
IN=FALL
P(INTEREST=NOT FALL) = .5
WHAT IS THE PROBABILITY OF STOCKS RISING IF INTEREST RATES FALL? .7
WHAT IS THE PROBABILITY OF STOCKS RISING IF INTEREST RATES DO NOT FALL? .5
P(STOCK=RISE) = .6
ST=RISE
*** SUCCESS
Break in 68
0
```

# Expert Systems:
# Knowledge Plus Inference

*Section 3 discusses three actual expert systems. We examine
the different ways each system represents its solution. To
further develop your understanding we have provided
programming examples. This sets the stage for you to
construct your own expert systems.*

# 8

# Financial Planning
# Expert System

Now that you understand some of the concepts of artificial intelligence and expert systems, you are ready to learn how to construct a knowledge base for an actual expert system.

We will now describe a simple financial planning system that anyone can use for making financial decisions. This system is not comprehensive and we certainly don't recommend that you plan your financial future using the limited database supplied here. What we have attempted to give you is a framework for creating a thorough financial planning expert system or another decision-making system based upon the same principles. To put it simply, we can't make you a financial planning expert, but we can make you a knowledge engineer.

We must first address three questions:

1. How do you choose a domain?

2. How do you research your domain?

3. How do you represent (organize) the relevant facts for the chosen domain?

The simplest way to answer these questions is to lead you through the development of an actual system and then write an expert system with you. We will take you step by step, just as we have done up until now.

First, let us review the basic definition of an expert system. Remember the description in Chapter 3 of how to create a domain of knowledge for an expert system? As described, the goals can be reached via facts, rules, pruning, and an inference mechanism. You select, as your domain, a special area of interest within the subject matter. You then collect all the goals, facts, and rules related to that small domain and put all this knowledge together with an inference mechanism and a pruning structure to create an expert system.

## How Do You Choose a Domain?

Two things go into choosing a domain. One, of course, is that it be of interest to you. Two is that the knowledge base be small enough so that a manageable amount of information can be gathered. This chapter is devoted to a specific domain within the broad field of financial planning. We chose this topic because it affects just about everyone. Managing your money wisely may be the single most important thing you can do today. In the complex age in which we live, with the unpredictable rise and fall of the dollar, it is essential to learn to make the most out of what you have. Besides, everyone is interested in making money.

So let's get started. Your first step is to visit the local library and bookstore and think of any professionals you know who are knowledgeable in this area. Before reviewing the research and/or interviewing knowledgeable people, keep in mind what aspect of the topic is of personal interest to you. In other words, always think about your own goals.

## How Do You Research Your Topic?

At this point you are probably thinking that financial planning is a vast topic, much too difficult for a simple computer program. Not so. Let's move along the following path. We went to our local library and took out several books on the topic—about five or six comprehensive ones were enough. We then thought of professionals that we knew, chose two that we felt were competent, and spent some time with each of them. At first, we came away with a lot of information but without a solid form. We had learned about stocks, real estate, and money market funds. We had learned about various financial services, such as discount brokerage services offered by the banks. We had learned about the many types of professionals that offer services. Some books analyzed the world financial situation from various angles. For example, some books advocated different creative means for investing money. Others stressed investment in real estate as the most profitable means of making money. One book stressed "crisis investment," that is, how to handle your money strategically in the event of an economic crisis. With all this deluge of information, we again asked ourselves the more specific question, "What would be of personal interest to us, what would be most beneficial for us to learn about?" When we thought about it at some length, we realized that professionals and the literature were both saying the same thing: Explore your own financial needs because that is what is most important.

So we decided the best approach would be to take much of the information we had learned and combine it into a meaningful whole. More specifically, we studied our financial needs and tailored a financial program to suit these needs based upon age and life-style. One of the best books we found that addressed the topic was *The Lifetime Book of Money Management* by Grace Weinstein (New American Library, 1983). The book describes a typical person's life cycle in terms of finances in four to five stages and outlines the most salient aspects of each stage. The goal that we chose for our expert system was to learn the best financial strategies available for a given age group.

## Organizing the Relevant
## Facts for the Domain

Once the goal had been established, the next step was to organize or partition that data into several primary but independent categories. For example, age groups would be one category. This partitioning would allow us to prune irrelevant categories from consideration by our inference mechanism. For example, by partitioning our knowledge base into age groups, we could eliminate (prune) age groups not included in our expert analysis of a specific person's financial needs. If the person's age is 50, for example, we would not consider the age 18 to 24 knowledge base. Based on literature suggestions, we have established the following age categories:

Ages 18 to 24 (young adult)

Ages 25 to 45 (adult)

Ages 46 to 64 (mature adult)

Ages 65 and over (senior adult)

This partition divides a life span into four different age groups. The goal for each age group is to determine where investments should be made. What are the facts associated with each age group? Knowing what our goal is, we can sort out the facts related to our goal. Compiling all of our research, we now listed from our notes various pieces of gathered information from a wide variety of sources.

Let us now begin to list these facts. Under the first age group, 18 to 24, we reviewed our research and listed the following facts in the form of a taxonomy, which is a classification of similar items into a system. This will be elaborated on after we list the facts for this age group.

A. Ages 18 to 24
    A-1  Train for a career
    A-2  Enter a vocational program
    A-3  Enter a college or graduate school
    A-4  Establish plan for a personal life
        A-4.1  Remain single
            A-4.1.1  Start savings plan with money devoted to own needs
            A-4.1.2  Establish credit identity
            A-4.1.3  Establish financial record-keeping system
        A-4.2  Marry with no children
            A-4.2.1  Start savings plan with joint goals
            A-4.2.2  Establish credit identity
            A-4.2.3  Establish financial record-keeping system
            A-4.2.4  Establish residential plans for life-style
        A-4.3  Marry with children
            A-4.3.1  Start savings plans with long-range plan to include children
            A-4.3.2  Establish credit identity for large future investments
            A-4.3.3  Establish financial record-keeping system
            A-4.3.4  Establish residential plans for life-style

Let us take a moment to explain the other structure used. Notice that the numbers to the left of the facts highlight the categories and subdivisions. For example, "Establish plans for a personal life" is numbered A-4 and all the supporting points related to "Establish plans for a personal life" are numbered A-4.1, A-4.2, etc. "Establish credit identity" is numbered A-4.1.2, a further subdivision of "Remain single" which is numbered A-4.1, which is a subdivision of "Establish plans for a personal life," which is numbered A-4. This numerical system (also called taxonomy) will be utilized later on in the chapter in order to guide us in the creation of a decision tree structure.

We now move on to the next age group, 25 to 45. What are the facts associated with this group? It is within this age group that a lot of planning is put into motion since these are the years when adult life-styles are established. These are the child-rearing years, years for putting aside money for educational needs of children, and years for expanded residential planning. These are also the years that people begin to earn larger incomes and must allocate their money in different directions. For this reason we have devoted more attention to this age group than to the others. First, we divided this age group into four categories of life-style in order to make it more manageable. Then we expanded on each category, listing all the pertinent facts. A taxonomy of the facts follows.

B. Ages 25 to 45
  B-1  Single adult
      B-1.1  Expand career goals
      B-1.2  Invest for capital growth
          B-1.2.1  Money market
          B-1.2.2  Time securities
          B-1.2.3  Savings bonds
      B-1.3  Plan for housing investment—buy apartment, condominium, or small house
  B-2  Single adults living together
      B-2.1  Expand career goals
      B-2.2  Invest for capital growth
          B-2.2.1  Joint accounts
          B-2.2.2  Separate accounts
      B-2.3  Plan for housing investment—buy apartment, condominium, or small house
          B-2.3.1  Joint ownership
              B-2.3.1.1  Draw up legal contracts
              B-2.3.1.2  Spell out obligations and responsibilities
  B-3  Single parent families
      B-3.1  Establish new career goals for former nonearning spouse
      B-3.2  Invest for capital growth
          B-3.2.1  Obtain credit for new purchases
          B-3.2.2  Meet insurance needs—insure supplementary income in the event of death of spouse, etc.
      B-3.3  Plan for housing
          B-3.3.1  Establish who will remain in house of origin (which divorced spouse)
          B-3.3.2  Establish what happens if house is sold
  B-4  Husband and wife families with children
      B-4.1  Provide for child-bearing and child-care expenses
          B-4.1.1  Provide for health insurance (1982 statistics show birth costs from $3,000 to $4,000.)
          B-4.1.2  Assess child-care expenses (They depend on whether mother works outside house or not.)
      B-4.2  Provide for expanded housing needs
          B-4.2.1  Apartments—rent stabilized (more control over living expenses)
          B-4.2.2  Private homes—more space, tax deductions, equity
              B-4.2.2.1  Assess schools in neighborhood to determine if school taxes will rise
              B-4.2.2.2  Estimate taxes and interest costs
      B-4.3  Increase insurance to meet expanding costs
          B-4.3.1  Working couples need to provide for income replacement to protect one another

              B-4.3.2  Buy life insurance that can later meet college needs
              B-4.3.3  Insurance to plan for retirement needs
    B-4.4  Build an education fund
              B-4.4.1  Determine specific costs
              B-4.4.2  Determine what your options are, based on income
                        B-4.4.2.1  Low income—financial aid
                        B-4.4.2.2  Middle income
                                  B-4.4.2.2.1  Savings plan—put away monthly
                                  B-4.4.2.2.2  Tax shelter
                                  B-4.4.2.2.3  Tax scholarship-custodial account to save in child's name
                                  B-4.4.2.2.4  Income splitting—sharing income with a family member in lower income bracket

The last two age groups have been divided into ages 46 to 64 and ages 65 and over. We have limited the facts for these age groups to a few basic ones as our intention is to focus more on the 25 to 45 age group. In addition, financial planning in later years tends to be a natural outgrowth of that which was done in earlier years and therefore involves fewer new financial planning considerations.

C. Ages 46 to 64
    C-1  Continue career development
    C-2  Diversify investments
    C-3  Develop estate plans
    C-4  Explore retirement goals
D. Ages 65 and over
    D-1  Re-evaluate budget to meet retirement needs
    D-2  Investigate part-time or volunteer work for retirement
    D-3  Review will

Let's review for a moment and see how the steps we have taken so far apply to *your* needs:

1. Choose your topic to create a knowledge base—one that is of personal interest to you and in so doing specify your goals.

2. Research your topic; read books on the topic, talk with respected professionals, and use your own expertise if you are also knowledgeable.

3. Categorize your information and properly organize your facts into a taxonomy.

As you will soon see, we will create a decision tree from the taxonomy of facts from which we will create the actual knowledge base.

## Decision Tree

So far we have a list of facts organized into a taxonomy. The next step we must take is to design a decision tree. A decision tree, as we saw in the chapter on backward chaining, is a grouping of questions that are related to the facts and that follow a path. The path may take us in several directions and explore several possibilities for those facts, but once we have reached the end of the path, we have come to a decision about those facts and thereby reached our goal. A path may move in several directions, and therefore several decisions will be made. As you will see on the decision tree in Figure 8-1, the end of the path is signified by a square, surrounding the statement, at the end of the path. Since we do not have enough space in this book to develop a decision tree for all the possible combinations of age groups and sub-divisions within those age groups, we will take a part of the taxonomy and develop a small portion of the whole tree. You will be able to fill in the rest very easily.

Let's now take two hypothetical cases. The first is a single adult, the second is single adult living together (living with another single adult). How should the single adult, age 25 to 45, handle investments for capital growth? Under this category we've suggested that a person in that age group and life-style consider money market funds (B-1.2.1), time deposit securities (B-1.2.2), and savings bonds (B-1.2.3).

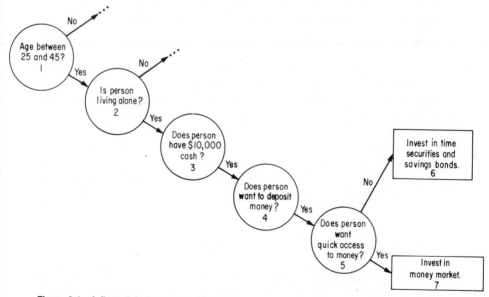

Figure 8-1   A financial planning decision tree.

The following questions will help us make decisions about the facts:

1. How much money does this single adult have?

2. Does this single adult want to deposit money for savings?

3. Does this single adult want quick access to money or is single adult willing to put money away for a longer period of time to accumulate interest?

4. Does single adult want security in investments?

The decision tree in Figure 8-1 illustrates these facts and the questions that will help reach our goal.

Notice that a few paths (the ones ending in three dots) are started but then trail off into space. These are included to give you an idea of how several paths are often interwoven into a decision tree and to show you how you might expand on this small tree if you wished to.

Now let us take the second hypothetical person, who is a single adult living together between the ages of 25 and 45. How would this person decide upon housing? Under the category "plan for housing investment" (B-2.3) we listed buy apartment, condominium, private house (B-2.3); joint ownership (B-2.3.1); draw up legal contracts (B-2.3.1.1); and spell out obligations and responsibilities (B-2.3.1.2). The following important questions are related to the facts:

1. How much money does the single adult living together have?

2. Does the single adult living together want to buy assets?

3. Does the single adult living together believe in joint ownership?

A larger portion of our small decision tree is shown in Figure 8-2.

From the decision tree we can directly write the rules for our knowledge base. This is done by tracing *all* paths leading to each terminated node of the tree. A terminated node is one that has a square drawn around it and one that does not have any branches leaving. For example, we have labeled some of our nodes with numbers. The node marked no. 6, invest in money market, is a terminated node. The path leading to this node is via the nodes labeled 1, 2, 3, 4, and 5. We can write a rule for arriving at this node as follows:

```
IF AGE >= (is more than or equal to) 25 AND          (Node 1)
   AGE <= (is less than or equal to) 45 AND           (Node 1)
   PERSON'S LIFE-STYLE = LIVING ALONE AND             (Node 2)
   PERSON'S CASH > $10,000 AND                        (Node 3)
   PERSON DEPOSIT CASH = YES                           (Node 4)
THEN PERSON INVEST = MONEY MARKET         (Terminal Node 6)
```

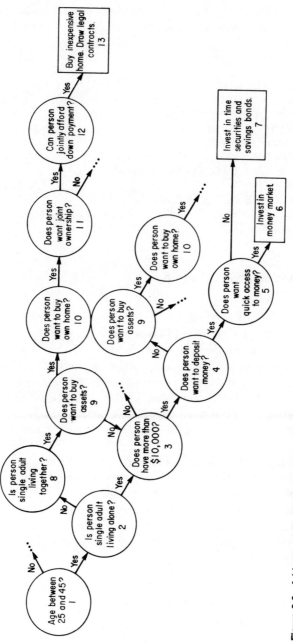

**Figure 8-2** A bigger portion of the decision tree.

Notice that we invented simple variable names such as PERSON INVEST. Remember to always be consistent with variable names and use them in other rules in which they apply. For example, terminal node 13 has the following rule that is generated by the path 1, 2, 8, 9, 10, 11, and 12:

| | |
|---|---|
| IF AGE >= 25 AND | (Node 1) |
| AGE <= 45 AND | (Node 1) |
| PERSON LIFE-STYLE = SINGLE ADULT | |
| LIVING TOGETHER | (Node 2 and 8) |
| PERSON BUY ASSETS = YES AND | (Node 9) |
| PERSON WANT OWN HOME = YES AND | (Node 10) |
| PERSON WANT JOINT OWNERSHIP | |
| = YES AND | (Node 11) |
| PERSON HAS DOWN PAYMENT = YES | (Node 12) |
| THEN PERSON INVEST = INEXPENSIVE HOME AND DRAW | |
| LEGAL CONTACT | |

## Backward and Forward Chaining Considerations

We can now place these rules in a knowledge base of either a backward or forward chaining system and then arrive at certain decisions. We would use a backward chaining system to see if a particular financial plan—or goal—is appropriate to a particular individual. We select a goal, such as finding the type of investments a person should make for capital growth. This is the one called PERSON INVEST. Once the goal has been identified, we search the THEN part of all the rules for the first instance of the goal's name. In our example of the single adult (living alone) we would study the rule related to PERSON INVEST: IF a person is more than age 25 *and* less than age 45 *and* is a single adult *and* has more than $10,000 cash *and* wants to deposit cash *and* wants to have quick access to cash, THEN PERSON INVEST in money market. All of the clauses after the IF statement and after the AND statements are clause variables that cannot be determined by invoking other rules (that is, they are not conclusion variables of other rules). We therefore must instantiate the variables by asking specific questions:

Is person more than age 25?

Is person less than age 45?

Is person single adult (living alone)?

Does person have more than $10,000 cash?

Does person want to deposit cash?

Does person want quick access to money?

A value (yes or no) must be provided for each question. Once this is done, each clause variable has been instantiated. If any of the questions are answered no, the statement for this goal is false. We then scan the rules for another statement that contains the conclusion variable PERSON INVEST. Since there are no other instances of that goal in our example, we are finished with this goal. In other words, such an investment is not a good idea for this individual. Of course, in a larger system there might be many other rules with instances of this goal.

If, however, all of the answers to our questions are yes, we have met this goal and the user can make a decision based upon the answer invest in money market.

In a forward chaining system rather than trying to satisfy a conclusion, we would try to recommend a financial path for an individual to take based upon that person's age, life-style, etc. We would do this by asking questions to satisfy the IF part of the rules in order to arrive at the conclusions generated by the THEN part. If we take the example of the single adult living together who is age 42 and is considering buying a home, we would ask the following questions:

Is person more than age 25?

Is person less than age 45?

Is this a single adult living together?

Does person want to buy assets?

Does person want to buy own home?

Does person want joint ownership?

Can person jointly afford down payment?

If all of the above conditions are met for this rule, that is, yes is answered to each question, the decision would be made to "buy an inexpensive home and draw up a legal agreement." If all the conditions are not met, that is, no is provided as an answer to at least one of the questions, we would have to look for another IF-THEN rule in which the conditions could be satisfied and an appropriate decision made.

From what you have read in this chapter, along with the chapters on the implementation theories of backward and forward chaining structures, you are now ready to undertake the development of a full-blown financial planning system.

## Programming Applications

The rules for financial planning as derived from the decision tree can be inserted into either the forward or backward chaining tools outlined in the previous chapters. The user, of course, should remove the sample knowledge base used for backward chaining and replace it with the knowledge base for financial planning. A discussion of the statements to be replaced follows.

Let us consider one of the rules to show how this is done.

```
IF AGE > = 25 AND
   AGE < = 45 AND
   LIFE-STYLE = LIVING ALONE AND
   CASH > $10,000 AND
   DEPOSIT = YES
THEN INVEST = MONEY MARKET
```

The first thing we must do is abbreviate each variable, as for example

AG for AGE      (No $ symbol as this will be a number)

LF$ for LIFE-STYLE

CA$ for CASH

DE$ for DEPOSIT

IN$ for INVEST

If we now refer to either the backward or forward chaining listing (Listings 5-1 and 6-1), we can replace statement 367 with

```
367  V$(1)="AG":V$(2)="LF":V$(3)="CA":V$(4)="DE"
```

This places the condition variables of the rule into the variable list. We can now insert the rule into the IF-THEN statement section starting at statement 1500 for either the backward or forward chaining program as follows:

```
1500  IF (AG>=25) AND (AG<=45) AND (LF$="LIVING ALONE") THEN T=1
1501  IF (T=1) AND (CA>10,000) AND (DE$="YES") THEN S=1
1502  RETURN
```

The reason the rule was separated into two parts at statements 1500 and 1501 has to do with the limitation of the length of a BASIC statement on some popular computers. Some computers limit a statement length to 80 characters. Briefly, the way the two statements tie together is

1. All three clauses of statement 1500 must be true for T = 1.
2. All three clauses of statement 1501, including T = 1 and the last two clauses, must be true for S = 1.
3. Therefore all five clauses of the rule must be true for S = 1, which is what we require.

For the backward chaining program the THEN part at statement 1510 would look like

```
1510   IN$="MONEY MARKET":PRINT"IN=MONEY MARKET":RETURN
```

For the forward chaining program the THEN part at statement 1510 would look like

```
1510   IN$="MONEY MARKET":PRINT"IN=MONEY MARKET":V$="IN"

1511   GOSUB 3100:RETURN
```

In addition, the following lists must be filled in. For backward chaining the conclusion variable list must contain the conclusion variable IN. This is done at statement number 305 as GL$(1) = "IN." In addition, the input statements starting at line 1700 must be modified to contain the condition variables. For example

```
1700   INPUT"INPUT AGE NUMBER FOR AG-";AG:RETURN

1705   INPUT"INPUT LIFE-STYLE (e.g., "LIVING ALONE") FOR LF$-";LF$:RETURN

1710   INPUT"INPUT A DOLLAR NUMBER FOR CA-";CA:RETURN

1715   INPUT"INPUT YES OR NO FOR DE$-";DE$:RETURN
```

For both backward and forward chaining the clause variable list must be filled in at statement 407. Unfortunately both tools have a limitation of four variables per clause. As an exercise, it will be very instructive for you to do the following:

> Expand both the forward and backward chaining tools so that the clause variable list can hold nine variables per statement. Then enter the rule into the knowledge base for both tools and run the program.

# Sales Expert System

The success of any business depends on how well it sells its product to its customers, be it automobiles, consulting services, feed grain, or insurance policies. The one-to-one relationship between a salesperson and a customer is still the basic unit of our sales-oriented economic system. Selling is anything but an exact science; the salesperson and the customer are individuals with different needs, different aspirations, and different considerations on their minds. Personalities play a major role in sales success. A poor mix of personalities has been known to ruin a sale to someone who was genuinely in need of the offered product, while just the right blend of characters often clinches a sale to a customer who probably didn't even need the product.

In business, computers are too often seen as no more than a tool for the most objective tasks: keeping records, compiling data, organizing statistical information. But in reality, computers can help make business more efficient even in an intangible and subjective area such as the effect of personality on sales performance.

The expert system we are about to describe is designed to assess the likelihood of a sale being closed based upon the personalities of both the salesperson and the customer. This assessment can help the salesperson determine what sort of approach should be taken with a particular customer and how much time and energy should reasonably be applied given the likelihood of a successful sale being made.

Needless to say, the variability of the human character is too complex a subject to be rendered neatly into an expert domain. But it is possible to include enough personality traits that are related to this specific area of human interrelationship to create a simple expert system that will give well-founded guidance to the salesperson.

## Establishing the Facts

The first thing that must be done in designing an expert system for the salesperson-customer personality domain is to collect all the relevant facts. The personality facts domain will be divided into its two component parts: the salesperson's personality and the customer's personality. For each personality, a set of facts will be recorded that will allow the expert system to classify a salesperson or a customer into one of a number of personality categories. The facts were gathered for this expert system through extensive research in the most current marketing and psychological studies available on the subject of sales performance and sales and customer personality traits.

## Salesperson Personality Types

What personality categories are there? In order to categorize sales personalities, we took from the literature various attributes that appeared to surface continually and formed them into general groupings. They were grouped into three main personality types which are

1. Dominant-aggressive
2. Submissive-pleasant
3. Assertive

We then made note of the most salient attributes (or characteristics) associated with these three personality types. In collecting attributes for a personality type we used both attributes that contributed greatly and those that contributed somewhat less. Naturally, there were also some attributes that belonged to more than one personality type. From this research we drew the following list of facts for each personality type. Each fact is assigned an identification number, such as 1-1, so we can refer to it for our later discussions. In addition, to the right of each fact in parenthesis is a weighting factor. The meaning of the weighting factor will be explained later.

Personality type 1—dominant-aggressive
  1-1  Likes to compete for a sale (5)
  1-2  Presentation is energetic and dynamic (5)
  1-3  Absorbed with own advancement (5)
  1-4  Hates to fail or lose a sale (10)
  1-5  Ambitious about moving up in company or meeting sales productivity demands (2.5)
  1-6  Decisive (2.5)

Personality type 2—submissive-pleasant
  2-1   Lacks assertiveness with customers (10)
  2-2   Feels the best offense is a good defense (5)
  2-3   Looks for security within job structure (5)
  2-4   Displays warm and affectionate behavior (5)
  2-5   Tries to be agreeable (2.5)
  2-6   Frequently wants to be available (2.5)

Personality type 3—assertive
  3-1   Likes to compete for a sale (2.5)
  3-2   Makes decisions easily (5)
  3-3   Open and honest with coworkers and customers (10)
  3-4   Ambitious to meet productivity demands (2.5)
  3-5   Presentation is energetic and dynamic (5)
  3-6   Welcomes another's opinion (5)

For purposes of simplicity, and to explain in clear, precise terms how to construct this sort of system, we have limited ourselves to only six attributes per personality type. In reality, of course, there are many more.

## Instantiating the Facts

The next step is to develop a set of questions that will instantiate the facts relating to the personality type attributes. These questions are shown below.

Do you like to compete for a sale?

Is your presentation energetic and dynamic?

Are you absorbed with your own advancement?

Do you hate to fail or lose a sale?

Are you ambitious about moving up in the company or meeting sales productivity demands?

Are you decisive?

Do you lack assertiveness with customers?

Do you feel that the best offense is a good defense?

Do you look for security within your job structure at all cost?

Do you display warm and affectionate behavior?

Do you always try to be agreeable?

Do you frequently want to be available?

Do you make decisions easily?

Are you open and honest with coworkers and customers?

Do you welcome another's opinion?

## Weighting Factors

Within a personality type, certain attributes are more important than others in determining whether an individual has that personality type. For example, when considering the dominant-aggressive personality, the attribute "hates to fail or lose a sale" (1-4) is more important than "decisive" (1-6). What is meant by the term "important?" A person with the attribute "hates to fail or lose a sale" would be more likely to be identified as a dominant-aggressive personality than one with the attribute "decisive." We can therefore rate each attribute on an importance scale of 1 to 10. The higher the number, the greater the importance. We call this number a weighting factor. Therefore "hates to fail or lose a sale" with a weighting factor of 10 has a higher value than "decisive" with a weighting factor of 2.5.

## How Are the Weighting Factors Used?

When an answer to a question is yes, the fact associated with the question also becomes yes. In order to get a weighting factor score for each personality, we sum those weighting factors instantiated to yes. The score is called the "sum weighting factor." If all the facts are instantiated to yes, the sum weighting factor we get is called the "maximum sum weighting factor." In our example, the maximum sum weighting factor is 30 and occurs when all facts for a given salesperson's personality are yes. For example, the sum weighting factors of all the facts in the dominant-aggressive personality are

$$5 + 5 + 5 + 10 + 2.5 + 2.5 = 30$$

## An Example of the System at Work

Since pictures are worth a thousand words, we will use an example to show you how those concepts we have already explained, plus additional concepts that will be explained in the following example, are used by the expert system.

The user, who in this case is the salesperson, sits at the computer terminal to answer all the personal questions. Our hypothetical salesperson's responses are indicated after the question mark.

1-1  Do you like to compete for a sale?   YES
1-2  Is your presentation energetic and dynamic?   YES

1-3  Are you absorbed with your own advancement?   NO
1-4  Do you hate to fail or lose a sale?   YES
1-5  Are you ambitious about moving up in the company or meeting sales productivity demands?   NO
1-6  Are you decisive?   NO
2-1  Do you lack assertiveness with customers?   NO
2-2  Do you feel that the best offense is a good defense?   NO
2-3  Do you look for security within your job structure at all cost?   NO
2-4  Do you display warm and affectionate behavior?   NO
2-5  Do you always try to be agreeable?   YES
2-6  Do you frequently want to make yourself available?   NO
3-2  Do you make decisions easily?   YES
3-3  Are you open and honest with coworkers and customers?   NO
3-6  Do you welcome another's opinions?   NO

You should note that question 3-1 is identical to question 1-1 and therefore does not have to be repeated. But it is also important to note that question 1-1 has a weighting of 5 and question 3-1 has a weighting factor of 2.5. The difference is their relative importance within the personality type they are included in. This is an important point. Similarly, questions 3-4 and 3-5 are already answered in questions 1-5 and 1-2, respectively. Table 9-1 summarizes the responses and provides the weighting factor calculations.

It is now quite apparent that people do not fit neatly into one type of personality structure but may contain characteristics of several types. There is obviously a great deal of overlap and variability within individuals, and this simple system highlights only a small degree of it.

We have now drawn a picture of the following salesperson's personality:

Likes to compete (personality 1 and 3)

Presentation is energetic and dynamic (personality 1 and 3)

Hates to fail or lose a sale (personality 1)

Always tries to be agreeable (personality 2)

Makes decisions easily (personality 3)

## Assessing the Salesperson Personality Scores

As seen in Table 9-1, the sum weighting factors for the three personality types are

| Sales personality 1 | Dominant-aggressive | 20.0 |
| Sales personality 2 | Submissive-pleasant | 2.5 |
| Sales personality 3 | Assertive | 12.5 |
| Total | | 35.0 |

Table 9.1 Results of Example Expert System for
Sales

| Personality attributes | Answers to questions | Weighting factor |
|---|---|---|
| Dominant-aggressive | | |
| 1-1 | Yes | 5.0 |
| 1-2 | Yes | 5.0 |
| 1-3 | No | 0 |
| 1-4 | Yes | 10.0 |
| 1-5 | No | 0 |
| 1-6 | No | 0 |
| Sum weighting factor | | 20.0 |
| Submissive-pleasant | | |
| 2-1 | No | 0 |
| 2-2 | No | 0 |
| 2-3 | No | 0 |
| 2-4 | No | 0 |
| 2-5 | Yes | 2.5 |
| 2-6 | No | 0 |
| Sum weighting factor | | 2.5 |
| Assertive | | |
| 3-1 | Yes | 2.5 |
| 3-2 | Yes | 5.0 |
| 3-3 | No | 0 |
| 3-4 | No | 0 |
| 3-5 | Yes | 5.0 |
| 3-6 | No | 0 |
| Sum weighting factor | | 12.5 |

We see that a salesperson may have a tendency to exhibit any one of
the personalities. The higher the sum weighting factors for a given
personality, the greater the tendency to exhibit that personality. For
example, there is a much greater tendency to exhibit a dominant-
aggressive personality with a sum weighting factor of 20 than to exhibit a submissive-pleasant one with a sum weighting factor of 2.5. If
these two personalities were the only personalities we had to deal with,
we could say that the possibility of this salesperson exhibiting a dominant-aggressive versus submissive-pleasant personality would be 20.0
divided by 22.5. The value 22.5 is the total of both sum weighting
factors. The possibility of being submissive-pleasant would be 2.5/22.5.
We have in effect compared one personality with another. This has
been accomplished by comparing the score of the individual personality with the combined scores of both personalities. In our example we
have three personalities. The same procedure would hold true for any

number of personalities considered. We will define the possibility that the salesperson will exhibit a particular personality with the following equation:

$$POS = \frac{\text{Sum weighting factor for a personality}}{\begin{array}{c}\text{Total of all sum weighting factors} \\ \text{for all three personalities}\end{array}}$$

Therefore for each salesperson personality we get the following possibility

POS 1 = 20/35 = .571 = 57.1%
POS 2 = 2.5/35 = .071 = 7.1%
POS 3 = 12.5/35 = .357 = 35.7%

These possibility values will be combined with the customer's personality possibility value to determine the likelihood of a successful sale.

## The Customer

We now move on to assess the various types of customer personalities. Again, we sort out all our research of the various customer personalities from the literature. Once again, for purposes of simplicity, we have organized our research into four customer personalities and listed those facts—four facts per personality—that we judged to belong to each of the personalities. They are listed with their associated weighting factors in parenthesis to the right of the fact:

Personality type 1—motivated by needs for independence and self-esteem
    1-1  Conversation is filled with reference to oneself (5)
    1-2  Is self-congratulatory or boastful (3)
    1-3  Does not seek advice of salesperson (2)
    1-4  Thinks he knows better than anyone else (5)
Personality type 2—motivated by needs for security
    2-1  Cautious (5)
    2-2  Slow to make decisions (5)
    2-3  Unwilling to share or provide information (3)
    2-4  Unwilling to reveal opinions or feelings (2)
Personality type 3—motivated by needs for social acceptance
    3-1  Goes out of way to please (5)
    3-2  Is very submissive (5)
    3-3  Dodges any hint of disagreement or argument (2)
    3-4  Comes across as pleasant, cooperative, sympathetic (3)
Personality type 4—motivated by needs for independence and self-realization
    4-1  Gets involved with presentation (5)
    4-2  Offers ideas and opinions freely (2)

4-3   Wants involvement as codecision-maker with salesperson (3)

4-4   Flexible approach (5)

A maximum sum weighting factor of 15 has been assigned to each customer personality type. For each customer, the salesperson will answer the following questions according to how the customer is observed:

1-1   Is customer's conversation filled with references to oneself?

1-2   Is customer self-congratulatory or boastful?

1-3   Does customer seek advice of salesperson?

1-4   Does customer think he knows better than anyone else?

2-1   Is customer cautious?

2-2   Is customer slow to make decisions?

2-3   Is customer unwilling to share or provide information?

2-4   Is customer unwilling to reveal opinions or feelings?

3-1   Does customer go out of way to please?

3-2   Is customer very submissive?

3-3   Does customer dodge any hint of disagreement or argument?

3-4   Does customer come across as pleasant, cooperative, or sympathetic?

4-1   Does customer get involved with presentation?

4-2   Does customer offer ideas and opinions freely?

4-3   Does customer want involvement as codecision-maker with salesperson?

4-4   Does customer have a flexible approach?

Each customer personality question is used to instantiate a fact in the same way the salesperson personality questions were used. A yes answer causes the weighting associated with that question to be evaluated. A no causes the weighting factor to be ignored. As an example, Table 9-2 was constructed for a particular customer based on the customer personality questions listed above.

It is apparent that customers, as well as salespersons, have personalities that can overlap into more than one personality type. For the customer example, these are sum weighting factors for customer personalities 2 and 3.

We have now drawn a picture of the following customer personality.

Cautious (personality 2)

Slow to make decisions (personality 2)

Goes out of way to please (personality 3)

Very submissive (personality 3)

Dodges any hint of disagreement or argument (personality 3)

Comes across as pleasant, cooperative, and sympathetic (personality 3)

**Table 9-2    Results of Example Expert System for Customer**

| Personality attributes | Answers to questions | Weighting factor |
|---|---|---|
| Customer type 1 | | |
| 1-1 | No | 0 |
| 1-2 | No | 0 |
| 1-3 | No | 0 |
| 1-4 | No | 0 |
| Sum weighting factor | | 0 |
| Customer type 2 | | |
| 2-1 | Yes | 5 |
| 2-2 | Yes | 5 |
| 2-3 | No | 0 |
| 2-4 | No | 0 |
| Sum weighting factor | | 10 |
| Customer type 3 | | |
| 3-1 | Yes | 5 |
| 3-2 | Yes | 5 |
| 3-3 | Yes | 2 |
| 3-4 | Yes | 3 |
| Sum weighting factor | | 15 |
| Customer type 4 | | |
| 4-1 | No | 0 |
| 4-2 | No | 0 |
| 4-3 | No | 0 |
| 4-4 | No | 0 |
| Sum weighting factor | | 0 |

## Assessing Customer Personality Scores

In summary the sum weighting factor for each customer personality is

| | | |
|---|---|---|
| Customer personality 1 | Conversation is filled with references to oneself | 0 |
| Customer personality 2 | Motivated by need for security | 10 |
| Customer personality 3 | Motivated by need for social acceptance | 15 |
| Customer personality 4 | Motivated by need for independence and self-realization | 0 |
| Total | | 25 |

Therefore using

$$POS = \frac{\text{Sum weighting factor}}{\text{Total of all sum weighting factors}}$$

we can calculate the possibilities of the customer being

POS 1 =   0/25 = 0.00 =   0%
POS 2 = 10/25 = 0.40 = 40%
POS 3 = 15/25 = 0.60 = 60%
POS 4 =   0/25 = 0.00 =   0%

## Assessing the Possible Sales and Customer Combinations

Now that we have values for the possibilities of a person being a particular sales type and a customer being a particular customer type, we
must determine the possibilities of having a specific combination when
the two interact with one another. It is quite clear that salesperson
personality 1 and customer personality 3 are the most likely for our
two examples. But what if the values were closer or there was a tie?
What if there was disagreement with the values? We must therefore
consider all possibilities and allow the expert system user to make the
final decision. To do this, we arrive at the combination possibilities by
multiplying the possibility of the salesperson being a particular sales
type by the possibility of the customer being a particular customer
type for all the personality types. In normal probability-possibility
theory when we have two events that are mutually exclusive of the
other and we want to find out the possibility of event 1 and event 2
occurring together, we multiply the probability-possibility of each individual event.

This product is shown in Table 9-3.

Table 9.3    Table of Combination Possibilities

| Sales type | Customer type | Sales possibility | Customer possibility | Combination possibility |
|---|---|---|---|---|
| 1 | 1 | 0.571 | 0 | 0 |
| 1 | 2 | 0.571 | 0.4 | 0.2284 |
| 1 | 3 | 0.571 | 0.6 | 0.3426 |
| 1 | 4 | 0.571 | 0 | 0 |
| 2 | 1 | 0.071 | 0 | 0 |
| 2 | 2 | 0.071 | 0.4 | 0.0284 |
| 2 | 3 | 0.071 | 0.6 | 0.0426 |
| 2 | 4 | 0.071 | 0 | 0 |
| 3 | 1 | 0.355 | 0 | 0 |
| 3 | 2 | 0.357 | 0.4 | 0.1428 |
| 3 | 3 | 0.357 | 0.6 | 0.2142 |
| 3 | 4 | 0.357 | 0 | 0 |

The system user can now study the combination possibilities to determine which sales and customer personalities are present and make corresponding decisions.

## Expert System Assessments

The user of the expert system may now want to assess, in simple narrative, what happens when a specific type of sales personality encounters a specific customer type. For example, since the possibility is highest that salesperson personality 1 and customer personality 3 are present, we might want to know the computer's "sales outcome" prediction for this combination. For this combination the expert system would print the following:

```
Sales result: Above average; salesperson dominates, customer admires
salesperson and complies.
```

This assessment by the expert system would come from the following list, which gives sales assessments by a human expert of each personality combination. SP (number) and CP (number) is a shorthand notation for salesperson personality (number) and customer personality (number).

| | |
|---|---|
| SP 1 and CP 1 | Sales result: Average; high mutual regard, interaction seen as a contest. |
| SP 1 and CP 2 | Sales result: Below average; salesperson disdains, customer withdraws. |
| SP 1 and CP 3 | Sales result: Above average; salesperson dominates, customer admires salesperson and complies. |
| SP 1 and CP 4 | Sales result: Average; salesperson respects customer, but customer suspicious of salesperson's forcefulness. |
| SP 2 and CP 1 | Sales result: Below average; salesperson withdraws, customer in control, low mutual regard. |
| SP 2 and CP 2 | Sales result: Below average; both withdraw, low-key interaction. |
| SP 2 and CP 3 | Sales result: Average; salesperson neutral toward customer, customer is eager to be nice guy. |
| SP 2 and CP 4 | Sales result: Below average; salesperson is aloof and passive; customer tries to gain information; salesperson has high regard for customer, but customer has mixed regard for salesperson. |
| SP 3 and CP 1 | Sales result: Above average; high mutual regard. |
| SP 3 and CP 2 | Sales result: Average; rapport easily established, salesperson patient, and customer trusts salesperson. |

SP 3 and CP 3    Sales result: Above average; salesperson responds to customer's social needs, customer responds.

SP 3 and CP 4    Sales result: Above average; excellent rapport, both function as partners, high mutual regard.

Let us now summarize the procedure for designing the expert system that is described in this chapter:

1. Research and organize gathered information.

2. List categories and the facts associated with each category.

3. List questions in order to attain the information for each fact.

4. Assign weighting factors.

5. Compute the sum weighting factor.

6. Assess possibilities based on the sum weighting factors.

7. Provide combination possibilities based on each category.

8. Provide strategic predictions based on the decision made.

You have just finished reading about one approach to creating an expert system for the salesperson-customer domain. You are now ready to expand upon this system or create another one within this domain but with a different thrust.

## Programming Applications

Let us examine a methodology for implementing this expert system in BASIC. Listing 9-1 is used to determine the sum weighting factors and possibilities for all of the personalities discussed.

### Program Explanation

The program is organized into four parts which are

1. Initialization

2. Salesperson, data acquisition, analysis

3. Customer, data acquisition, analysis

4. A combined salesperson-customer analysis

### Program Listing

Listing 9-1 is followed by a sample run.

**Listing 9-1 Sales expert system.**

```
1 REM ************** SALES EXPERT SYSTEM *********************
5 REM *********************************************************
10 REM ** INITIALIZATION SECTION
15 REM SALESMAN PERSONALITY NAME
20 DIM S$(3)
25 S$(1)="DOMINANT/AGRESSIVE"
30 S$(2)="SUBMISSIVE/PLEASANT"
35 S$(3)="ASSERTIVE"
40 REM CUSTOMER PERSONALITY NAME
45 DIM C$(4)
50 C$(1)="MOTIVATED BY NEEDS FOR INDEPENDENCE AND SELF ESTEEM"
55 C$(2)="MOTIVATED BY NEEDS FOR SECURITY"
60 C$(3)="MOTIVATED BY NEEDS FOR SOCIAL ACCEPTANCE"
65 C$(4)="MOTIVATED BY NEEDS FOR INDEPENDENCE AND SELF-REALIZATION"
70 REM SUM WEIGHTING FACTOR ARRAY FOR SALESPERSON
75 DIM SW(3)
80 REM SUM WEIGHTING FACTOR ARRAY FOR CUSTOMER
85 DIM CW(4)
90 REM SALESPERSONS WEIGHTING FACTORS
95 DIM SF(18)
100 SF(1)=5:SF(2)=5:SF(3)=5:SF(4)=10:SF(5)=2.5:SF(6)=2.5
105 SF(7)=10:SF(8)=5:SF(9)=5:SF(10)=5:SF(11)=2.5:SF(12)=2.5
110 SF(13)=2.5:SF(14)=5:SF(15)=10:SF(16)=2.5:SF(17)=5:SF(18)=5
115 REM CUSTOMERS WEIGHTING FACTORS
120 DIM CF(16)
125 CF(1)=5:CF(2)=3:CF(3)=2:CF(4)=5
130 CF(5)=5:CF(6)=5:CF(7)=3:CF(8)=2
135 CF(9)=5:CF(10)=5:CF(11)=2:CF(12)=3
140 CF(13)=5:CF(14)=2:CF(15)=3:CF(16)=5
145 REM *********************************************************
150 REM ************** DATA ACQUISITION SECTION ****************
155 DIM A$(20) :REM ANSWER ARRAY
160 REM ************** SALESPERSONS DATA ***********************
162 PRINT"**** SALESPERSONS DATA ****"
165 INPUT"DO YOU LIKE TO COMPETE FOR A SALE";A$(1)
170 INPUT"IS YOUR PRESENTATION ENERGETIC AND DYNAMIC";A$(2)
175 INPUT"ARE YOU ABSORBED WITH YOUR OWN ADVANCEMENT";A$(3)
180 INPUT"DO YOU HATE TO FAIL OR LOSE A SALE";A$(4)
185 PRINT"ARE YOU AMBITIOUS ABOUT MOVING UP IN THE COMPANY OR"
190 INPUT" MEETING SALES PRODUCTIVITY DEMANDS";A$(5)
195 INPUT"ARE YOU DECISIVE";A$(6)
200 INPUT"DO YOU LACK ASSERTIVENESS WITH CUSTOMERS";A$(7)
205 INPUT"DO YOU FEEL THAT THE BEST OFFENSE IS A GOOD DEFENSE";A$(8)
210 PRINT"DO YOU LOOK FOR SECURITY WITHIN YOUR JOB STRUCTURE"
215 INPUT" AT ALL COSTS";A$(9)
220 INPUT"DO YOU DISPLAY WARM AND AFFECTIONATE BEHAVIOR";A$(10)
225 INPUT"DO YOU ALWAYS TRY TO BE AGREABLE";A$(11)
230 INPUT"DO YOU FREQUENTLY WANT TO BE AVAILABLE";A$(12)
235 A$(13)=A$(1)
240 INPUT"DO YOU MAKE DECISIONS EASILY";A$(14)
245 INPUT"ARE YOU OPEN AND HONEST WITH CO-WORKERS AND CUSTOMERS";A$(15)
250 A$(16)=A$(5)
255 A$(17)=A$(2)
260 INPUT"DO YOU WELCOME ANOTHER'S OPINION";A$(18)
265 REM CALCULATE SUM-WEIGHTING FACTOR AND POSSIBILITY FACTOR
270 FOR I=1 TO 3:REM CALCULATE SUM WEIGHTING FACTOR
275 S=0:REM TEMPORARY SUM WEIGHTING FACTOR
280 FOR J=1 TO 6
285 K=(I-1)*6+J
290 IF A$(K)="Y" THEN S=S+SF(K)
295 NEXT J
300 SW(I)=S
305 NEXT I
310 REM CALCULATE THE POSSIBILITIES OF BEING A PERSONALITY TYPE
315 DIM PS(3)
320 S=SW(1)+SW(2)+SW(3):REM TOTAL SUM WEIGHTING FACTORS
330 FOR I=1 TO 3: REM PRINT RESULTS
335 PRINT S$(I)
340 PRINT"SUM WEIGHTING FACTOR=";SW(I)
345 PS(I)=SW(I)/S:PRINT"POSSIBILITY=";PS(I)
350 PRINT
355 NEXT I
500 REM *********************************************************
505 REM ********** CUSTOMERS DATA ******************************
507 PRINT"**** CUSTOMERS DATA ****"
```

```
510 INPUT"IS CUSTOMERS CONVERSATION FILLED WITH REFERENCE TO ONESELF";A$(1)
515 INPUT"IS CUSTOMER SELF CONGRATULATORY/BOASTFUL";A$(2)
520 INPUT"DOES CUSTOMER SEEK ADVICE OF SALESPERSON";A$(3)
525 INPUT"DOES CUSTOMER THINK HE KNOWS BETTER THAN ANYONE ELSE";A$(4)
530 INPUT"IS CUSTOMER CAUTIOUS";A$(5)
535 INPUT"IS CUSTOMER SLOW TO MAKE DECISIONS";A$(6)
540 INPUT"IS CUSTOMER UNWILLING TO SHARE OR PROVIDE INFORMATION";A$(7)
545 INPUT"IS CUSTOMER UNWILLING TO REVEAL OPINIONS OR FEELINGS";A$(8)
550 INPUT"DOES CUSTOMER GO OUT OF WAY TO PLEASE";A$(9)
555 INPUT"IS CUSTOMER VERY SUBMISSIVE";A$(10)
560 INPUT"DOES CUSTOMER DODGE ANY DISAGREEMENT OR ARGUMENT";A$(11)
565 PRINT"DOES CUSTOMER COME ACROSS AS PLEASANT-COOPERATIVE OR"
570 INPUT" SYMPATHETIC";A$(12)
575 INPUT"DOES CUSTOMER GET INVOLVED WITH PRESENTATION";A$(13)
580 INPUT"DOES CUSTOMER OFFER IDEAS AND OPINIONS FREELY";A$(14)
585 PRINT"DOES CUSTOMER WANT INVOLVEMENT AS CO-DECISION MAKER WITH"
590 INPUT" SALESPERSON";A$(15)
595 INPUT"DOES CUSTOMER HAVE FLEXIBLE APPROACH";A$(16)
700 REM CALCULATE SUM-WEIGHTING FACTOR AND POSSIBILITY FACTOR
705 FOR I=1 TO 4:REM CALCULATE SUM WEIGHTING FACTOR
710 S=0:REM TEMPORARY SUM WEIGHTING FACTOR
715 FOR J=1 TO 4
720 K=(I-1)*4+J
725 IF A$(K)="Y" THEN S=S+CF(K)
730 NEXT J
735 CW(I)=S
740 NEXT I
742 INPUT"ENTER RETURN TO CONTINUE";K$
745 REM CALCULATE THE POSSIBILITIES OF BEING A PERSONALITY TYPE
750 DIM PC(4)
755 S=CW(1)+CW(2)+CW(3):REM TOTAL SUM WEIGHTING FACTORS
760 FOR I=1 TO 4: REM PRINT RESULTS
765 PRINT C$(I)
770 PRINT"SUM WEIGHTING FACTOR=";CW(I)
775 PC(I)=CW(I)/S:PRINT"POSSIBILITY=";PC(I)
780 PRINT
785 NEXT I
900 REM ****************************************
905 REM POSSIBILITY COMBINATIONS
910 FOR I=1 TO 3
915 FOR J=1 TO 4
920 PRINT"SALES ";I;"  CUSTOMER ";J;" POSSIBILITY=";PS(I)*PC(J)
925 NEXT J
930 INPUT"ENTER RETURN TO CONTINUE";K$
935 NEXT I:STOP
```

## Sample Run

```
RUN
**** SALESPERSONS DATA ****
DO YOU LIKE TO COMPETE FOR A SALE? Y
IS YOUR PRESENTATION ENERGETIC AND DYNAMIC? Y
ARE YOU ABSORBED WITH YOUR OWN ADVANCEMENT? N
DO YOU HATE TO FAIL OR LOSE A SALE? Y
ARE YOU AMBITIOUS ABOUT MOVING UP IN THE COMPANY OR
 MEETING SALES PRODUCTIVITY DEMANDS? N
ARE YOU DECISIVE? N
DO YOU LACK ASSERTIVENESS WITH CUSTOMERS? N
DO YOU FEEL THAT THE BEST OFFENSE IS A GOOD DEFENSE? N
DO YOU LOOK FOR SECURITY WITHIN YOUR JOB STRUCTURE
 AT ALL COSTS? N
DO YOU DISPLAY WARM AND AFFECTIONATE BEHAVIOR? N
DO YOU ALWAYS TRY TO BE AGREEABLE? Y
DO YOU FREQUENTLY WANT TO BE AVAILABLE? N
DO YOU MAKE DECISIONS EASILY? Y
ARE YOU OPEN AND HONEST WITH CO-WORKERS AND CUSTOMERS? N
DO YOU WELCOME ANOTHER'S OPINION? N
```

```
DOMINANT/AGGRESSIVE
SUM WEIGHTING FACTOR= 20
POSSIBILITY= .5714286

SUBMISSIVE/PLEASANT
SUM WEIGHTING FACTOR= 2.5
POSSIBILITY= .0714285

ASSERTIVE
SUM WEIGHTING FACTOR= 12.5
POSSIBILITY= .3571429


**** CUSTOMERS DATA ****
IS CUSTOMERS CONVERSATION FILLED WITH REFERENCE TO ONESELF? N
IS CUSTOMER SELF CONGRATULATORY/BOASTFUL? N
DOES CUSTOMER SEEK ADVICE OF SALESPERSON? N
DOES CUSTOMER THINK HE KNOWS BETTER THAN ANYONE ELSE? N
IS CUSTOMER CAUTIOUS? Y
IS CUSTOMER SLOW TO MAKE DECISIONS? Y
IS CUSTOMER UNWILLING TO SHARE OR PROVIDE INFORMATION? N
IS CUSTOMER UNWILLING TO REVEAL OPINIONS OR FEELINGS? N
DOES CUSTOMER GO OUT OF WAY TO PLEASE? Y
IS CUSTOMER VERY SUBMISSIVE? Y
DOES CUSTOMER DODGE ANY DISAGREEMENT OR ARGUMENT? Y
DOES CUSTOMER COME ACROSS AS PLEASANT-COOPERATIVE OR
 SYMPATHETIC? Y
DOES CUSTOMER GET INVOLVED WITH PRESENTATION? N
DOES CUSTOMER OFFER IDEAS AND OPINIONS FREELY? N
DOES CUSTOMER WANT INVOLVEMENT AS CO-DECISION MAKER WITH
 SALESPERSON? N
DOES CUSTOMER HAVE FLEXIBLE APPROACH? N

ENTER RETURN TO CONTINUE?
MOTIVATED BY NEEDS FOR INDEPENDENCE AND SELF ESTEEM
SUM WEIGHTING FACTOR= 0
POSSIBILITY= 0

MOTIVATED BY NEEDS FOR SECURITY
SUM WEIGHTING FACTOR= 10
POSSIBILITY= .4

MOTIVATED BY NEEDS FOR SOCIAL ACCEPTANCE
SUM WEIGHTING FACTOR= 15
POSSIBILITY= .6

MOTIVATED BY NEEDS FOR INDEPENDENCE AND SELF-REALIZATION
SUM WEIGHTING FACTOR= 0
POSSIBILITY= 0
SALES  1   CUSTOMER  1   POSSIBILITY= 0
SALES  1   CUSTOMER  2   POSSIBILITY= .2285714
SALES  1   CUSTOMER  3   POSSIBILITY= .3428572
SALES  1   CUSTOMER  4   POSSIBILITY= 0
ENTER RETURN TO CONTINUE?
SALES  2   CUSTOMER  1   POSSIBILITY= 0
SALES  2   CUSTOMER  2   POSSIBILITY= .0285714
SALES  2   CUSTOMER  3   POSSIBILITY= .0428571
SALES  2   CUSTOMER  4   POSSIBILITY= 0
ENTER RETURN TO CONTINUE?
SALES  3   CUSTOMER  1   POSSIBILITY= 0
SALES  3   CUSTOMER  2   POSSIBILITY= .1428572
SALES  3   CUSTOMER  3   POSSIBILITY= .2142857
SALES  3   CUSTOMER  4   POSSIBILITY= 0
ENTER RETURN TO CONTINUE?
Break in 935
Ok
```

# 10

# Learning Evaluation Expert System

This chapter will describe how an expert system can be used to pinpoint the existence of an educational problem. Statistics show that a large number of English-speaking native born American adults read or write so poorly that they have trouble holding jobs. Some of them may suffer from specific learning disorders. Statistics also show that many children in this country also suffer from some organically based learning disability.

A learning problem or disability can most profitably be seen as spanning a continuum from mild to severe. We will use the term "learning disability" to define the more severe and the term "learning problem" to define the milder educational problem. The severity of the learning problem depends on the number and severity of processes affected.

Reading and other academic skills are not the only issues to address when studying the field of educational problems. Katrina De Hirsch, in her article, "Learning Disabilities, an Overview," states

> Psychological and physiological factors, the child's genetic endowment, including his vulnerability to stress, his prenatal, neonatal, and postnatal history, the emotional climate in which he is reared, and the social milieu of which he is a part, all interact in complex ways.

The literature therefore makes it clear that disabilities or learning problems are the result of complex interacting forces. Assessment and evaluation, which is the accepted method of diagnosis in the field today, must therefore take into account many factors in order to make a correct evaluation.

Today, the accepted method of educational assessment is implemented by administering standardized tests and gathering pertinent data. In general these tests evaluate specific academic skills such as reading, spelling, and arithmetic. They also assess vocabulary and expressive writing skills. In addition the evaluator gathers background information related to preschool history and present functioning. The testee's school and home environment is assessed as are those psychological and social attributes that relate to the learning process. The evaluator computes the educational test scores, studies the responses on the test in order to pinpoint educational deficits, summarizes all the data gathered regarding background information and present social and psychological functioning, and forms an overall assessment of the person's total learning capacity.

An expert system that assesses the incidence of a learning problem must take all these procedures into consideration. We have created such a system called the Learning Evaluating System (LES). It organizes the process of evaluation systematically so that a thorough and exact analysis is made. As you can well understand, evaluations that are administered by human beings, i.e., professional evaluators, can often be very subjective. People too often consider one or two facts and draw final conclusions swiftly and erroneously. This is not to say that human beings do not evaluate professionally or that computers do a better job. But a system like LES can guide the evaluator in a carefully constructed process by highlighting all of the important facts to be assessed and providing guidelines on how to make decisions about those collected facts. The human mind simply cannot process all of that information simultaneously or as systematically as a computer can.

LES does not make any black and white decisions. It pinpoints specific areas of educational dysfunction and appraises the extent of the deficit, but it allows the evaluator to make the final decisions and recommendations.

This was accomplished via the following format:

1. Organizing the data into topics and subtopics
2. Listing facts associated with each subtopic
3. Assigning weighting factors to the facts and establishing decision levels
4. Verifying the data

## Organizing the Data into Topics and Subtopics

Via a literature search, extensive experience, and the collaboration of several professionals, the system has been divided into the following topics:

Educational

Biological and physical

Psychological

Social

These topics represent some of the determinants or causative contributors to learning problems and disabilities. Since they encompass a great deal of material, several subtopics were devised for each general topic. The topics and subtopics are as follows:

A. Educational
   A-1  Reading
   A-2  Arithmetic
B. Biological and physical
   B-1  Hereditary factors
C. Psychological
   C-1  Self-confidence

## Listing the Facts

We took the topics and subtopics and listed the facts associated with each. Please remember that there are many more topics and facts associated with an educational evaluation than the ones listed below. These facts are but a very small sample of those used in the Learning Evaluation System.

The number in parentheses after each fact is the weighting factor, which will be discussed later in this chapter.

A. Educational
   A-1  Reading
      A-1.1  Pronunciation
         A-1.1.1  Recognizes letters of the alphabet (1)
         A-1.1.2  Pronounces words without reversing or omitting letters (1)
         A-1.1.3  Knows where to place the accent (1)
         A-1.1.4  Breaks different words into proper syllable division (1)
         A-1.1.5  Retains and evokes sound equivalent of letters in words (1)
      A-1.2  Comprehension
         A-1.2.1  Retains facts (1)
         A-1.2.2  Draws inferences (1)
         A-1.2.3  Familiar with vocabulary (1)
         A-1.2.4  Familiar with concepts presented (1)
   A-2  Arithmetic
      A-2.1  Adds numbers in a single column (1)
      A-2.2  Adds numbers in multiple columns (1)

A-2.3   Subtracts with single-column borrowing (1)
A-2.4   Subtracts with multiple-column borrowing (1)
A-2.5   Multiplies single digits (1)
A-2.6   Multiplies multiple digits (1)
A-2.7   Divides and finds a quotient without remainders (1)
A-2.8   Divides and finds a quotient with remainders (1)

B. Biological and physical
  B-1   Hereditary factors
      B-1.1   Parents with learning disabilities (1)
      B-1.2   Sibling (not a twin) with learning disabilities (1)
      B-1.3   Twin with learning disabilities (1)
      B-1.4   Incidence of chromosome anomalies or hereditary disorders in family (1)

C. Psychological
  C-1   Self-confidence
      C-1.1   Withdraws from activities (1)
      C-1.2   Lacks motivation (1)
      C-1.3   Exhibits defeatism (1)

## Assigning Weighting Factors and Establishing Decision Levels

The numbers in parentheses following each of the facts are the weighting factors. Weighting factors help us make decisions because they assign specific values to the facts. Notice that in this system all the factors have been given the weight 1. Since weighting factors are equivalent to importance in their contribution to a problem or lack of one, this means that all the listed facts have equal importance. How do we then make decisions as to whether there is an educational problem? In this system we have established decision levels. Each fact can contribute to a learning problem or disability. If there are many contributing facts, we say the student has a learning problem. If a small number of facts contribute, we might say the student is just missing the point. The way we determine this is by adding the weighting factors of each fact that contributes to that topic, i.e., arithmetic, attention span, etc., being a problem. We call the sum of these facts the sum weighting factor. The lowest sum weighting factor within a subtopic that we determine causes a learning problem is the decision level. If a person scores a sum weighting factor within a subtopic that equals or exceeds the decision level, we assert that there is a problem in that area. For example, the decision level for hereditary factors is 1. If a person received a score of 2 or more in that subtopic, there is probably a problem. Since each fact has a weighting factor of 1, any one or more facts in this topic will cause the decision level to be reached.

The values that we assign to decision levels are determined by testing and research. By testing a sample population, the researcher learns what degree of difficulty indicates a problem area. Of course ongoing, more comprehensive research might modify our selection of weighting factors and decision levels. We have designed an expert system which uses the best guesses of present-day experts and experimentation, but its simple organization will allow us to make easy modifications, should they be needed in the future.

Now that we have the facts and our inference mechanism in hand— the weighting factors and decision levels—let's start out with the implementation.

The procedure for implementing this system is as follows. We formulate questions for each fact of each topic. The questions are formulated so that a yes answer indicates that the fact contributes to a learning problem or deficiency. A no answer indicates that there is no problem or deficiency. The evaluator will sit at the computer and answer specific questions about a subject's performance. The evaluator's response of yes will indicate that the weighting factor, which in this case is always 1, is to be added to the score. A response of no does not add anything to the score. Within a subtopic the final sum weighting factor is tabulated. If the sum weighting factor equals or exceeds the decision level for that subtopic, we state that this subtopic constitutes a problem and inform the evaluator. We may find, of course, that several subtopics are problem areas. We therefore note the number of subtopics that equaled or exceeded the decision levels. If too many exceeded, we definitely have a learning problem. For our simplistic purposes, we can hypothetically establish that if three subtopics exceed the weighting factors, there is a severe problem; if two, there is a mild learning problem; and if one or zero, either there is no learning problem or there is a need for future exploration. To summarize

1. We compute the sum weighting factor by adding the weighting factor of all of the questions that received a yes within a subtopic.

2. We establish whether the sum weighting factor for a subtopic equals or exceeds the decision level for that same subtopic.

3. We print the number and the names of those subtopics that equal or exceed the decision levels.

4. Depending on the number of topics that indicate a problem, we determine whether an individual has a learning problem, a learning disability, or neither.

## An Example of the System at Work

We will now show you how the system works with the following example of a sample case. The evaluator's responses are contained after the question marks below.

Name of person to be evaluated?    Sara Green
Age of person to be evaluated?    12 years, 8 months
Grade level (if applicable)?    7th grade, 10th month
Date of evaluation?    June 7, 1985
Name of evaluator?    Diane Drang

A. Educational
  A-1  Reading
    A-1.1  Pronunciation
      Is person unable to
      A-1.1.1  Recognize letters of the alphabet?  No
      A-1.1.2  Pronounce words without reversing and omitting letters?  Yes
      A-1.1.3  Know where to place the accent?  Yes
      A-1.1.4  Break difficult words into proper syllable division? Yes
      A-1.1.5  Retain and evoke sound equivalent of letters in words?  Yes
           Sum weighting factor = 4
           Decision level = 2
           Test score = Grade 5 years, 8 months
    A-1.2  Comprehension
      Is person unable to
      A-1.2.1  Retain facts?  No
      A-1.2.2  Draw inferences?  Yes
      A-1.2.3  Handle difficult vocabulary?  No
      A-1.2.4  Handle concepts presented?  Yes
           Sum weighting factor = 2
           Decision level = 1
           Test score = Grade 4 years, 8 months
  A-2  Arithmetic
    Is person unable to
    A-2.1  Add numbers in a single column?  No
    A-2.2  Add numbers in multiple columns?  No
    A-2.3  Subtract with single column borrowing?  No
    A-2.4  Subtract with multiple column borrowing?  No
    A-2.5  Multiply single digits?  No
    A-2.6  Multiply multiple digits?  No
    A-2.7  Divide to find quotient without remainders?  No
    A-2.8  Divide to find quotient with remainders?  No
         Sum weighting factor = 0
         Decision level = 2
         Test score = Grade 8 years, 2 months
B. Biological and physical
  B-1  Hereditary factors
    B-1.1  Does either parent have a learning disability?  Yes
    B-1.2  Is there a sibling (not a twin) with a learning disability?  No
    B-1.3  Is there a twin with a learning disability?  No

    B-1.4   Is there any familial history of chromosome anomalies or he-
            reditary disorders in family?   No
                Sum weighting factor = 1
                Decision level = 1
C. Psychological
    C-1   Self-confidence
    Does person
    C-1.1   Withdraw from activities?   No
    C-1.2   Lack motivation?   Yes
    C-1.3   Exhibit defeatism?   No
                Sum weighting factors = 1
                Decision level = 3
Summary of evaluation:
    Names of subtopics that equal or exceed decision level:
    1. Reading pronunciation        2. Reading comprehension
    3. Hereditary factors
Total of subtopics that equal or exceed decision level:   3
    A score of 3 indicates possible incidence of severe learning disability.
    A score of 2 indicates possible incidence of mild learning problem.
    A score of 1 or 0 indicates no learning disability or learning problem.
Sara Green displays a problem in 3 subtopics and therefore shows evidence of
having a severe learning disability.


## Verification Using the Inference Mechanism

Once we have totaled the sum weighting factors and assessed which
subtopics are problem areas, we can say that we have reached our goal.
But to further determine if it was reached accurately, we must check
one more thing. We must create some method for verifying the yes and
no responses that we provided. In other words, how do we know that
the answers we have provided are correct? We need some measure of
verification. Verification is achieved by taking new data and matching
it with original data. The mechanism that matches the two sets of data
is part of the inference mechanism.

As noted earlier in the chapter, one of the important aspects of an
educational evaluation is the administering of educational tests. The
test scores are in the form of age levels and grades. Naturally a person
is expected to score at appropriate grade or age levels chronologically.
An 8-year-old, for example, should achieve an equivalent score of
grade 3 or age 8. If a person scores below age or grade level, we can
state that the person has some problem in that area. The lower the
score, the greater the problem. Consequently the higher the score, the
fewer the problems. It is then safe to say that if a test score falls below
age and grade expectation, there must be deficiencies in that area. For
example, our 12-year-old testee scored grade 4.8 in reading com-

prehension. That score is much lower than her chronological grade level. This means that there must be deficiencies in reading comprehension and *at least* one fact associated with reading comprehension must be answered with a yes. Remember, yes signifies a deficiency.

Verification has a dual purpose. We are trying to verify whether or not a deficiency exists. The verification that a deficiency exists will occur for a specific subtopic when a test score for that specific subtopic shows a deficiency *and* the sum weighting factor for that specific subtopic equals or exceeds the decision level. A deficiency does not exist if the test score does not show a deficiency *and* the decision level has not been achieved. If we are inconsistent in our judgment, i.e., we note a deficient test score and the decision level is not achieved, or we note a high test score and the decision level *is* achieved, the system will tell us that we have made an error. We can use IF-THEN rules to make our verification determination. The rules are the new data which will be matched with the sum weighting factors.

The following are examples of these rules:

1. IF a person scores below age and/or grade level on tests of reading pronunciation, THEN there must be at least one deficiency noted in reading pronunciation.

2. IF a person scores below age and/or grade level on tests of reading comprehension, THEN there must be at least one deficiency noted in reading comprehension.

3. IF a person scores more than 2 years below age and/or grade level on tests for reading pronunciation, THEN that person will equal or exceed the decision level for reading pronunciation.

4. IF a person scores more than 2 years below age and/or grade level on tests for reading comprehension, THEN that person will equal or exceed the decision level for reading comprehension.

The same kinds of rules can be written for all of the educational subtopics. If the evaluator makes an error (for example, suppose all the questions in reading pronunciation are answered no, which indicates no problem, but the score fell below age or grade level on the test for reading pronunciation), the system will print the following error message:

```
Error: Go back and check response to the questions
       related to reading pronunciation.
```

The user would then return to that section and re-evaluate the responses to the questions. Once the errors were corrected, the system would then proceed to evaluate the responses to the questions as described at the end of the sample program.

## Additional Applications

Although this system was designed for the learning specialist or professional, it can serve another purpose as well. A parent, for example, concerned about a child who is not achieving good grades in school observes troubling behavior patterns but is not sure what they mean. The parent might suspect the child has some sort of learning problem or disability but wants more information before seeking help. A parent may simply feel uninformed about the subject matter and would like to gain some vital information on this topic. The better informed one is before seeking professional help, the better equipped one is for making wise selective decisions. A modified system could provide assessment and information rather than diagnosis. It could then be used to determine if there is a need to seek help for a learning problem or disability. The methodology could serve as a model for other kinds of informative self-test systems as well.

Of course a system designed for at-home use would not include standardized testing because parents or people using it for self-education are not familiar with, nor are they trained in, this area. The system would contain questions pertaining to observed behaviors, background information, and some educational issues. It could include the following modified topics and subtopics that were used for LES.

A. Biological and physical
    A-1  Hereditary factors
B. Psychological and social
    B-1  Self-confidence
    B-2  Attention span
    B-3  Social awareness
C. Educational
    C-1  Academic achievement
    C-2  Language and thought development

The following is the taxonomy of facts and their weighting factors for the modified system:

A. Biological and physical
    A-1  Hereditary factors
        A-1.1  Parents with learning disabilities (1)
        A-1.2  Sibling (not a twin) with learning disability (1)
        A-1.3  Twin with learning disability (1)
        A-1.4  Chromosome anomalies or hereditary disorder in family (1)

The facts associated with the next subtopics are different from LES. They pertain more to behaviors that parents observe about their children.

B. Psychological and social
    B-1   Self-confidence
         B-1.1  Exhibits defeatism (1)
         B-1.2  Lacks motivation (1)
         B-1.3  Behaves sluggishly or apathetically (1)
         B-1.4  Downgrades self continuously (1)
    B-2   Attention span
         B-2.1  Appears restless and distracted (1)
         B-2.2  Daydreams excessively (1)
         B-2.3  Responds impulsively (1)
         B-2.4  Relies on others continuously for help with school work (1)
         B-2.5  Hands in assignments late (1)
    B-3   Social awareness
         B-3.1  Appears inept in social situations (1)
         B-3.2  Behaves excessively (loud, comical, aggressive) (1)
         B-3.3  Withdraws from social encounters (1)
         B-3.4  Disorganized about personal belongings and appearance (1)
C. Educational
    C-1   Academic achievement
         C-1.1  Has low school achievement in reading pronunciation of words or paragraphs (1)
         C-1.2  Has low school achievement in reading comprehension (1)
         C-1.3  Has low school achievement in arithmetic (1)
         C-1.4  Has poor handwriting (1)
         C-1.5  Has difficulty with expressive writing skills in school (1)
    C-2   Language and thought development
         C-2.1  Does not speak fluently (1)
         C-2.2  Has difficulty explaining self in full sentences (1)
         C-2.3  Has difficulty understanding what is said in order to follow directions (1)
         C-2.4  Has difficulty linking words with the objects the words refer to (1)
        Has poor memory for
         C-2.5  Remembering numbers (1)
         C-2.6  Remembering names (1)
         C-2.7  Recalling information in sequence presented (1)
         C-2.8  Remembering months of the year (1)
         C-2.9  Remembering days of the week (1)

A sample of how the program works follows. The answers are indicated after the question marks. Notice that the questions are phrased somewhat differently than in the previous section, although some of the content overlaps. The format for using the sum weighting factors and decision levels is the same. The educational section is last (in the previous section it was first) because the emphasis of this assessment is not on standardized testing but on a generalized study of observed behaviors.

Name of child?      Steven Jones
Age?      9 years, 2 months
Grade?      4th
Date of assessment?      June 17, 1985

A. Biological and physical
  A-1  Hereditary factors
      A-1.1  Does either parent have a learning disability?  No
      A-1.2  Is there a sibling not a twin with a learning disability?  No
      A-1.3  Is there a twin with a learning disability?  No
      A-1.4  Are there any chromosome anomalies or hereditary disorders in family?  No
          Sum weighting factor = 0
          Decision level = 1
B. Psychological and social
  B-1  Self-confidence
      Does your child
      B-1.1  Exhibit defeatism?  Yes
      B-1.2  Lack motivation?  Yes
      B-1.3  Behave sluggishly or apathetically?  Yes
      B-1.4  Downgrade self continuously?  Yes
          Sum weighting factor = 4
          Decision level = 3
  B-2  Attention span:
      B-2.1  Is your child restless and easily distractible?  No
      B-2.2  Does your child daydream excessively?  No
      B-2.3  Does your child respond impulsively?  Yes
      B-2.4  Does your child rely continuously on school help from others?  Yes
      B-2.5  Does your child hand in school assignments late?  Yes
          Sum weighting factor = 3
          Decision level = 3
  B-3  Social awareness
      Does your child
      B-3.1  Appear inept in social situations?  No
      B-3.2  Behave excessively?  No
      B-3.3  Withdraw from social encounters?  Yes
      B-3.4  Exhibit disorganization about personal belongings or appearances?  Yes
          Sum weighting factor = 2
          Decision level = 3
C. Educational
  C-1  Academic achievement
      Does school report your child has low achievement in
      C-1.1  Reading pronunciation?  Yes
      C-1.2  Reading comprehension?  Yes

C-1.3   Arithmetic?   Yes
C-1.4   Handwriting?   No
C-1.5   Expressive writing skills?   Yes
        Sum weighting factor = 4
        Decision level = 2

C-2   Language and thought development
Does your child
C-2.1   Have difficulty speaking fluently and clearly?   No
C-2.2   Have limited vocabulary?   No
C-2.3   Have difficulty explaining self in full sentences?   No
C-2.4   Have difficulty understanding what is said in order to follow
        directions?   No
C-2.5   Have difficulty remembering numbers?   No
C-2.6   Have difficulty remembering names?   No
C-2.7   Have difficulty recalling information in sequence?   No
C-2.8   Have difficulty recalling months of the year?   No
C-2.9   Have difficulty recalling days of the week?   No
        Sum weighting factor = 0
        Decision level = 3

Summary of evaluation:
   Names of subtopics that equal or exceed decision levels:
      Self-confidence
      Attention span
      Academic achievement
   Total number of subtopics that equal or exceed decision levels:
      A score of 5 or 6 indicates that there is evidence of a learning problem or
      learning disability, and professional help should be sought.
      A score of 3 or 4 indicates that there is little evidence of a learning prob-
      lem, but professional help might be sought temporarily.
      A score of 1 or 2 indicates that there is no problem indicated here that
      requires professional help.
Steven Jones displays a problem in three subtopics and therefore shows evidence of a learning problem that requires professional help.


It should be noted that these decision levels are not absolute. They
are, in reality, hypothetical examples of how they may be used to
assess learning problems. As the use of expert systems in education is
new and experimental, decision levels are open to further research and
discussion.

If you compare the evaluations of Sara Green and Steven Jones, you
will observe that both exhibit some serious indication that a learning
problem or disability exists. However, a look at the names of the subtopics shows that although both exhibit problems, Sara displays strong
symptoms educationally and biologically but very little psychologically. Steven Jones displays strong symptoms psychologically along
with academic underachievement. Thus the organization of facts into
subtopics enables the professional evaluator or the parent to pinpoint

the specific problem areas. The number of subtopics that equal or exceed the decision level indicates the extent or the severity of the problem.

## Summary

This chapter has described the use of an expert system to evaluate the extent of an educational problem. Educational problems are of particular interest at this time because many American adults and children lack elementary skills. Discussion of how the current conventional methods of educational assessment can be transferred to an expert system has now been introduced. Topics, subtopics, and a list of facts comprise the basic structure. A format for arriving at sum weighting factors and comparing them with decision levels was established. The next step was verification of the data. The use of an expert system to provide a method of evaluation for the professional educational evaluator was extended to use by parents who are concerned about their children's levels of achievement. Programming examples were provided.

## Programming Applications

The LES program, Listing 10-1, is provided so that you can study the concepts of this chapter with your own computer. The program is written in BASIC.

### Program Explanation

The program is divided into four segments which are

1. The initialization section in which weighting factors are supplied, statements 20 and 25
2. The acquisition of personal data, statements 60 through 85
3. The data to be used in making the evaluation, statements 100 through 240
4. The inference mechanism for making the evaluation, statements 5015 through 5140

You are encouraged to modify any of the first three sections as a means of constructing an individual evaluation system.

### Program Listing

Listing 10-1 is followed by sample runs.

**Listing 10-1   Learning evaluation expert system.**

```
1 REM ********** LEARNING EVALUATION (EXPERT) SYSTEM ********************
5 REM WEIGHTING FACTOR ARRAY
10 DIM W(100)
15 REM INSERT WEIGHTING FACTOR
20 FOR I=1 TO 100
25 W(I)=1:NEXT I
30 DIM A$(10):REM ANSWER ARRAY
35 DIM D$(20):REM DEFFICIENCY ARRAY
40 FOR I=1 TO 20
45 D$(I)="":NEXT I
50 DP=1:REM DEFICIENCY POINTER
55 WP=1:REM WEIGHTING FACTOR POINTER
60 REM *** PERSONAL DATA ***
65 INPUT"NAME OF PERSON TO BE EVALUATED ";NP$
70 INPUT"AGE OF PERSON TO BE EVALUATED YEAR-MONTH ";AY,AM
75 INPUT"PERSONS SCHOOL GRADE LEVEL (IF APPLICABLE) YEAR-MONTH ";GY,GM
80 INPUT"DATE OF EVALUATION MONTH-DAY-YEAR ";DM,DD,DY
85 INPUT"NAME OF EVALUATOR ";NE$
90 REM ** DATA ACQUISITION SECTION **
95 REM ***********************************
100 REM READING PRONUNCIATION SECTION
105 INPUT"ENTER READING PRONUNCIATION GRADE TEST SCORE..YEAR-MONTH ";TY,TM
110 INPUT"ENTER DECISION LEVEL";DL
115 PRINT"* IS PERSON UNABLE TO:"
120 INPUT"RECOGNIZE LETTERS OF THE ALPHABET";A$(1)
125 INPUT"PRONOUNCE WORDS WITHOUT REVERSING OR OMITTING LETTERS";A$(2)
130 INPUT"KNOW WHERE TO PLACE THE ACCENT";A$(3)
135 INPUT"BREAK DIFFICULT WORDS INTO PROPER SYLLABLE DIVISION";A$(4)
140 INPUT"RETAIN/EVOKE SOUND EQUIVALENT OF LETTERS IN WORDS";A$(5)
145 PRINT"** READING PRONUNCIATION **"
150 REM GOTO INFERENCE MECHANISM..DETERMINE IF DECISION LEVEL IS
155 REM EXCEEDED..VERIFY THE DATA AS COMPARED TO THE TEST SCORE
160 K$="READING PRONUNCIATION":SE=5:GOSUB 5000:REM NUMBER OF QUESTIONS
195 REM ***********************************
200 REM READING COMPREHENSION SECTION
205 INPUT"ENTER READING COMPREHENSION GRADE TEST SCORE..YEAR-MONTH ";TY,TM
210 INPUT"ENTER DECISION LEVEL";DL
215 PRINT"* IS PERSON UNABLE TO:"
220 INPUT"RETAIN FACTS";A$(1)
225 INPUT"DRAW INFERENCES";A$(2)
230 INPUT"HANDLE DIFFICULT VOCABULARY";A$(3)
235 INPUT"HANDLE CONCEPTS PRESENTED";A$(4)
240 K$="READING COMPREHENSION":SE=4:GOSUB 5000:REM NUMBER OF QUESTIONS
4000 REM ***********************************
4005 PRINT"DEFICIENT RESPONSES"
4010 FOR I=1 TO 20
4015 IF D$(I)="" THEN GOTO 4025
4020 PRINT D$(I)
4025 NEXT I
4999 STOP:REM ******** END OF RUN
5000 REM ***********************************
5005 REM ** INFERENCE MECHANISM **
5010 REM ************************
5015 REM IS TEST SCORE ABOVE OR BELOW GRADE
5020 TB=0:REM TEST SCORE BELOW GRADE IF TB=1
5025 Y=GY-TY:M=GM-TM
5030 IF Y>0 THEN TB=1
5035 IF (Y=0) AND (M>0) THEN TB=1
5040 IF TB=1 THEN PRINT"** TEST SCORE BELOW AVERAGE"
5045 REM ***********************************
5050 REM IF ANSWERS PRODUCE A SUM WEIGHTING  FACTOR AT LEAST EQUAL TO
5055 REM THE DECISION LEVEL THEN THERE IS A PROBLEM
5060 S=0:REM INITIALIZE SUM WEIGHTING FACTOR
5063 REM
5065 REM ADD ALL WEIGHTING FACTORS CORRESPONDING TO A Y
5070 FOR I=1 TO SE
5075 IF A$(I)="Y" THEN S=W(WP)+S:WP=WP+1
5080 NEXT I
5085 PRINT"** SUM WEIGHTING FACTOR IS ";S
5090 REM ***********************************
5095 REM IS DECISION LEVEL REACHED
5100 IF S>=DL THEN PRINT"** DECISION LEVEL IS REACHED"
5105 IF S>=DL THEN D$(DP)=K$:DP=DP+1
5110 REM ***********************************
5115 REM INCONSISTENCY DETERMINATION
5120 REM DEFICIENCY LEVEL REACHED BUT TEST SCORE ABOVE AVERAGE
5125 IF (S>=DL) AND (TB=0) THEN PRINT"** DEFICIENCY REACHED/GOOD SCORE"
5130 IF (S<DL) AND (TB=1) THEN PRINT"** DEFICIENCY NOT REACHED/BAD SCORE"
5135 RETURN
```

## Sample Runs

```
RUN
NAME OF PERSON TO BE EVALUATED ? SARA GREEN
AGE OF PERSON TO BE EVALUATED YEAR-MONTH ? 12,8
PERSONS SCHOOL GRADE LEVEL (IF APPLICABLE) YEAR-MONTH ? 7,10
DATE OF EVALUATION MONTH-DAY-YEAR ? 6,7,1985
NAME OF EVALUATOR ? DIANE DRANG
ENTER READING PRONUNCIATION GRADE TEST SCORE..YEAR-MONTH ? 5,8
ENTER DECISION LEVEL? 2
* IS PERSON UNABLE TO:
RECOGNIZE LETTERS OF THE ALPHABET? N
PRONOUNCE WORDS WITHOUT REVERSING OR OMITTING LETTERS? Y
KNOW WHERE TO PLACE THE ACCENT? Y
BREAK DIFFICULT WORDS INTO PROPER SYLLABLE DIVISION? Y
RETAIN/EVOKE SOUND EQUIVALENT OF LETTERS IN WORDS? Y
** READING PRONUNCIATION **
** TEST SCORE BELOW AVERAGE
** SUM WEIGHTING FACTOR IS  4
** DECISION LEVEL IS REACHED

ENTER READING COMPREHENSION GRADE TEST SCORE..YEAR-MONTH ? 4,8
ENTER DECISION LEVEL? 1
* IS PERSON UNABLE TO:
RETAIN FACTS? N
DRAW INFERENCES? Y
HANDLE DIFFICULT VOCABULARY? N
HANDLE CONCEPTS PRESENTED? Y
** TEST SCORE BELOW AVERAGE
** SUM WEIGHTING FACTOR IS  2
** DECISION LEVEL IS REACHED
DEFICIENT RESPONSES
READING PRONUNCIATION
READING COMPREHENSION
Break in 4999
Ok
```

The sample run for Sara Green was taken directly from this chapter.

```
RUN
NAME OF PERSON TO BE EVALUATED ? JOHN SMITH
AGE OF PERSON TO BE EVALUATED YEAR-MONTH ? 12,8
PERSONS SCHOOL GRADE LEVEL (IF APPLICABLE) YEAR-MONTH ? 7,10
DATE OF EVALUATION MONTH-DAY-YEAR ? 6,7,1985
NAME OF EVALUATOR ? DIANE DRANG
ENTER READING PRONUNCIATION GRADE TEST SCORE..YEAR-MONTH ? 7,11
ENTER DECISION LEVEL? 2
* IS PERSON UNABLE TO:
RECOGNIZE LETTERS OF THE ALPHABET? N
PRONOUNCE WORDS WITHOUT REVERSING OR OMITTING LETTERS? Y
KNOW WHERE TO PLACE THE ACCENT? Y
BREAK DIFFICULT WORDS INTO PROPER SYLLABLE DIVISION? Y
RETAIN/EVOKE SOUND EQUIVALENT OF LETTERS IN WORDS? Y
** READING PRONUNCIATION **
** SUM WEIGHTING FACTOR IS  4
** DECISION LEVEL IS REACHED
** DEFICIENCY REACHED/GOOD SCORE
ENTER READING COMPREHENSION GRADE TEST SCORE..YEAR-MONTH ? 4,8
ENTER DECISION LEVEL? 1
```

```
* IS PERSON UNABLE TO:
RETAIN FACTS? N
DRAW INFERENCES? Y
HANDLE DIFFICULT VOCABULARY? N
HANDLE CONCEPTS PRESENTED? Y
** TEST SCORE BELOW AVERAGE
** SUM WEIGHTING FACTOR IS  2
** DECISION LEVEL IS REACHED
DEFICIENT RESPONSES
READING PRONUNCIATION
READING COMPREHENSION
Break in 4999
Ok
```

Notice that under reading pronunciation the printed output "Deficiency Reached/Good Score" means that although the decision level indicated a deficiency, the test score exceeded grade level. This constitutes a contradiction and therefore instructs the user to re-examine the answers and results.

# Advanced Programming Techniques for Powerful Systems

*Section 4 discusses the concepts of object-oriented programming and how it is used in the design of expert systems. In order to further clarify the concepts, a program is provided which will allow you to set up your own system. If you wish to expand your conceptual understanding, you can use the subroutines provided in the program to develop more sophisticated systems.*

# Fundamentals of Object-Oriented Programming

Imagine that you have a box that has a lot of pigeon holes—like an old-fashioned box for hand-sorting mail. Each hole contains a piece of information written on a piece of paper. A hole labeled "union activities" contains the latest information concerning arbitration and grievances of the union members; a hole labeled "pensions" describes options for investing money in company-sponsored financial plans, and so on. Such a box that has a lot of holes or spaces for inserting, removing, and changing information is called a structure. A structure gathers together many pieces of information into a fixed pattern.

How is a structure built and the labeling of the holes determined? As an example, suppose someone of high authority, such as the president of a company, wishes to define and categorize all the information needed to run the business. This individual might create a plan for building the actual structure and deciding how many holes are needed and what they should be called according to the size and nature of the company. The plan would then be given to a carpenter who actually builds the structure to the plan's specifications.

Structures are also used to gather and sort information in artificial intelligence programs. In AI terminology, the holes in the box are called "slots" and the labels on the holes are called "attributes." The pieces of information placed in the slots are called "values." When values are placed into the slots, the actual "object" comes into being.

For example, suppose many people constantly want to reserve a conference room. In order to accommodate all these people, we must have a formal procedure for reserving the room. We must build a conference room structure. One of the slots of the structure must have the attribute "time the conference room is needed." After all, we cannot schedule two conferences in the same room at the same time. Another slot must have as an attribute "the person's name who is reserving the conference room," and so on, for all the pertinent attributes of this structure. When someone wishes to actually reserve a room, the values (time and name) needed to construct an object from the conference room structure would be provided.

Let's review these definitions:

1. Structure—a plan for constructing an object

2. Object—a structure that contains information

3. Slot—a place to store information

4. Attribute—a labeled slot

5. Value—information associated with an attribute and placed in a labeled slot

Let's consider the conference room example in more detail. Suppose a company has a number of very busy conference rooms and is in need of a system for assigning time in each of the rooms. The structure the company would use is a general form that employees must fill out when they need the use of a conference room. We'll call this structure the conference room form. By filling out the form, a specific instance of the structure is created, which is called an object. In this case, the object will contain a person's name and all the other items that were filled in to complete the form. During the course of a single day there may be more than one conference; each individual conference represents a separate object. Let's say it again to be sure it's absolutely clear: A structure defines attributes that are important in doing something, and an object is a specific instance of that structure.

The conference room structure should allow any employee to reserve a room and also provide enough information so that all other employees can know what is going on in the room at any time. A typical conference room structure might look like this:

1. Conference room number

2. Subject of discussion

3. Speaker's name

4. Start-time of conference

5. End-time of conference

There are five attributes that we have chosen in the conference room structure for this example. Assume there are 12 different conference rooms in the company's office building. An employee who wishes to use a conference room fills out a form that contains all the attributes of the conference room structure and provides all the required information. That conference room is now reserved for that time. An example of a conference room object that was created by filling out the form would be

1. 10                                  (conference room number)
2. Employee overtime rules     (subject of discussion)
3. Daniel Drang                     (speaker's name)
4. 10:00                             (start-time of conference)
5. 11:00                             (end-time of conference)

The object's first value, 10, corresponds to the attribute "conference room number," and the second value, employee overtime rules, corresponds to the attribute "subject of the discussion." The other values also correspond to the attributes of the structure.

In both small and large companies, there are many different activities going on at all times. Each of these activities might require employees to follow a specific procedure for engaging in that activity. The procedure may in fact be as simple as a checklist. Airplane mechanics have checklists of items they must verify as working before a plane can take off. These checklists are all derived from a structure. For example, the mechanic has to determine that the plane has enough fuel and that the tires have enough air in them. Airlines have many things to do; therefore they may have many forms, each of which is a specific structure for doing something. Each structure must have an identification number, or name, so that a form for that structure can be requested and located. The name of the mechanic's checklist structure may be called "preparation for take-off." This immediately tells us something important about some needed structure properties, which are

1. Name, so that the structure can be referred to
2. Attributes, which define the structure's contents

Let's continue with the mechanic's work. After obtaining a form of the structure preparation for take-off, the mechanic goes through the checklist, fills it out, signs the form, and hands it in, thereby creating an object from the form. This object is given an identification number (which is really its name). Since there may be many of these forms filled out in a single day—at least one for each plane taking off—this particular form can be retrieved at a later time by knowing its name (identification number).

From this discussion we can conclude that an object must have the following properties:

1. Structure name, so that we know the meaning of the rules given to the objects

2. Object name, so that it can be referred to

3. Attributes, which define its items of importance

4. Values, which are pieces of information corresponding to the attributes

Another thing that must accompany a structure and its objects is a set of "procedures." For example, what is the procedure to be followed if a tire is flat? Do we fix it with all the passengers still on the plane? Are there any procedures for dealing with a leaky fuel line? Procedures are therefore an integral part of a structure.

Some procedures must be carried out before other procedures. For example, before checking various gauges on a plane, the plane's electrical power must be turned on. Therefore, we must have a procedure for turning on the power before we follow the gauge-checking procedure. The before procedure, which is not directly referred to but still must be carried out, is called a "before demon." (Procedures that exist but are not invoked directly by the user are referred to as demons.) Similarly, there might be procedures that have to be invoked after a main procedure is completed. These procedures are also not directly referred to but must be done. They are called "after demons." An example of an after demon would be a procedure for filing the preparation for take-off form after all the gauges have been checked.

Procedures can be stated directly in the structure or made known to the user of the structure in other ways. In the mechanic example, a portion of the checklist might look like this:

1. Read fuel gauge and record it.

2. If fuel gauge is less than 2000 gallons, invoke procedure on form 34555.

3. Check tire pressure and record it.

4. If tire pressure is less than . . . , invoke procedure on form 34556.

Slots 2 and 4 are references to procedures for handling certain occurrences. But the actual methods for reading the fuel gauge and checking tire pressure are part of the mechanic's training and are contained perhaps in separate forms with which the mechanic is already familiar. They are not detailed in this checklist.

## Creating a Structure

Each of the properties that we described for structures and objects must be available to the programmer for constructing an object-oriented system. In review, these properties are

1. The ability to create a structure
2. The ability to create objects from that structure
3. The ability to create procedures for doing things with objects

As we discussed earlier, a structure must have a name, so that it can be referred to, and attributes, which describe the structure's makeup. By giving names to structures, the user can easily refer to a required structure by name, assign values to its attributes, and thereby create an object. This is just what mechanics might do when they go to the room where all the forms are kept: request the needed form by name, fill in the blanks, and in the process create an object.

To create an object-oriented program, we must have a procedure for creating a structure and for specifying each of the attributes. Here is the format that we will use to describe how a structure subroutine is created in a computer program. The actual BASIC instructions are shown in Listing 11-1 at the end of the chapter.

```
CREATE-STRUCTURE (SNAME  = name of the structure
                  NATTR  = number of attributes for this
                           structure
            ATTR  = first attribute name
            ATTR  = second attribute name
              .
              .
              .
            ATTR   = last attribute name)
```

To illustrate how a structure is created, let's consider the following conference room structure:

1. Conference room number    (ROOM)
2. Subject of discussion      (SUBJECT)
3. Speaker's name             (SPEAKER)
4. Start-time of conference   (START)
5. End-time of conference     (END)

In order to make our discussion of the conference room structure easier to follow, we have abbreviated the attributes as shown in the list in parentheses following each one. The conference room structure has five attributes whose abbreviated names are ROOM, SUBJECT, SPEAKER, START, and END. Since the conference room structure must have a name, we'll call it CONF. Whenever we refer to CONF in our program, the system will understand that we mean the conference room structure together with the five attributes associated with it. The way in which these things are put together is

```
CREATE-STRUCTURE(SNAME = CONF, NATTR = 5, ATTR =
                 ROOM, ATTR = SUBJECT, ATTR =
                 SPEAKER, ATTR = START, ATTR = END)
```

Using the conference room structure, let's now consider the CREATE-STRUCTURE subroutine. As you can see, each attribute is preceded by a keyword. This tells the object-oriented system which attribute is being passed to it. The keyword SNAME = tells the system to use the name following this keyword as the name of the structure. In this case, it is CONF. The keyword NATTR = tells the system what the number of attributes it will get follows. In this case it is five. The keyword ATTR = tells the system to accept the following name as the name of the attribute. In this case there are five ATTR keywords, one for each attribute. The object-oriented system now knows the form of the conference room structure.

## Creating an Object

Whenever we want to create an object of a structure, all we have to do is tell the system the name of the structure and then provide the values that should be given to each attribute. This is like applying for a job, getting a form to fill out, and then detailing your previous job history on the form. You have in essence requested a structure (the job application form) and given the attributes values (name, address, previous employment, etc.), thereby creating an object. The form you filled out is filed by your name (object name) for future reference. Let's see how this is done by the programmer. The general format for creating an object subroutine is

```
CREATE-OBJECT(SNAME  = name of structure from which object is
                        derived
              ONAME  = name of this particular object
              ATTRI1 = attribute's value
              ATTRI2 = attribute's value


              ATTRIn = attribute's value)
```

SNAME = is followed by the structure name, ONAME = is followed by the object name, and ATTRI1 = is followed by the value you have given to that particular attribute. There can be one of these for each attribute defined in the structure. If you leave out an attribute name, the object will have a space in that attribute's location when the object is created. We can provide this value at a later time, just as you might leave blank spaces on a form and come back and fill them in later.

As an example, let's assume that Susan Bard needs conference room number 10 for 1 hour beginning at 10 A.M. to discuss employee overtime rules. She will create an object and give it a name that is not already used—such as TEN1—as follows:

CREATE-OBJECT (SNAME = CONF, ONAME = TEN1, ROOM = 10, SUBJECT = EMPLOYEE OVERTIME RULES, SPEAKER = Susan Bard, START = 10:00, END = 11:00)

By referring to the object by the object name, TEN1, the object can be accessed.

What we have done up to this point is develop a general form (structure specification) for the CREATE-STRUCTURE subroutine and one object of this form (the object being an instance of a structure), also part of the CREATE-OBJECT subroutine.

## Overview of Objects and Their Operations

What we have done in creating a specific structure and objects conforming to that particular structure is in reality create a database. The objects are records in the database, and the structure specifies the format of a record and its components. (In database terminology, records consist of fields, which we have chosen to call attributes.) Some of the things we normally do with a database are

1. Place and modify values in the fields (or attributes) of each record (or object).

2. Get statistics from the database, such as the number of conferences going on at a given time.

3. Provide procedures for operations on one or more fields (attributes) of a record (object).

4. Be able to view the database as is.

## Operations on Objects

Before we discuss some of the operations we can apply to objects, let's create two more objects so that we can facilitate our explanation:

CREATE-OBJECT (SNAME = CONF, ONAME = TEN2, ROOM =
            10, SUBJECT = PAY RAISES, SPEAKER = Marc
            Stone, START = 13:00, END = 14:00)

CREATE-OBJECT (SNAME = CONF, ONAME = ELE1, ROOM =
            11, SUBJECT = SALES PROJECTIONS,
            SPEAKER = Andy Rome, START = 10:00, END
            = 12:00)

You should be able to read these objects easily by now: Marc Stone has
reserved conference room 10 from 1 to 2 P.M. (equivalent to 13:00 and
14:00) to discuss pay raises (object name TEN2), and Andy Rome has
reserved conference room 11 from 10:00 to 12:00 to discuss sales projections (object name ELE1).

## Viewing Objects and Structures

Sometimes we would just like to view the structures and objects to find
out which ones are in the system at a given time. This is done by
sitting down at the console and typing certain commands. To list all
objects, you would call up a subroutine named, for example, LIST-
ALL-OBJECT-NAMES. In our example, the computer would respond
with

```
TEN1
TEN2
ELE1
```

To get a listing of all structure names, we could call up subroutine
LIST-ALL-STRUCTURE-NAMES. We have only created one structure so far, so the computer will respond with

```
CONF
```

We can list all the values of the attributes of a specific object by going
to the LIST-OBJECT subroutine. For our example, if we wanted to
view the object ELE1, we would enter the following responses to program queries:

```
LIST-OBJECT, SNAME=CONF, ONAME=ELE1
```

and would obtain

```
ROOM=11
SUBJECT=SALES PROJECTIONS
SPEAKER=Andy Rome
START=10:00
END=12:00
```

## Object Operations

In addition to creating objects, we might also have occasion to remove them. For example, when Andy Rome's sales projections meeting is over in conference room 11, we would want to eliminate that object from our database because he finished using the room. We do that with a REMOVE subroutine. We would remove object ELE1 and then verify the removal of ELE1 with subroutine LIST-ALL-OBJECT-NAMES. We would get as a response

```
TEN1
TEN2
```

ELE1, as desired, is missing from the list.

There are times when we will want to change the value of an attribute in an object. A SEND subroutine can be used to insert a value in an object's attribute. In our example, the following responses to program queries will change the starting time (START) for object TEN1 from 10:00 to 9:00:

```
SEND (SNAME=CONF, ONAME=TEN1, START=9:00)
```

If we now ran the LIST-OBJECT subroutine, we would get

```
ROOM=10
SUBJECT=EMPLOYEE OVERTIME RULES
SPEAKER=Susan Bard
START=9:00
END=11:00
```

Notice that the starting time, as we wanted, has been changed from 10:00 to 9:00.

The last subroutine we will discuss allows us to copy the value of an object's attribute into a variable. Once the value is in the form of a variable, a whole set of operations can be performed on the variable. To do this, we use the COPY subroutine. Let's take the SPEAKER attribute of TEN2 as an example. We could use the subroutine to copy SPEAKER to the variable y$ and then use the BASIC command

```
PRINT y$
```

and we will get

```
Marc Stone
```

If, for example, we wished to write a report for management on conference room activities, we can do it by merely "copying" and "printing" the values of the attributes into a report.

Let's review what we have learned:

1. We can create a structure via CREATE-STRUCTURE.
2. We can create objects of the structure via CREATE-OBJECT.
3. We can change an object's attribute via SEND.
4. We can obtain the value of an object's attribute via COPY.
5. We can remove an object from the database via REMOVE.
6. We can view structures and objects via LIST-ALL-STRUCTURE-NAMES, LIST-OBJECT, and LIST-ALL-OBJECTS.

## Invoking Procedures

When we discussed the plane mechanic's checklist in relation to the tire pressure, we said a procedure would be invoked to reinflate the tire if the pressure was too low. The procedure might simply be to attach an air hose to the tire. In any event, the mechanic would know what the procedure is for doing that. Let's examine what we are saying on a more general level:

1. We have a procedure for checking a slot of an object for a specific value (in our example, it was a minimum tire pressure).
2. If the value exceeded some boundary condition, we invoked a procedure to deal with it (in our example, it was a procedure for reinflating the tire if the pressure was too low).

Let's examine one more example to make sure the concept of procedures is clear. In our conference room example, we described how the SEND subroutine was used to change the START time of Susan Bard's conference from 10:00 to 9:00 A.M. What would have happened if someone else had scheduled a conference in that same room between the hours of 9:00 and 10:00 A.M.? If we allowed the change to take place without any further actions, two groups would have arrived at the conference room at 9. What should have happened is this: When Susan changed the conference room time, a procedure should automatically have been invoked to check the conference room number and starting and ending times of all objects with the same conference room number in order to see if there was a conflict. If there was, Susan could then have been notified, allowing her to make appropriate arrangements.

On the other hand, if Susan simply wanted to change the title of her discussion (attribute SUBJECT) there would be no need to invoke a procedure because the change has no effect on other objects. The essential procedure philosophy is

> When certain attributes are modified, procedures may be invoked to see if any action should be taken.

## A Method for Invoking Procedures

When we discussed operations on objects, we showed how a value is inserted in the slot of an object by the SEND subroutine. As we will see in the programming considerations section of this chapter, the SEND subroutine is composed of a series of instructions that locates an object of a structure and then stores a value into an attribute slot of the object. For example:

```
SEND (SNAME=CONF, ONAME=TEN1, START=9:00)
```

will create a set of instructions that will first search the computer's memory for the location of the structure CONF and object within the structure called TEN1. Then, the value 9:00 would be inserted into the slot assigned to the attribute START. The question is, How is the procedure invoked? The answer is that an indication must be provided to the SEND subroutine that when a specific attribute has a value assigned to it, a procedure must automatically be invoked. Since it is the SEND subroutine that is changing the value, it is therefore logical for the SEND subroutine to be connected to the invoking of a procedure.

What we must do is find a way of telling the SEND subroutine that the attribute whose value is changing should invoke a procedure. For example, when we change the start-time attribute of TEN1, we want to invoke a procedure to tell us when a conflict arises. Changing the title of the attribute SUBJECT, on the other hand, should *not* invoke a procedure.

Well, the answer is very simple. When, in defining a structure, we come upon an attribute that should invoke a procedure, we do the following:

1. Precede the name of the attribute with an asterisk.

2. When the SEND subroutine "sees" this attribute, it knows a procedure should be invoked because of the asterisk.

3. The procedure name should be the very next attribute.

For example, we want to invoke a procedure if either the start- or end-time of a conference is changed. This procedure would ensure that there is no conflict when employees sign up to use the rooms. The way we accomplish all this is via the CREATE-STRUCTURE subroutine, which contains the following:

CREATE-STRUCTURE (SNAME = CONF, NATTR = 7, ATTR = ROOM, ATTR = SUBJECT, ATTR = SPEAKER, ATTR = *START, ATTR = PRO-CEDURE, ATTR = *END, ATTR = PRO-CEDURE)

Note the asterisk before the START and END attributes. Following these asterisked attributes are two additional attributes with the keyword PROCEDURE (also note that the total number of attributes have been increased to seven—NATTR = 7—as a result). These procedure slots will be used, when creating an object of the structure CONF, to specify the procedure to be invoked when the SEND subroutine changes the START or END value. Let's see how this works. The CONF object created for Susan Bard would look like this:

CREATE-OBJECT (SNAME = CONF, ONAME = TEN1, ROOM = 10, SUBJECT = EMPLOYEE OVERTIME RULES, SPEAKER = Susan Bard, START = 10:00, PRO-CEDURE = name of procedure, END = 11:00, PROCEDURE = name of procedure)

If we were implementing the CREATE-OBJECT subroutine in BASIC, we would use a number in place of "name of procedure." (In other languages, such as LISP, we could use a symbolic name such as START-PROC.) The number in BASIC would be used to identify the statement number of the procedure. Now when we view the object with the LIST-OBJECT subroutine, this is where we stand:

```
ROOM=10
SUBJECT=EMPLOYEE OVERTIME RULES
SPEAKER=Susan Bard
*START=10:00
PROCEDURE=1
*END=11:00
PROCEDURE=1
```

The PROCEDURE = 1 signifies that the same procedure is used when the SEND subroutine changes either the START or END time. If Susan now wanted to change the starting time, she would do so with the SEND subroutine. It would invoke procedure 1. This procedure would check all objects with the attribute value ROOM = 10 to see if there is an overlap with another conference being held in the same room. The sequence of events taken by the SEND subroutine to accomplish all this is

1. Find the location in computer memory where the structure is located. It is the structure that tells us if an asterisk precedes an attribute name.

2. Scan the structure's attributes for the name of the attribute whose value is changing.

3. If there is an asterisk preceding the name, get ready to invoke a procedure.

4. Now that we know if an object's attribute invokes a procedure, we can locate the object in memory.

5. Next, we invoke the procedure of the attribute that is changed if there is an asterisk preceding it. If there is no asterisk, simply change the value.

The ability to use the SEND subroutine in conjunction with the procedure invocation is one of the most important features of object-oriented programming. Since different objects have different tasks, it is this feature that allows objects with varied responsibilities to communicate with each other via a method of sending messages. This procedure is initially set up when the system is created. For example, if the procedure invoked by a conference room time change detected a time overlap with another conference for the same room causing a conflict for both conference room space and speaker time, the SEND subroutine would direct a message to a speaker object. This message would invoke another procedure that would cause a message to be triggered at the terminal, which would then inform the speaker of the conflict overlap. Now that we have journeyed through object-oriented programming, put down your pencil and paper and run the program in Listing 11-1. It will solidify all the concepts you have learned.

## Programming Applications

The purpose of this portion of the chapter is to provide a set of subroutines, written in BASIC, for doing object-oriented programming. You can use these subroutines to set up your own object-oriented system. The program is divided into two parts. One part contains the object-oriented subroutines, which are located in statements 2999 through 5240. The other part is an application program designed to acquaint you with the methodology for using these subroutines. The application part is contained in statements 2 through 905. The application part is divided into eight object-oriented operations, each having a similar design in the way it interacts with the subroutines. Understanding how one works should give you a clue as to how all the

operations work. Each of the eight operations can be selected by a
menu. Let's see how the program works in creating a structure.

### Programming Explanation

The first thing we must do is enter the RUN command at the console.
At statement 2, the program will create the structure-object array
SO$, which will contain the structure definitions and the objects. Then
statements 2 through 55 will cause the following menu to appear on
the screen:

```
ENTER A NUMBER TO DO ONE OF THE FOLLOWING
1-CREATE A STRUCTURE
2-CREATE AN OBJECT
3-NAME OF ALL STRUCTURES
4-NAME OF ALL OBJECTS
5-VIEW A STRUCTURE
6-VIEW AN OBJECT
7-SEND A VALUE TO AN OBJECT
8-COPY A VALUE TO Z$ FROM AN OBJECT'S ATTRIBUTE
9-EXIT
? 1
```

In our sample runs, the user response appears after the question mark.
When the user entered a 1 at the console, the program executed statement 60, causing transfer of control to the subroutine at statement
100. Statements 105 and 110 were then executed, resulting in the
following screen-user dialogue:

```
ENTER STRUCTURE NAME ? CONF
ENTER NUMBER OF ATTRIBUTES ? 5
```

This resulted in the execution of statement 115 to assign 5 to N and 7
to E. The FOR loop at statements 120 through 135 caused the following
screen-user dialogue:

```
ATTRIBUTE  1 -? ROOM
ATTRIBUTE  2 -? SUBJECT
ATTRIBUTE  3 -? SPEAKER
ATTRIBUTE  4 -? START
ATTRIBUTE  5 -? END
```

The last seven user responses are stored in the temporary array T$.
The structure-creating subroutine was then entered indirectly via
statement 145, which transferred control to the subroutine at statement 3000. The program as written can only contain two structures in
SO$. Of course, it can be modified to contain more. One structure can
start at SO$(1) and the other at SO$(101). The structure locations are

assigned in the order of creation, with the first at SO$(1). The CREATE STRUCTURE subroutine located at statements 3000 through 3080 determines in which half of SO$ to store the structure definition contained in the temporary array T$. The RETURN from the subroutine is to statement 150, which then displays the menu on the screen, allowing the user to select other options.

The other menu selections work in a very similar way, making it easy to follow their program sequences.

### Program Listing

Listing 11-1 is followed by a sequence of sample runs that correspond to the conference room discussion.

**Listing 11-1   Object-oriented programming.**

```
1 REM ************* OBJECT ORIENTED PROGRAMMING ****************
2 DIM FO$(200):REM STRUCTURE ARRAY
5 PRINT"ENTER A NUMBER TO DO ONE OF THE FOLLOWING"
10 PRINT"1-CREATE A STRUCTURE"
15 PRINT"2-CREATE AN OBJECT"
20 PRINT"3-NAME OF ALL STRUCTURES"
25 PRINT"4-NAME OF ALL OBJECTS"
30 PRINT"5-VIEW A STRUCTURE"
35 PRINT"6-VIEW AN OBJECT"
40 PRINT"7-SEND A VALUE TO AN OBJECT"
45 PRINT"8-COPY A VALUE TO Z$ FROM AN OBJECT'S ATTRIBUTE"
50 PRINT"9-EXIT"
55 INPUT N
60 ON N GOSUB 100,200,300,400,500,600,700,800,900
65 GOTO 5
100 REM **** CREATE A STRUCTURE
105 INPUT"ENTER STRUCTURE NAME ";T$(1)
110 INPUT"ENTER NUMBER OF ATTRIBUTES ";T$(2)
115 N=VAL(T$(2)):E=3+N-1
120 FOR I=3 TO E
125 PRINT"ATTRIBUTE ";I-2;"-";
130 INPUT T$(I)
135 NEXT I
140 REM CREATE STRUCTURE CALLING SEQUENCE
145 GOSUB 3000
150 RETURN
200 REM ***** CREATE AN OBJECT
205 INPUT"ENTER STRUCTURE NAME ";T$(1)
210 INPUT"ENTER OBJECTS NAME ";T$(2)
215 INPUT"ENTER NUMBER OF ATTRIBUTES ";T$(3)
220 N=VAL(T$(3)):E=4+N-1
225 FOR I=4 TO E
230 PRINT"ATTRIBUTE ";I-3;"-";
235 INPUT T$(I)
240 NEXT I
245 REM CREATE OBJECT CALLING SEQUENCE
250 GOSUB 3200
255 RETURN
300 REM **** NAME OF ALL STRUCTURES
310 REM PRINT NAMES OF ALL STRUCTURES
315 GOSUB 4400
320 RETURN
400 REM **** NAME OF ALL OBJECTS
405 INPUT"ENTER STRUCTURE NAME ";T$(1)
410 REM PRINT ALL OBJECTS NAMES IN A STRUCTURE
415 GOSUB 4200
420 RETURN
500 REM **** VIEW A STRUCTURE
505 INPUT"ENTER A STRUCTURE NAME ";T$(1)
510 REM PRINT STRUCTURE ATTRIBUTES
515 GOSUB 3400
520 RETURN
600 REM **** VIEW AN OBJECT
605 INPUT"ENTER A STRUCTURE NAME ";T$(1)
610 INPUT"ENTER AN OBJECT NAME ";T$(2)
615 REM VIEW AN OBJECT
620 GOSUB 4000
625 RETURN
700 REM **** SEND A VALUE TO AN OBJECT
705 INPUT"ENTER A STRUCTURE NAME ";T$(1)
710 INPUT"ENTER AN OBJECT NAME ";T$(2)
715 INPUT"ENTER ATTRIBUTE NAME ";T$(3)
720 INPUT"ENTER VALUE ";T$(4)
725 REM **** SEND A VALUE TO AN OBJECTS ATTRIBUTE
730 GOSUB 5000
735 RETURN
800 REM **** COPY A VALUE TO Z$ FROM AN OBJECTS ATTRIBUTE
805 INPUT"ENTER A STRUCTURE NAME ";T$(1)
810 INPUT"ENTER AN OBJECT NAME ";T$(2)
815 INPUT"ENTER ATTRIBUTE NAME ";T$(3)
820 REM COPY AN OBJECTS ATTRIBUTE TO Z$
825 GOSUB 5200
830 PRINT"ATTRIBUTE VALUE IS ";Z$
835 RETURN
900 REM EXIT
905 STOP
```

```
999 REM ****************** USER WRITTEN ROUTINES ******************************
2999 REM ************** SYSTEM ROUTINES ******************
3000 REM ********** CREATE STRUCTURE
3010 REM STRUCTURE NAME T$(1)
3015 REM NUMBER OF ATTRIBUTES T$(2)
3020 REM ATTRIBUTE 1..AN * MEANS A NAME THEN A ROUTINE NUMBER FOLLOWS T$(3)
3025 REM .....
3030 REM ATTRIBUTE N T$(N+2)
3035 REM SEARCH FOR THE STRUCTURE NAME IN EITHER THE TOP OR BOTTOM HALF.
3040 REM THEN STORE THE STRUCTURE ARGUMENTS IN THAT LOCATION
3045 Y=1:REM POINT TO LOWER HALF
3050 IF FO$(1) <> "" THEN Y=101:REM POINT TO TOP HALF BOTTOM NOT EMPTY
3055 N=VAL(T$(2)):N=N+2:REM NUMBER OF ELEMENTS IN STRUCTURE IS NUMBER ARG+2
3060 FOR Z=1 TO N
3065 FO$(Y)=T$(Z):Y=Y+1
3070 NEXT Z
3080 RETURN
3200 REM ************ CREATE OBJECT CALLING SEQUENCE
3210 REM STRUCTURE NAME T$(1)
3215 REM OBJECT NAME T$(2)
3220 REM NUMBER OF VALUES OF ATTRIBUTES T$(3)
3225 REM VALUE OF ATTRIBUTE 1 T$(4)
3230 REM VALUE OF ATTRIBUTE .......
3235 REM VALUE OF ATTRIB N T$(N+3)...INCLUDES STRUCTURE + OBJECT NAME + NO OF
     ATTRIBUTE
3240 REM POINT TO THE STRUCTURE
3245 Z=1
3250 IF T$(1) = FO$(101) THEN Z=101
3255 E=Z+99:REM LAST LOCATION IN THAT STRUCTURE SPACE
3260 REM FIND FIRST FREE OBJECT SPACE
3265 FOR I=Z TO E
3270 IF FO$(I) = "" THEN GOTO 3280
3275 NEXT I
3280 REM STORE OBJECT HERE
3285 L=I:FO$(L)=T$(2):L=L+1:REM STORE OBJECT NAME
3290 REM GET NUMBER OF ATTRIBUTES
3295 N=VAL(T$(3)):FO$(L)=T$(3):L=L+1:REM STORE NUMBER
3300 E=L+N-1:REM LAST ATTRIBUTE LOCATION
3305 K=4:REM FIRST ATTRIBUTE LOCATION
3310 FOR I=L TO E
3315 FO$(I)=T$(K):K=K+1
3320 NEXT I
3325 RETURN
3400 REM ************ PRINT THE STRUCTURE ATTRIBUTES
3405 REM STRUCTURE NAME T$(1)
3410 REM POINT TO THE STRUCTURE
3415 Z=1
3420 IF T$(1)=FO$(101) THEN Z=101
3425 PRINT"STRUCTURE IS ";T$(1):Z=Z+1
3430 PRINT"NUMBER OF ATTRIBUTES ARE ";FO$(Z)
3435 N=VAL(FO$(Z)):Z=Z+1
3440 E=Z+N-1
3445 K=1:REM ATTRIBUTE NUMBER
3450 FOR I=Z TO E
3455 PRINT"ATTRIBUTE NUMBER ";K;"IS ";FO$(I)
3460 K=K+1
3465 NEXT I
3470 RETURN
3600 REM ************** FIND THE ATTRIBUTE NUMBER OF AN ATTRIBUTE IN AN OBJECT
3603 REM   Z=ATTRIBUTE NUMBER, A=0 IF NO *, A=1 IF *
3605 REM STRUCTURE NAME T$(1)
3610 REM ...RESERVED
3615 REM ATTRIBUTE NAME T$(3)
3630 REM POINT TO THE STRUCTURE
3635 Z=1
3640 IF T$(1)=FO$(101) THEN Z=101
3645 Z=Z+2:N=1:REM START THE SEARCH
3650 IF T$(3)=FO$(Z) THEN GOTO 3665
3655 Z=Z+1:N=N+1
3660 GOTO 3650 :REM TRY AGAIN
3665 REM DOES ATTRIBUTE HAVE AN *
3670 A=0:Z=Z-1:REM POINT TO ASTERISK LOCATION
3675 IF FO$(Z)="*" THEN A=1
3680 Z=N+1:RETURN
3800 REM ********** POINT TO AN OBJECT
3805 REM STRUCTURE NAME T$(1)
```

Listing 11-1 *(Continued)*

```
3810 REM OBJECT NAME T$(2)
3815 REM POINT TO THE STRUCTURE
3820 Z=1
3825 IF T$(1)=FO$(101) THEN Z=101
3830 REM NUMBER OF STRUCTURE ATTRIBUTES
3835 Z=Z+1:N=VAL(FO$(Z))
3840 Z=Z+N+1:REM FIRST OBJECT IN STRUCTURE
3845 REM IS THIS OBJECT LOCATION BLANK
3850 IF FO$(Z)<>"" THEN GOTO 3865
3855 REM BLANK SPACE SEARCH FOR FIRST NON-BLANK OBJECT SPACE
3860 Z=Z+1:GOTO 3850
3865 REM GET THE NUMBER OF OBJECT ATTRIBUTES
3870 Z=Z+1:N=VAL(FO$(Z)):Z=Z-1:REM RESET POINTER TO OBJECT NAME
3875 REM IS THIS THE OBJECT
3880 IF T$(2)=FO$(Z) THEN RETURN:REM *** Z IS THE LOCATION OF THE OBJECT
3885 REM NEXT OBJECT
3890 Z=Z+N+2:GOTO 3880
4000 REM ************* VIEW AN OBJECT
4005 REM STRUCTURE NAME T$(1)
4010 REM OBJECT NAME T$(2)
4015 REM POINT TO AN OBJECT Z IS THE VALUE OF THE POINTER. N IS THE
4020 REM NUMBER OF ATTRIBUTES IN THE OBJECT
4025 GOSUB 3800
4030 PRINT"OBJECT IS ";FO$(Z):Z=Z+1
4035 PRINT"NUMBER OF ATTRIBUTES IS ";FO$(Z):Z=Z+1
4040 E=Z+N-1:P=1
4045 FOR I=Z TO E
4050 PRINT"ATTRIBUTE NUMBER ";P;"IS ";FO$(I):P=P+1
4055 NEXT I
4060 RETURN
4200 REM ********** PRINT ALL OBJECTS NAMES IN A FRAME
4205 REM STRUCTURE NAME T$(1)
4210 REM POINT TO THE STRUCTURE
4215 Z=1
4220 IF T$(1)=FO$(101) THEN Z=101
4225 E=Z+99 :REM END OF STRUCTURE ARRAY
4230 REM NUMBER OF STRUCTURE ATTRIBUTES
4235 Z=Z+1:N=VAL(FO$(Z))
4240 REM GET NUMBER OF OBJECTS ATTRIBUTES
4245 Z=Z+N+2:N=VAL(FO$(Z)):Z=Z-1:REM FIRST OBJECT
4250 FOR I=Z TO E STEP N+2
4255 IF FO$(I)<>"" THEN PRINT"OBJECT NAME-";FO$(I)
4260 NEXT I
4265 RETURN
4400 REM ************* PRINT NAMES OF ALL STRUCTURES
4405 PRINT"STRUCTURE"
4410 PRINT FO$(1)
4415 PRINT FO$(101)
4420 RETURN
4600 REM ************** DELETE AN OBJECT
4605 REM STRUCTURE NAME T$(1)
4610 REM OBJECT NAME T$(2)
4615 REM POINT TO AN OBJECT..Z=LOCATION..N=NUMBER OF ATTRIBUTES
4620 GOSUB 3800
4625 E=Z+N+2:OBJECTS END LOCATION
4630 FOR I=Z TO E
4635 FO$(I)=""
4640 NEXT I
4645 RETURN
4800 REM ************* POINT TO AN OBJECT'S ATTRIBUTE
4805 REM STRUCTURE NAME T$(1)
4810 REM OBJECT'S NAME T$(2)
4815 REM ATTRIBUTES NAME T$(3)
4820 REM FIND THE ATTRIBUTE NUMBER OF THE ATTRIBUTE (Z),IF ATTRIBUTE=* A=1
4825 GOSUB 3600:AN=Z
4830 REM POINT TO AN OBJECT (Z)
4835 GOSUB 3800
4840 REM POINT TO THE ATTRIBUTE
4845 Z=Z+AN-1
4850 RETURN
5000 REM ************* SEND A VALUE TO AN OBJECT'S ATTRIBUTE
5005 REM STRUCTURE NAME T$(1)
5010 REM OBJECT NAME T$(2)
5015 REM ATTRIBUTE NAME T$(3)
5020 REM VALUE T$(4)
5025 REM POINT TO AN OBJECTS ATTRIBUTE (Z)
```

```
5030 GOSUB 4800
5035 REM STORE VALUE INTO ATTRIBUTE,IF NO ASTERISK,*, A=0
5040 IF A=0 THEN GOTO 5060:REM NO *
5045 REM AN * CALL USER WRITTEN ROUTINE
5050 Z=Z+1:N=VAL(FO$(Z)):ON N GOSUB 10000
5055 Z=Z-1:FO$(Z)=T$(4):RETURN:REM POINT TO THE ATTRIBUTE AGAIN
5060 Z=Z+1:FO$(Z)=T$(4)
5065 RETURN
5200 REM ************** COPY AN OBJECT'S ATTRIBUTE TO Z$
5205 REM STRUCTURE NAME T$(1)
5210 REM OBJECT NAME T$(2)
5215 REM ATTRIBUTE NAME T$(3)
5220 REM VALUE Z$
5225 REM POINT TO AN OBJECTS ATTRIBUTE (Z)
5230 GOSUB 4800
5235 Z$=FO$(Z)
5240 IF A=0 THEN GOTO 5260:REM NO *
5245 REM AN * CALL USER WRITTEN ROUTINE
5255 Z$=FO$(Z):RETURN:REM POINT TO THE ATTRIBUTE AGAIN
5260 Z=Z+1:Z$=FO$(Z)
5265 RETURN
9000 REM PSEUDO VOLTAGE CHECKER
9002 REM THE PSEUDO VOLTAGE VIA RND(X) IS CHECKED AT THE PSEUDO TIME INTERVALS
9004 REM VIA FOR QB LOOP
9020 T$(1)="VOLTAGE":T$(2)="EQUIP":T$(3)="TIME":T$(4)="5"
9040 FOR QA=1 TO 30:GOSUB 5000
9060 FOR QB=1 TO 1000:NEXT QB:REM PSEUDO TIME DELAY
9080 NEXT QA:RETURN
9999 REM ***************** USER WRITTEN ROUTINES ****************************
10000 QQ=RND(Z):IF QQ>.7 THEN PRINT"VOLTAGE TOO HIGH=";QQ
10005 RETURN
```

## Sample Runs

Sample runs for each menu item in Listing 11-1 are shown below. Remember, the user responses follow the question marks.

```
ENTER A NUMBER TO DO ONE OF THE FOLLOWING
1-CREATE A STRUCTURE
2-CREATE AN OBJECT
3-NAME OF ALL STRUCTURES
4-NAME OF ALL OBJECTS
5-VIEW A STRUCTURE
6-VIEW AN OBJECT
7-SEND A VALUE TO AN OBJECT
8-COPY A VALUE TO Z$ FROM AN OBJECT'S ATTRIBUTE
9-EXIT
$ 1
ENTER STRUCTURE NAME ? CONF
ENTER NUMBER OF ATTRIBUTES ? 5
ATTRIBUTE   1 -? ROOM
ATTRIBUTE   2 -? SUBJECT
ATTRIBUTE   3 -? SPEAKER
ATTRIBUTE   4 -? START
ATTRIBUTE   5 -? END

ENTER A NUMBER TO DO ONE OF THE FOLLOWING
1-CREATE A STRUCTURE
2-CREATE AN OBJECT
3-NAME OF ALL STRUCTURES
4-NAME OF ALL OBJECTS
5-VIEW A STRUCTURE
6-VIEW AN OBJECT
7-SEND A VALUE TO AN OBJECT
```

```
8-COPY A VALUE TO Z$ FROM AN OBJECT'S ATTRIBUTE
9-EXIT
? 3
STRUCTURES
CONF

ENTER A NUMBER TO DO ONE OF THE FOLLOWING
1-CREATE A STRUCTURE
2-CREATE AN OBJECT
3-NAME OF ALL STRUCTURES
4-NAME OF ALL OBJECTS
5-VIEW A STRUCTURE
6-VIEW AN OBJECT
7-SEND A VALUE TO AN OBJECT
8-COPY A VALUE TO Z$ FROM AN OBJECT'S ATTRIBUTE
9-EXIT
? 5
ENTER A STRUCTURE NAME ? CONF
STRUCTURE IS CONF
NUMBER OF ATTRIBUTES ARE 5
ATTRIBUTE NUMBER  1 IS ROOM
ATTRIBUTE NUMBER  2 IS SUBJECT
ATTRIBUTE NUMBER  3 IS SPEAKER
ATTRIBUTE NUMBER  4 IS START
ATTRIBUTE NUMBER  5 IS END

ENTER A NUMBER TO DO ONE OF THE FOLLOWING
1-CREATE A STRUCTURE
2-CREATE AN OBJECT
3-NAME OF ALL STRUCTURES
4-NAME OF ALL OBJECTS
5-VIEW A STRUCTURE
6-VIEW AN OBJECT
7-SEND A VALUE TO AN OBJECT
8-COPY A VALUE TO Z$ FROM AN OBJECT'S ATTRIBUTE
9-EXIT
? 2
ENTER STRUCTURE NAME ? CONF
ENTER OBJECTS NAME ? TEN1
ENTER NUMBER OF ATTRIBUTES ? 5
ATTRIBUTE  1 -? 10
ATTRIBUTE  2 -? EMPLOYEE OVERTIME RULES
ATTRIBUTE  3 -? SUSAN BARD
ATTRIBUTE  4 -? 10:00
ATTRIBUTE  5 -? 11:00

ENTER A NUMBER TO DO ONE OF THE FOLLOWING
1-CREATE A STRUCTURE
2-CREATE AN OBJECT
3-NAME OF ALL STRUCTURES
4-NAME OF ALL OBJECTS
5-VIEW A STRUCTURE
6-VIEW AN OBJECT
7-SEND A VALUE TO AN OBJECT
8-COPY A VALUE TO Z$ FROM AN OBJECT'S ATTRIBUTE
9-EXIT
? 2
ENTER STRUCTURE NAME ? CONF
ENTER OBJECTS NAME ? TEN2
ENTER NUMBER OF ATTRIBUTES ? 5
ATTRIBUTE  1 -? 10
ATTRIBUTE  2 -? PAY RAISES
```

```
ATTRIBUTE  3 -? MARC STONE
ATTRIBUTE  4 -? 13:00
ATTRIBUTE  5 -? 14:00

ENTER A NUMBER TO DO ONE OF THE FOLLOWING
1-CREATE A STRUCTURE
2-CREATE AN OBJECT
3-NAME OF ALL STRUCTURES
4-NAME OF ALL OBJECTS
5-VIEW A STRUCTURE
6-VIEW AN OBJECT
7-SEND A VALUE TO AN OBJECT
8-COPY A VALUE TO Z$ FROM AN OBJECT'S ATTRIBUTE
9-EXIT
? 2
ENTER STRUCTURE NAME ? CONF
ENTER OBJECTS NAME ? ELE1
ENTER NUMBER OF ATTRIBUTES ? 5
ATTRIBUTE  1 -? 11
ATTRIBUTE  2 -? SALES PROJECTIONS
ATTRIBUTE  3 -? ANDY ROME
ATTRIBUTE  4 -? 10:00
ATTRIBUTE  5 -? 11:00

ENTER A NUMBER TO DO ONE OF THE FOLLOWING
1-CREATE A STRUCTURE
2-CREATE AN OBJECT
3-NAME OF ALL STRUCTURES
3-NAME OF ALL STRUCTURES
4-NAME OF ALL OBJECTS
5-VIEW A STRUCTURE
6-VIEW AN OBJECT
7-SEND A VALUE TO AN OBJECT
8-COPY A VALUE TO Z$ FROM AN OBJECT'S ATTRIBUTE
9-EXIT
? 4
ENTER STRUCTURE NAME ? CONF
OBJECT NAME-TEN1
OBJECT NAME-TEN2
OBJECT NAME-ELE1

ENTER A NUMBER TO DO ONE OF THE FOLLOWING
1-CREATE A STRUCTURE
2-CREATE AN OBJECT
2-CREATE AN OBJECT
3-NAME OF ALL STRUCTURES
4-NAME OF ALL OBJECTS
5-VIEW A STRUCTURE
6-VIEW AN OBJECT
7-SEND A VALUE TO AN OBJECT
8-COPY A VALUE TO Z$ FROM AN OBJECT'S ATTRIBUTE
9-EXIT
? 6
ENTER A STRUCTURE NAME ? CONF
ENTER AN OBJECT NAME ? TEN2
OBJECT IS TEN2
NUMBER OF ATTRIBUTES IS 5
ATTRIBUTE NUMBER  1 IS 10
ATTRIBUTE NUMBER  2 IS PAY RAISES
ATTRIBUTE NUMBER  3 IS MARC STONE
ATTRIBUTE NUMBER  4 IS 13:00
ATTRIBUTE NUMBER  5 IS 14:00
```

```
ENTER A NUMBER TO DO ONE OF THE FOLLOWING
1-CREATE A STRUCTURE
2-CREATE AN OBJECT
3-NAME OF ALL STRUCTURES
4-NAME OF ALL OBJECTS
5-VIEW A STRUCTURE
6-VIEW AN OBJECT
7-SEND A VALUE TO AN OBJECT
8-COPY A VALUE TO Z$ FROM AN OBJECT'S ATTRIBUTE
9-EXIT
? 6
ENTER A STRUCTURE NAME ? CONF
ENTER AN OBJECT NAME ? TEN1
OBJECT IS TEN1
NUMBER OF ATTRIBUTES IS 5
ATTRIBUTE NUMBER  1 IS 10
ATTRIBUTE NUMBER  2 IS EMPLOYEE OVERTIME RULES
ATTRIBUTE NUMBER  3 IS SUSAN BARD
ATTRIBUTE NUMBER  4 IS 10:00
ATTRIBUTE NUMBER  5 IS 11:00

ENTER A NUMBER TO DO ONE OF THE FOLLOWING
1-CREATE A STRUCTURE
2-CREATE AN OBJECT
3-NAME OF ALL STRUCTURES
4-NAME OF ALL OBJECTS
5-VIEW A STRUCTURE
6-VIEW AN OBJECT
7-SEND A VALUE TO AN OBJECT
8-COPY A VALUE TO Z$ FROM AN OBJECT'S ATTRIBUTE
9-EXIT
? 7
ENTER A STRUCTURE NAME ? CONF
ENTER AN OBJECT NAME ? TEN1
ENTER ATTRIBUTE NAME ? START
ENTER VALUE ? 09:00

ENTER A NUMBER TO DO ONE OF THE FOLLOWING
1-CREATE A STRUCTURE
2-CREATE AN OBJECT
3-NAME OF ALL STRUCTURES
4-NAME OF ALL OBJECTS
5-VIEW A STRUCTURE
6-VIEW AN OBJECT
7-SEND A VALUE TO AN OBJECT
8-COPY A VALUE TO Z$ FROM AN OBJECT'S ATTRIBUTE
9-EXIT
? 6
ENTER A STRUCTURE NAME ? CONF
ENTER AN OBJECT NAME ? TEN1
OBJECT IS TEN1
NUMBER OF ATTRIBUTES IS 5
ATTRIBUTE NUMBER  1 IS 10
ATTRIBUTE NUMBER  2 IS EMPLOYEE OVERTIME RULES
ATTRIBUTE NUMbER  3 IS SUSAN BARD
ATTRIBUTE NUMBER  4 IS 09:00
ATTRIBUTE NUMBER  5 IS 11:00
```

We will now create a new conference room structure. This time we will include procedures with the start- and end-time attributes.

```
ENTER A NUMBER TO DO ONE OF THE FOLLOWING
1-CREATE A STRUCTURE
2-CREATE AN OBJECT
3-NAME OF ALL STRUCTURES
4-NAME OF ALL OBJECTS
5-VIEW A STRUCTURE
6-VIEW AN OBJECT
7-SEND A VALUE TO AN OBJECT
8-COPY A VALUE TO Z$ FROM AN OBJECT'S ATTRIBUTE
9-EXIT
? 1
ENTER STRUCTURE NAME ? CONF1
ENTER NUMBER OF ATTRIBUTES ? 7
ATTRIBUTE  1 -? ROOM
ATTRIBUTE  2 -? SUBJECT
ATTRIBUTE  3 -? SPEAKER
ATTRIBUTE  4 -? *
ATTRIBUTE  5 -? START
ATTRIBUTE  6 -? *
ATTRIBUTE  7 -? END

ENTER A NUMBER TO DO ONE OF THE FOLLOWING
1-CREATE A STRUCTURE
2-CREATE AN OBJECT
3-NAME OF ALL STRUCTURES
4-NAME OF ALL OBJECTS
5-VIEW A STRUCTURE
6-VIEW AN OBJECT
7-SEND A VALUE TO AN OBJECT
8-COPY A VALUE TO Z$ FROM AN OBJECT'S ATTRIBUTE
9-EXIT
? 2
ENTER STRUCTURE NAME ? CONF1
ENTER OBJECTS NAME ? TEN1
ENTER NUMBER OF ATTRIBUTES ? 7
ATTRIBUTE  1 -? 10
ATTRIBUTE  2 -? EMPLOYEE OVERTIME RULES
ATTRIBUTE  3 -? SUSAN BARD
ATTRIBUTE  4 -? 10:00
ATTRIBUTE  5 -? 1
ATTRIBUTE  6 -? 11:00
ATTRIBUTE  7 -? 1

ENTER A NUMBER TO DO ONE OF THE FOLLOWING
1-CREATE A STRUCTURE
2-CREATE AN OBJECT
3-NAME OF ALL STRUCTURES
4-NAME OF ALL OBJECTS
5-VIEW A STRUCTURE
6-VIEW AN OBJECT
7-SEND A VALUE TO AN OBJECT
8-COPY A VALUE TO Z$ FROM AN OBJECT'S ATTRIBUTE
9-EXIT
? 8
ENTER A STRUCTURE NAME ? CONF1
ENTER AN OBJECT NAME ? TEN1
ENTER ATTRIBUTE NAME ? START
ATTRIBUTE VALUE IS 10:00

ENTER A NUMBER TO DO ONE OF THE FOLLOWING
1-CREATE A STRUCTURE
2-CREATE AN OBJECT
3-NAME OF ALL STRUCTURES
```

```
4-NAME OF ALL OBJECTS
5-VIEW A STRUCTURE
6-VIEW AN OBJECT
7-SEND A VALUE TO AN OBJECT
8-COPY A VALUE TO Z$ FROM AN OBJECT'S ATTRIBUTE
9-EXIT
? 7
ENTER A STRUCTURE NAME ? CONF1
ENTER AN OBJECT NAME ? TEN1
ENTER ATTRIBUTE NAME ? START
ENTER VALUE ? 08:00
***** USER ROUTINE **** 1
```

The SEND subroutine was used to change the value of the START attribute. The START attribute is preceded by an asterisk in the structure CONF1. This means that the number 1 in the fifth attribute that follows the START attribute of the object TEN1 will direct us to a subroutine that is invoked. This is done in the program's SEND sequence at statement numbers 5040 through 5055. Statement 5050, ON N GOSUB 10000, will enter a user-written subroutine at statement number 10000. This will cause the ****USER ROUTINE**** message to be printed.

```
ENTER ATTRIBUTE NAME ? START
ATTRIBUTE VALUE IS 10:00
ENTER A NUMBER TO DO ONE OF THE FOLLOWING
1-CREATE A STRUCTURE
2-CREATE AN OBJECT
3-NAME OF ALL STRUCTURES
4-NAME OF ALL OBJECTS
5-VIEW A STRUCTURE
6-VIEW AN OBJECT
7-SEND A VALUE TO AN OBJECT
8-COPY A VALUE TO Z$ FROM AN OBJECT'S ATTRIBUTE
9-EXIT
? 6
ENTER A STRUCTURE NAME ? CONF1
ENTER AN OBJECT NAME ? TEN1
OBJECT IS TEN1
NUMBER OF ATTRIBUTES IS 7
ATTRIBUTE NUMBER  1 IS 10
ATTRIBUTE NUMBER  2 IS EMPLOYEE OVERTIME RULES
ATTRIBUTE NUMBER  3 IS SUSAN BARD
ATTRIBUTE NUMBER  4 IS 08:00
ATTRIBUTE NUMBER  5 IS 1
ATTRIBUTE NUMBER  6 IS 11:00
ATTRIBUTE NUMBER  7 IS 1
```

## Exercise

You can include a REMOVE OBJECT option in the menu using the DELETE AN OBJECT subroutine at statements 4600 through 4645.

# 12

# Object-Oriented Programming: An Engineering Example

Now that you have a clear picture of the fundamentals of object-oriented programming, you are ready to consider an engineering example. Although the topic is somewhat complex, we will make the explanations simple enough for you to follow easily. By the time we're finished, you will be able to apply object-oriented programming to sampling data in electronic systems. This chapter will also set the stage for your understanding of object-oriented expert systems.

### Analog-to-Digital Conversion

We all know, from using ordinary household appliances, that the ac voltage in a wall socket reaches 120 volts at a frequency of 60 cycles. What does this mean? Figure 12-1 should help make the matter clear. AC stands for "alternating current," which means that the current reverses its direction at regular intervals. In our example, the current moves from $+120$ volts to $-120$ volts and back again, moving toward 0 volts in between. Each cycle takes $\frac{1}{60}$ of a second, so that after 60 cycles, 1 second has elapsed. That is what is meant by a frequency of 60 cycles. As the voltage goes between $+120$ volts and $-120$ volts, it takes on a continuous set of values; that is, at one moment in time it is 36 volts, at another it is 112, and so on. This is known as an "analog" representation because the voltage can be represented by directly measurable quantities that visually reflect the movement of the current.

In order to perform any kind of analysis of the voltage in a computer, it must be presented to the "input channel." This is the place where everything outside a computer enters for analysis. Since a computer is an electrical device, the input channel can only interpret voltage levels. All the information in the world outside, therefore, must somehow be converted to a voltage before it is presented to the input channel. Once this is accomplished, and the information passes into the computer, the voltage's value is placed in a memory location so that it can be processed by a program.

However, life at the input channel is not so simple. Before any value can be input into the computer, its voltage must be presented in a binary digital format. What does this mean?

The basic unit of computer memory is a "bit," which is short for *binary digit*. A bit consists of either a 0 or a 1. (This system is a base 2 representation, as opposed to the base 10 representation upon which our standard counting system is founded. In base 2, the number 1 is written as 001, 2 is 010, 3 is 011, 4 is 100, and so on.) One bit represents a single line of voltage, which can take on only one of two voltage values. Every computer's basic circuitry is designed to work with two different voltage levels which can be represented by a 0 or 1.

A larger unit of computer memory is the "byte," which is an 8-bit number. The binary digital number representation of 1 volt is 0000 0001. The value of +9 volts is represented as 0000 1001. (An easy way to count in base 2 is to begin at the right. The first digit on the right has a weight of 1, the second a weight of 2, the third 4, then 8, 16, 32, 64, and 128. By simply adding up all the weights in the positions that contain 1s, you can figure out what number is represented. In this last example, 0000 1001, by adding the weight for the first digit from the right—1—to the weight of the fourth—8—we get the number 9.)

Many naturally occurring things that we may wish to analyze can be represented by an analog voltage. The continuously varying voltage in

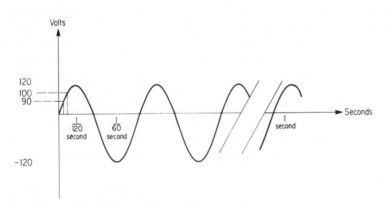

**Figure 12-1    120 volts at 60 cycles.**

a wall socket is one example; the oscillating picture of a heartbeat on a cardiac monitor is another. In order to analyze these analog voltages in a computer, we must ask the question: What is the methodology for converting an analog voltage to a binary digital representation?

The answer is to use a simple piece of hardware called an analog-to-digital converter, or ADC. The ADC automatically does the conversion by accepting analog voltages as its input and producing binary numbers as output. An example of how this is done is shown in Figure 12-2.

Before the ADC performs the conversion, the computer must somehow *instruct* the ADC to do it. This is accomplished by a signal that is sent by the computer to the ADC on the "convert" line, as shown in the figure. After the conversion takes place, the computer is ready to analyze the input.

For example, suppose we are analyzing the ac voltage supplied by your local power company. Let's assume that the people who run the utility are worried that the voltage may fall to unacceptably low levels, causing a brownout, or shoot up to unacceptably high voltages, ruining equipment and appliances. A picture of the ac voltage is shown in Figure 12-3. The graph shows how the voltage starts at 0 volts and passed through other voltages as it approaches 120; then it decreases, passing below 0. The cycle is repeated every ¹⁄₆₀ of a second.

The figure illustrates how the computer sent out convert signals at two different parts of the cycle. The first signal was sent to the ADC when the voltage value was at 30 volts and was converted to binary digital form as 0001 1110. The second convert signal, at 60 volts, resulted in the conversion to 0011 1100 by the ADC. To put it simply, the ADC takes *one* voltage line and converts it to *eight* binary voltage lines, which we refer to as a byte.

Let's review:

1. An ADC is a device that converts analog voltages to a binary digital representation.

Figure 12-2  Analog to digital conversion input channel.

2. A computer can only process binary digital representations.

3. A convert line into the ADC allows the computer to control exactly when the voltage at the ADC should be converted.

### An Engineering System Using Object-Oriented Programming

Now that you have a basic understanding of analog voltage, binary digital representation, and analog-to-digital conversion, you are ready to tackle an engineering problem.

The voltage supplied by a power company is going to a power supply which is supplying three pieces of sensitive electronic equipment. We want to devise a system that will prevent this sensitive equipment from becoming overloaded. If the power supply voltage exceeds 124 volts, the computer is to energize a circuit breaker that will remove the voltage from the sensitive equipment. A system that can do this is shown in Figure 12-4.

If the voltage exceeds 124 volts, the computer's input/output channel will recognize this event with the help of the ADC and will cause the circuit breaker to open, thereby removing the excess voltage and protecting the sensitive electronic equipment. We need to design an object-oriented system with a structure, objects, and procedures for monitoring the voltage.

### Structure

Although Figure 12-4 looks complicated, we can create a structure that will make it quite simple. The structure must contain all the

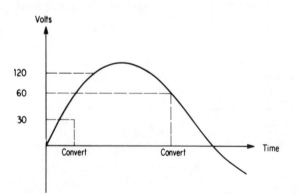

Figure 12-3   Voltages at two different convert times.

attributes that will enable us to represent the entire problem. The task at hand is to

1. Convert the voltage appearing at the sensitive equipment to binary representation and compare this voltage with a maximum acceptable limit. For example, we can tolerate a maximum of 124 volts (0111 1100).

2. If the voltage exceeds 124 volts, we want the circuit breaker to open.

3. The conversion should be done at a regular, safe time interval. For example, if we allow the time between conversions to be 60 seconds, what might happen? Let's say that at the last conversion the voltage was 123 volts, which is safe. But 20 seconds later the voltage rises to 125 volts, which is unsafe. Since we are not even looking at the voltage for another 40 seconds, the computer would never "see" the 125 volts and the equipment would be ruined. A conversion time of 2 seconds, however, *would* detect 125 volts, assuming a gradual transmission of voltage, and provides enough time to open the circuit breaker.

The structure for this problem should have the following attributes:

1. The voltage at which the circuit breaker is to be opened (VOLTAGE)

Figure 12-4   Computer controlled monitoring system.

2. The time interval for converting the voltage (CONVERT)

3. The last time we converted the voltage (LAST)

4. The present time (PRESENT)

5. The procedure for determining if we must open the circuit breaker (BREAKER)

The CREATE-STRUCTURE subroutine will create the structure. We will call the structure SENSOR because it is designed to sense excessive voltages. The sensor structure, using the format we introduced in Chapter 12, would look as follows:

```
CREATE-STRUCTURE (SNAME = SENSOR, NATTR = 5, ATTR =
                  VOLTAGE, ATTR = CONVERT, ATTR =
                  LAST, ATTR = *PRESENT, ATTR = PRO-
                  CEDURE)
```

Note the asterisk at the attribute PRESENT. This will cause a procedure to be invoked if a SEND subroutine changes the value of the attribute PRESENT. The object is created as follows:

```
CREATE-OBJECT (SNAME = SENSOR, ONAME = EQUIPMENT,
               VOLTAGE = 124, CONVERT = 2, LAST = 0,
               PRESENT = 0, PROCEDURE = name of
               the procedure)
```

How does the object-oriented system use the structure? Attribute 4 represents the present time, so that when the time is sent to the object via the SEND subroutine, a procedure is invoked to determine if the circuit breaker should be opened. This procedure is represented by attribute 5. This is how the procedure works. The present time, in attribute 4, is subtracted from the *last* time the voltage was converted, as represented by attribute 3, LAST. This time interval is compared to the desired time interval for converting, as represented by attribute 2, CONVERT. If the difference is equal to or greater than the time interval for converting, then a convert signal must be sent to the ADC. The converted voltage is compared to the voltage at which the circuit breaker is to be opened, which is attribute 1, VOLTAGE. If this voltage exceeds the VOLTAGE attribute, the circuit breaker is automatically opened to protect the equipment.

Since TIME is a standard command that is included in the BASIC computer language, the present time can be obtained simply via

```
Y$ = TIME
```

We can then send the time value to the object with the following responses to system questions:

```
SEND (SNAME=SENSOR, ONAME=EQUIPMENT, PRESENT=Y$)
```

This will invoke the routine specified in the object for checking the power supply voltage using the ADC.

## Real-Time Data Acquisition

The system we have just described, which depends upon conversion of voltages and possible subsequent action, is referred to as operating in "real time." This means that something is done at specific instances of time, which in our system was the conversion of voltages every 2 seconds. The term "real-time data acquisition" means that data is acquired at precise moments in time and processed right away. Our system is therefore a real-time data acquisition system that uses object-oriented programming.

## Process Control

We can use the same methods to monitor and control all kinds of processes, from plastics manufacture to egg laying to maintaining the temperature in a nuclear reactor. In these applications, we would include programs or devices that convert pressures or locations on a conveyer belt or temperatures into analog voltages. These voltages are fed in turn into an ADC so they can be processed by the computer. The computer can then make decisions that will control the pressures and temperatures or simply alert the user that not enough eggs are being laid in a given time interval. Such systems are known as "process control systems."

## Programming Applications

The object-oriented program, Listing 11-1, was modified to reflect the engineering example of checking a voltage. The time at which the voltage is checked is simulated in a subroutine starting at statement 9000. A FOR loop is used as a pseudotime interval. The SEND subroutine via GOSUB 5000 causes the invocation of a procedure, located at statement 10000, which checks a pseudovoltage via the RND (X) statement.

### Program Listing

Listing 12-1 is followed by a sample run.

**Listing 12-1  Engineering object-oriented programming.**

```
1 REM ************** ENG-OBJECT ORIENTED PROGRAMMING ***************
2 DIM FO$(200):REM STRUCTURE ARRAY
5 PRINT"ENTER A NUMBER TO DO ONE OF THE FOLLOWING"
10 PRINT"1-CREATE A STRUCTURE"
15 PRINT"2-CREATE AN OBJECT"
20 PRINT"3-NAME OF ALL STRUCTURES"
25 PRINT"4-NAME OF ALL OBJECTS"
30 PRINT"5-VIEW A STRUCTURE"
35 PRINT"6-VIEW AN OBJECT"
40 PRINT"7-SEND A VALUE TO AN OBJECT"
45 PRINT"8-COPY A VALUE TO Z$ FROM AN OBJECT'S ATTRIBUTE"
50 PRINT"9-PSEUDO VOLTAGE CHECKER"
55 INPUT N
60 ON N GOSUB 100,200,300,400,500,600,700,800,9000
65 GOTO 5
100 REM **** CREATE A STRUCTURE
105 INPUT"ENTER STRUCTURE NAME ";T$(1)
110 INPUT"ENTER NUMBER OF ATTRIBUTES ";T$(2)
115 N=VAL(T$(2)):E=3+N-1
120 FOR I=3 TO E
125 PRINT"ATTRIBUTE ";I-2;"-";
130 INPUT T$(I)
135 NEXT I
140 REM CREATE STRUCTURE CALLING SEQUENCE
145 GOSUB 3000
150 RETURN
200 REM ***** CREATE AN OBJECT
205 INPUT"ENTER STRUCTURE NAME ";T$(1)
210 INPUT"ENTER OBJECTS NAME ";T$(2)
215 INPUT"ENTER NUMBER OF ATTRIBUTES ";T$(3)
220 N=VAL(T$(3)):E=4+N-1
225 FOR I=4 TO E
230 PRINT"ATTRIBUTE ";I-3;"-";
235 INPUT T$(I)
240 NEXT I
245 REM CREATE OBJECT CALLING SEQUENCE
250 GOSUB 3200
255 RETURN
300 REM **** NAME OF ALL STRUCTURES
310 REM PRINT NAMES OF ALL STRUCTURES
315 GOSUB 4400
320 RETURN
400 REM **** NAME OF ALL OBJECTS
405 INPUT"ENTER STRUCTURE NAME ";T$(1)
410 REM PRINT ALL OBJECTS NAMES IN A STRUCTURE
415 GOSUB 4200
420 RETURN
500 REM **** VIEW A STRUCTURE
505 INPUT"ENTER A STRUCTURE NAME ";T$(1)
510 REM PRINT STRUCTURE ATTRIBUTES
515 GOSUB 3400
520 RETURN
600 REM **** VIEW AN OBJECT
605 INPUT"ENTER A STRUCTURE NAME ";T$(1)
610 INPUT"ENTER AN OBJECT NAME ";T$(2)
615 REM VIEW AN OBJECT
620 GOSUB 4000
625 RETURN
700 REM **** SEND A VALUE TO AN OBJECT
705 INPUT"ENTER A STRUCTURE NAME ";T$(1)
710 INPUT"ENTER AN OBJECT NAME ";T$(2)
715 INPUT"ENTER ATTRIBUTE NAME ";T$(3)
720 INPUT"ENTER VALUE ";T$(4)
725 REM **** SEND A VALUE TO AN OBJECTS ATTRIBUTE
730 GOSUB 5000
735 RETURN
800 REM **** COPY A VALUE TO Z$ FROM AN OBJECTS ATTRIBUTE
805 INPUT"ENTER A STRUCTURE NAME ";T$(1)
810 INPUT"ENTER AN OBJECT NAME ";T$(2)
815 INPUT"ENTER ATTRIBUTE NAME ";T$(3)
820 REM COPY AN OBJECTS ATTRIBUTE TO Z$
825 GOSUB 5200
830 PRINT"ATTRIBUTE VALUE IS ";Z$
835 RETURN
900 REM EXIT
905 STOP
```

```
999 REM ***************** USER WRITTEN ROUTINES *****************************
2999 REM ************** SYSTEM ROUTINES ****************+-
3000 REM ********** CREATE STRUCTURE
3010 REM STRUCTURE NAME T$(1)
3015 REM NUMBER OF ATTRIBUTES T$(2)
3020 REM ATTRIBUTE 1..AN * MEANS A NAME THEN A ROUTINE NUMBER FOLLOWS T$(3)
3025 REM .....
3030 REM ATTRIBUTE N T$(N+2)
3035 REM SEARCH FOR THE STRUCTURE NAME IN EITHER THE TOP OR BOTTOM HALF.
3040 REM THEN STORE THE STRUCTURE ARGUMENTS IN THAT LOCATION
3045 Y=1:REM POINT TO LOWER HALF
3050 IF.FO$(1) <> "" THEN Y=101:REM POINT TO TOP HALF BOTTOM NOT EMPTY
3055 N=VAL(T$(2)):N=N+2:REM NUMBER OF ELEMENTS IN STRUCTURE IS NUMBER ARG+2
3060 FOR Z=1 TO N
3065 FO$(Y)=T$(Z):Y=Y+1
3070 NEXT Z
3080 RETURN
3200 REM *********** CREATE OBJECT CALLING SEQUENCE
3210 REM STRUCTURE NAME T$(1)
3215 REM OBJECT NAME T$(2)
3220 REM NUMBER OF VALUES OF ATTRIBUTES T$(3)
3225 REM VALUE OF ATTRIBUTE 1 T$(4)
3230 REM VALUE OF ATTRIBUTE .......
3235 REM VALUE OF ATTRIB N T$(N+3)...INCLUDES STRUCTURE + OBJECT NAME + NO OF
     ATTR
3240 REM POINT TO THE STRUCTURE
3245 Z=1
3250 IF T$(1) = FO$(101) THEN Z=101
3255 E=Z+99:REM LAST LOCATION IN THAT STRUCTURE SPACE
3260 REM FIND FIRST FREE OBJECT SPACE
3265 FOR I=Z TO E
3270 IF FO$(I) = "" THEN GOTO 3280
3275 NEXT I
3280 REM STORE OBJECT HERE
3285 L=I:FO$(L)=T$(2):L=L+1:REM STORE OBJECT NAME
3290 REM GET NUMBER OF ATTRIBUTES
3295 N=VAL(T$(3)):FO$(L)=T$(3):L=L+1:REM STORE NUMBER
3300 E=L+N-1:REM LAST ATTRIBUTE LOCATION
3305 K=4:REM FIRST ATTRIBUTE LOCATION
3310 FOR I=L TO E
3315 FO$(I)=T$(K):K=K+1
3320 NEXT I
3325 RETURN
3400 REM *********** PRINT THE STRUCTURE ATTRIBUTES
3405 REM STRUCTURE NAME T$(1)
3410 REM POINT TO THE STRUCTURE
3415 Z=1
3420 IF T$(1)=FO$(101) THEN Z=101
3425 PRINT"STRUCTURE IS ";T$(1):Z=Z+1
3430 PRINT"NUMBER OF ATTRIBUTES ARE ";FO$(Z)
3435 N=VAL(FO$(Z)):Z=Z+1
3440 E=Z+N-1
3445 K=1:REM ATTRIBUTE NUMBER
3450 FOR I=Z TO E
3455 PRINT"ATTRIBUTE NUMBER ";K;"IS ";FO$(I)
3460 K=K+1
3465 NEXT I
3470 RETURN
3600 REM ************* FIND THE ATTRIBUTE NUMBER OF AN ATTRIBUTE IN AN OBJECT
3603 REM  Z=ATTRIBUTE NUMBER, A=0 IF NO *, A=1 IF *
3605 REM STRUCTURE NAME T$(1)
3610 REM ...RESERVED
3615 REM ATTRIBUTE NAME T$(3)
3630 REM POINT TO THE STRUCTURE
3635 Z=1
3640 IF T$(1)=FO$(101) THEN Z=101
3645 Z=Z+2:N=1:REM START THE SEARCH
3650 IF T$(3)=FO$(Z) THEN GOTO 3665
3655 Z=Z+1:N=N+1
3660 GOTO 3650 :REM TRY AGAIN
3665 REM DOES ATTRIBUTE HAVE AN *
3670 A=0:Z=Z-1:REM POINT TO ASTERISK LOCATION
3675 IF FO$(Z)="*" THEN A=1
3680 Z=N+1:RETURN
3800 REM *********** POINT TO AN OBJECT
3805 REM STRUCTURE NAME T$(1)
```

Listing 12-1 (Continued)

```
3810 REM OBJECT NAME T$(2)
3815 REM POINT TO THE STRUCTURE
3820 Z=1
3825 IF T$(1)=FO$(101) THEN Z=101
3830 REM NUMBER OF STRUCTURE ATTRIBUTES
3835 Z=Z+1:N=VAL(FO$(Z))
3840 Z=Z+N+1:REM FIRST OBJECT IN STRUCTURE
3845 REM IS THIS OBJECT LOCATION BLANK
3850 IF FO$(Z)<>"" THEN GOTO 3865
3855 REM BLANK SPACE SEARCH FOR FIRST NON-BLANK OBJECT SPACE
3860 Z=Z+1:GOTO 3850
3865 REM GET THE NUMBER OF OBJECT ATTRIBUTES
3870 Z=Z+1:N=VAL(FO$(Z)):Z=Z-1:REM RESET POINTER TO OBJECT NAME
3875 REM IS THIS THE OBJECT
3880 IF T$(2)=FO$(Z) THEN RETURN:REM *** Z IS THE LOCATION OF THE OBJECT
3885 REM NEXT OBJECT
3890 Z=Z+N+2:GOTO 3880
4000 REM ************* VIEW AN OBJECT
4005 REM STRUCTURE NAME T$(1)
4010 REM OBJECT NAME T$(2)
4015 REM POINT TO AN OBJECT Z IS THE VALUE OF THE POINTER. N IS THE
4020 REM NUMBER OF ATTRIBUTES IN THE OBJECT
4025 GOSUB 3800
4030 PRINT"OBJECT IS ";FO$(Z):Z=Z+1
4035 PRINT"NUMBER OF ATTRIBUTES IS ";FO$(Z):Z=Z+1
4040 E=Z+N-1:P=1
4045 FOR I=Z TO E
4050 PRINT"ATTRIBUTE NUMBER ";P;"IS ";FO$(I):P=P+1
4055 NEXT I
4060 RETURN
4200 REM ********** PRINT ALL OBJECTS NAMES IN A FRAME
4205 REM STRUCTURE NAME T$(1)
4210 REM POINT TO THE STRUCTURE
4215 Z=1
4220 IF T$(1)=FO$(101) THEN Z=101
4225 E=Z+99 :REM END OF STRUCTURE ARRAY
4230 REM NUMBER OF STRUCTURE ATTRIBUTES
4235 Z=Z+1:N=VAL(FO$(Z))
4240 REM GET NUMBER OF OBJECTS ATTRIBUTES
4245 Z=Z+N+2:N=VAL(FO$(Z)):Z=Z-1:REM FIRST OBJECT
4250 FOR I=Z TO E STEP N+2
4255 IF FO$(I)<>"" THEN PRINT"OBJECT NAME-";FO$(I)
4260 NEXT I
4265 RETURN
4400 REM ************* PRINT NAMES OF ALL STRUCTURES
4405 PRINT"STRUCTURE"
4410 PRINT FO$(1)
4415 PRINT FO$(101)
4420 RETURN
4600 REM ************* DELETE AN OBJECT
4605 REM STRUCTURE NAME T$(1)
4610 REM OBJECT NAME T$(2)
4615 REM POINT TO AN OBJECT..Z=LOCATION..N=NUMBER OF ATTRIBUTES
4620 GOSUB 3800
4625 E=Z+N+2:OBJECTS END LOCATION
4630 FOR I=Z TO E
4635 FO$(I)=""
4640 NEXT I
4645 RETURN
4800 REM ************* POINT TO AN OBJECT'S ATTRIBUTE
4805 REM STRUCTURE NAME T$(1)
4810 REM OBJECT'S NAME T$(2)
4815 REM ATTRIBUTES NAME T$(3)
4820 REM FIND THE ATTRIBUTE NUMBER OF THE ATTRIBUTE (Z),IF ATTRIBUTE=* A=1
4825 GOSUB 3600:AN=Z
4830 REM POINT TO AN OBJECT (Z)
4835 GOSUB 3800
4840 REM POINT TO THE ATTRIBUTE
4845 Z=Z+AN-1
4850 RETURN
5000 REM ************* SEND A VALUE TO AN OBJECT'S ATTRIBUTE
5005 REM STRUCTURE NAME T$(1)
5010 REM OBJECT NAME T$(2)
5015 REM ATTRIBUTE NAME T$(3)
5020 REM VALUE T$(4)
5025 REM POINT TO AN OBJECTS ATTRIBUTE (Z)
```

```
5030 GOSUB 4800
5035 REM STORE VALUE INTO ATTRIBUTE,IF NO ASTERISK,*, A=0
5040 IF A=0 THEN GOTO 5060:REM NO *
5045 REM AN * CALL USER WRITTEN ROUTINE
5050 Z=Z+1:N=VAL(FO$(Z)):ON N GOSUB 10000
5055 Z=Z-1:FO$(Z)=T$(4):RETURN:REM POINT TO THE ATTRIBUTE AGAIN
5060 Z=Z+1:FO$(Z)=T$(4)
5065 RETURN
5200 REM ************* COPY AN OBJECT'S ATTRIBUTE TO Z$
5205 REM STRUCTURE NAME T$(1)
5210 REM OBJECT NAME T$(2)
5215 REM ATTRIBUTE NAME T$(3)
5220 REM VALUE Z$
5225 REM POINT TO AN OBJECTS ATTRIBUTE (Z)
5230 GOSUB 4800
5235 Z$=FO$(Z)
5240 IF A=0 THEN GOTO 5260:REM NO *
5245 REM AN * CALL USER WRITTEN ROUTINE
5255 Z$=FO$(Z):RETURN:REM POINT TO THE ATTRIBUTE AGAIN
5260 Z=Z+1:Z$=FO$(Z)
5265 RETURN
9999 REM **************** USER WRITTEN ROUTINES ***************************
10000 PRINT"***** USER ROUTINE **** ";FO$(Z)
10005 RETURN
```

## Sample Run

```
RUN
ENTER A NUMBER TO DO ONE OF THE FOLLOWING
1-CREATE A STRUCTURE
2-CREATE AN OBJECT
3-NAME OF ALL STRUCTURES
4-NAME OF ALL OBJECTS
5-VIEW A STRUCTURE
6-VIEW AN OBJECT
7-SEND A VALUE TO AN OBJECT
8-COPY A VALUE TO Z$ FROM AN OBJECT'S ATTRIBUTE
9-PSEUDO VOLTAGE CHECKER
? 1
ENTER STRUCTURE NAME ? VOLTAGE
ENTER NUMBER OF ATTRIBUTES ? 2
ATTRIBUTE  1 -? *
ATTRIBUTE  2 -? TIME

ENTER A NUMBER TO DO ONE OF THE FOLLOWING
1-CREATE A STRUCTURE
2-CREATE AN OBJECT
3-NAME OF ALL STRUCTURES
4-NAME OF ALL OBJECTS
5-VIEW A STRUCTURE
6-VIEW AN OBJECT
7-SEND A VALUE TO AN OBJECT
8-COPY A VALUE TO Z$ FROM AN OBJECT'S ATTRIBUTE
9-PSEUDO VOLTAGE CHECKER
? 2
ENTER STRUCTURE NAME ? VOLTAGE
ENTER OBJECTS NAME ? EQUIP
ENTER NUMBER OF ATTRIBUTES ? 2
ATTRIBUTE  1 -? 9:00
ATTRIBUTE  2 -? 1

ENTER A NUMBER TO DO ONE OF THE FOLLOWING
1-CREATE A STRUCTURE
2-CREATE AN OBJECT
```

```
3-NAME OF ALL STRUCTURES
4-NAME OF ALL OBJECTS
5-VIEW A STRUCTURE
6-VIEW AN OBJECT
7-SEND A VALUE TO AN OBJECT
8-COPY A VALUE TO Z$ FROM AN OBJECT'S ATTRIBUTE
9-PSEUDO VOLTAGE CHECKER
? 9
VOLTAGE TOO HIGH=   .767173
VOLTAGE TOO HIGH=   .8798876
VOLTAGE TOO HIGH=   .8236365
VOLTAGE TOO HIGH=   .9229655
VOLTAGE TOO HIGH=   .8604398
VOLTAGE TOO HIGH=   .8269814
VOLTAGE TOO HIGH=   .7464719
VOLTAGE TOO HIGH=   .7312078
VOLTAGE TOO HIGH=   .9698101
```

**Chapter**

# 13

# Object-Oriented Expert Systems

Now that you understand objects and how to write programs using them, let's see how we can use them in an expert system. As an example, we will design an expert system that can predict when a town that is located along a river should be evacuated because there is a danger of flooding. The system will use a rule-based structure that utilizes objects. As we've said before, don't worry that the subject matter may sound complicated; we will lead you carefully through every step in the design of the flood-warning system.

### Designing the Structure

Since our problem deals with flood warning, the first thing we must do in designing the structure is to identify those things that must be considered to warn the people in a town of possible flooding. These things are the attributes of the structure. We will consider four crucial attributes and define the attributes' values in fuzzy terms such as high, hot, etc. The attribute names, with explanation of their meaning are

1. WATER-LEVEL   This is the water level of the river near the town. If it is high, there is danger of flooding. If it is low, it can absorb runoff of a heavy rain or swiftly melting snow.

2. RAIN   This is the weather forecast in terms of rain. If it is heavy and the water level is high, there is a chance of flooding. If no rain is forecast, then rain cannot contribute to a flood.

3. TEMPERATURE   If the weather forecast is for a hot day and there is a lot of snow in the mountains surrounding the river and the water level is high, there is a danger of flooding.

4. SNOW    The level of snow in the mountain. Melting snow can cause run-off into the river and increase the danger of flooding. A low level of snow contributes very little to danger of flooding no matter what the rain or temperature.

We can create the FLOOD structure via the Create-Structure subroutine, as follows:

> CREATE-STRUCTURE (SNAME = FLOOD, NATTR = 4, ATTR = WATER-LEVEL, ATTR = RAIN, ATTR = TEMPERATURE, ATTR = SNOW)

## Creating an Object

Remember, an object is an instance on a particular day, one in April 1985. We were working in the weather laboratory and decided to create objects to represent the weather status of our two towns, River City and Redwood City. Using the flood structure, we can create objects to represent the two towns at different locations along a river. We will name the objects according to the names of the towns. Let's call the towns and their objects names RIVER-CITY and REDWOOD-CITY. The created objects are

> CREATE-OBJECT (SNAME = FLOOD, ONAME = RIVER-CITY, WATER-LEVEL = HIGH RAIN = HEAVY RAIN, TEMPERATURE = HOT, SNOW = A LOT)

This object's name is RIVER-CITY. Today, the water level is high, the rain in the area is heavy, the temperature is hot, and there is a lot of snow in the mountains. The other object created is

> CREATE-OBJECT (SNAME = FLOOD, ONAME = REDWOOD-CITY, WATER-LEVEL = LOW RAIN = NO RAIN, TEMPERATURE = WARM, SNOW = A LOT)

This object is REDWOOD-CITY. Today, the water level is low, there is no rain, it is warm, and there is a lot of snow in the mountains.

## Building the Knowledge Base

As we have done previously, we will first represent the knowledge base by a decision tree and then convert this tree into a set of IF-THEN rules. The decision tree is shown in Figure 13-1.

Remember how we convert the decision tree to a set of rules? By following every path that leads to a conclusion. In this example there is

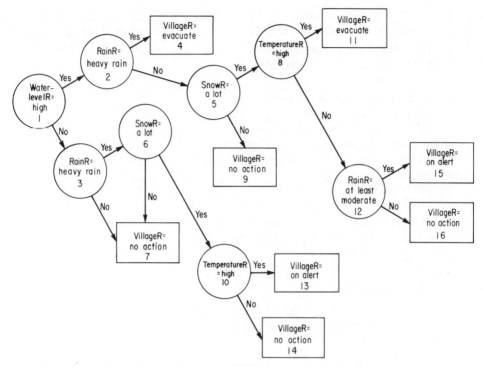

Figure 13-1   Decision tree for a flood alert system.

one conclusion, which is whether or not an evacuation should take place.

## Writing the Rules

The following nine paths can be drawn from the tree:

1. 1, 2, 4
2. 1, 2, 5, 8, 11
3. 1, 2, 5, 8, 12, 15
4. 1, 2, 5, 8, 12, 16
5. 1, 2, 5, 9
6. 1, 3, 6, 10, 13
7. 1, 3, 6, 10, 14
8. 1, 3, 6, 7
9. 1, 3, 7

From these paths we can write the corresponding rules for the knowledge base. Notice that we've added an R onto the end of the names of the following rule variables; we don't want to confuse a variable name with its corresponding attribute name.

1   IF WATER-LEVELR = HIGH AND
    RAINR = HEAVY RAIN
    THEN VILLAGER = EVACUATE

2   IF WATER-LEVELR = HIGH AND
    RAINR = NOT HEAVY RAIN AND
    SNOWR = A LOT AND
    TEMPERATURER = HIGH
    THEN VILLAGER = EVACUATE

3   IF WATER-LEVELR = HIGH AND
    RAINR = NOT HEAVY RAIN AND
    SNOWR = A LOT AND
    TEMPERATURER = NOT HIGH AND
    RAINR = AT LEAST MODERATE
    THEN VILLAGER = ON ALERT

4   IF WATER-LEVELR = HIGH AND
    RAINR = NOT HEAVY RAIN AND
    SNOWR = A LOT AND
    TEMPERTURER = NOT HIGH AND
    RAINR = LESS THAN MODERATE
    THEN VILLAGER = NO ACTION

5   IF WATER-LEVELR = HIGH AND
    RAINR = NOT HEAVY RAIN AND
    SNOWR = NOT A LOT
    THEN VILLAGER = NO ACTION

6   IF WATER-LEVELR = NOT HIGH AND
    RAINR = HEAVY RAIN AND
    SNOWR = A LOT AND
    TEMPERATURER = HIGH
    THEN VILLAGER = ON ALERT

7   IF WATER-LEVELR = NOT HIGH AND
    RAINR = HEAVY RAIN AND
    SNOWR = A LOT AND
    TEMPERATURER = NOT HIGH
    THEN VILLAGER = NO ACTION

8   IF WATER-LEVELR = NOT HIGH AND
    RAINR = HEAVY RAIN AND
    SNOWR = NOT A LOT
    THEN VILLAGER = NO ACTION

9   IF WATER-LEVELR = NOT HIGH AND
    RAINR = NOT HEAVY RAIN
    THEN VILLAGER = NO ACTION

## Using the Knowledge Base

In order to see how the rules use the objects, let us first rewrite the objects as follows:

| Name of attributes | River City | Redwood City |
|---|---|---|
| WATER-LEVEL | HIGH | LOW |
| RAIN | HEAVY RAIN | NO RAIN |
| TEMPERATURE | HOT | WARM |
| SNOW | A LOT | A LOT |

Let's take rule 1 as an example and see how it uses objects:

    1   IF WATER-LEVELR = HIGH AND
        RAINR = HEAVY RAIN
        THEN VILLAGER = EVACUATE

Assume we wish to know whether River City should be evacuated. We would instantiate WATER-LEVELR, and we have to instantiate all the condition variables (water level and rain). The way a variable is instantiated with the value in an object is via the COPY subroutine. If we provide the COPY subroutine with the structure name, object name, and the attribute of that object, it will reach into the object's attribute, take the value, and place it with the variable, shown here on the left side of the copy expression. For example, the COPY subroutine would do the following:

    WATER-LEVELR = COPY (SNAME = FLOOD, ONAME = RIVER-CITY, WATER-LEVEL)

(WATER-LEVEL is the name of the attribute, not the name of the variable WATER-LEVELR.)

What this subroutine does is find the object, RIVER-CITY, obtain the value in the attribute WATER-LEVEL, which in this case is HIGH, and pass it to the variable called WATER-LEVELR.

Returning to the first condition clause of rule 1, we see that it is satisfied because it says, "IF WATER-LEVELR IS HIGH." We must now see if the second condition clause, which is RAINR = HEAVY RAIN, is also true. We do this by using the COPY subroutine again:

    RAINR = COPY (SNAME = FLOOD, ONAME = RIVER-CITY, RAIN)

Since the RAIN attribute for RIVER-CITY is HEAVY RAIN, the COPY subroutine will cause RAINR to get the value HEAVY RAIN.

The THEN part of the rule will be invoked since both clauses of the

IF part are true. We must then evacuate the town. We could do the same thing, of course, for Redwood City. What these copy subroutines do is to transfer a factual situation about these towns, one day in April, into the rule variables so the reference technique can be applied to see if a flood warning is warranted.

## Backward or Forward Chaining

The only difference between executing a backward or forward chaining operation on objects as opposed to executing them on just variables is the way we access the attributes in the objects. That is, we use the SEND and COPY subroutines for setting or obtaining values of objects. All the other features are the same, allowing us to follow the explanations of the chapters describing backward and forward chaining for objects as well.

Briefly, when would we choose a backward chaining technique and when would we instead opt for forward chaining? As you've probably guessed already, this system would make the best use of a forward chaining technique because it is intended to predict the outcome (conclusion) from various factors (conditions). The conditions are, it is raining, the snow is low, etc. In terms of the system, that means we search the IF parts of the rules for conditions that will lead to the invoking of the THEN parts.

Don't count backward chaining out of this problem, though. It could be very useful in the aftermath of a flood in trying to determine the causes once the flood has occurred. This is the conclusion. In order to determine the condition that caused it, we would invoke backward chaining. The situation is very much like a criminal case or a mechanical problem in your car or any other backward chaining example we have previously discussed. In other words, once a particular situation exists, the task is to look for causes. In the backward chaining system, the rules are scanned for THEN parts that match the actual event—in this case, a flood—and the IF parts are then instantiated to see if the circumstances in the rule fit the actual occurrence.

Finding the causes of previous floods through backward chaining would be a very good way of setting up a flood-warning system based on forward chaining—once the factors that caused the flood are known, they can be carefully monitored to avoid a future disaster. Backward chaining discovers, forward chaining predicts.

# Advanced Knowledge Representation for Smart Systems

*Section 5 contains a potpourri of topics that briefly describe additional artificial intelligence representations, dealing with uncertainty and an introduction to automated learning. It is chock-full of examples and programs that will enhance your understanding of the topics.*

# 14

# Semantic Nets

In this chapter we will give you an introductory understanding of some other important artificial intelligence concepts used in expert systems. Semantic nets are graphical representations of knowledge. Like a decision tree, they consist of nodes that are represented by circles, and arcs that are represented by lines with arrows. The nodes contain pieces of information and the arcs show the relationship between them.

A semantic net illustrating a knowledge base for some form of bird and plane is shown in Figure 14-1. Every arc indicates some relationship between items contained in the nodes. For example, as you can see from the figure, the relationship between the node "gasoline" and the node "engine" is that the engine "uses" gasoline, as indicated on the arc.

### Structure and Objects of Semantic Nets

One of the ways we can use a semantic net is to create objects. Let's see how this works with the semantic net shown in Figure 14-1. First, we will concentrate on developing a structure for a bird. The objects of the structure, BIRD, that is, specific instances of the structure, are identified by the "is a" relationship. These are FALCON and EAGLE, meaning falcon is a bird, and eagle is a bird. Other arc relationships will provide us with the attributes of BIRD. From the "has" relationship, we see three of the attributes, which are WINGS, FEATHERS, and BEAK; in other words, BIRD has all of these, as shown in the semantic net. From the "does" relationship, we see an attribute, namely FLY; that is, a bird does fly, and from the "uses" relationship, we get the attribute AERODYNAMIC PRINCIPLES; the bird uses aerodynamic principles. From these attributes we can now create the STRUCTURE, BIRD:

> CREATE-STRUCTURE (SNAME = BIRD, NATTR = 5, ATTR = BEAK, ATTR = FEATHERS, ATTR = WINGS, ATR = FLY, ATTR = AERODYNAMIC PRINCIPLES)

Using the structure, we can now create the objects EAGLE and FALCON. For example, the object EAGLE is created by

> CREATE-OBJECT (SNAME = BIRD, ONAME = EAGLE, BEAK = LONG, FEATHERS = LIGHT, WINGS = WIDE, FLY = HIGH, AERODYNAMIC PRINCIPLES = GLIDING)

We could now use the objects to create a knowledge base that can help us to answer specific questions about the objects.

## Rule-Based System Using Semantic Nets

From the semantic net we can also set up a knowledge base that would enable us to identify whether a flying object is a bird or plane. The

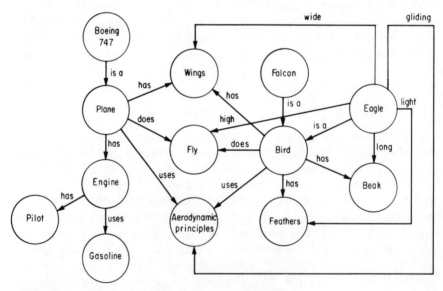

Figure 14-1   Semantic net showing relationships between parts of a bird and a plane.

following are some of the rules that can be part of the bird-plane knowledge base:

```
IF OBJECT-ATTRIBUTE = BEAK
THEN FLYING OBJECT = BIRD

IF OBJECT-ATTRIBUTE = WINGS
THEN FLYING-OBJECT = BIRD OR
        FLYING-OBJECT = PLANE

IF OBJECT-ATTRIBUTE = FALCON OR
    OBJECT-ATTRIBUTE = EAGLE
THEN FLYING-OBJECT = BIRD

IF OBJECT-ATTRIBUTE = FEATHERS AND
    OBJECT-ATTRIBUTE = BEAK AND
    OBJECT-ATTRIBUTE = WINGS
THEN FLYING-OBJECT = BIRD

IF FLYING-OBJECT = BIRD
THEN OBJECT-ATTRIBUTE = FEATHERS
```

Here is a summary of some of the principles of semantic nets:

1. Semantic nets describe relationships between things that are represented by nodes.
2. The nodes are circles that have names.
3. The relationships between nodes are represented by arcs that connect the circles.
4. A semantic net can be used to generate structures and objects.
5. A semantic net can be used to generate rules for a knowledge base.

## Programming Applications

Let's examine a program written in BASIC, Listing 14-1, which manipulates the semantic net shown in Figure 14-2. This semantic net is a subset of the one we used to describe the concepts.

### Program Explanation

Listing 14-1 is divided into three functional parts. Each part performs an operation that allows you to view a particular aspect of the semantic net. For example, we can obtain a list of all node pairs for a particular relationship. The "is a" relationship has node pairs FALCON-BIRD and EAGLE-BIRD. Each operation is simply understood by tracing through at most 15 BASIC statements. The semantic net is defined

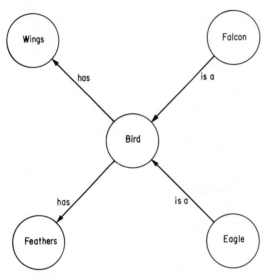

**Figure 14-2   A semantic net.**

within two arrays. One array contains the names of the nodes and is symbolically represented as N$. The other array is a two-dimensional array and contains the arc relationship names. This is symbolically represented as R$. We have given values to these two arrays in statement numbers 70 and 75 to correspond to Figure 14-3. We can alternately represent the semantic net with the N$ and R$ array values as shown in the matrix of Figure 14-3.

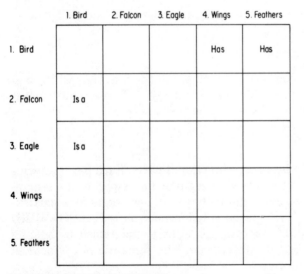

|            | 1. Bird | 2. Falcon | 3. Eagle | 4. Wings | 5. Feathers |
|------------|---------|-----------|----------|----------|-------------|
| 1. Bird    |         |           |          | Has      | Has         |
| 2. Falcon  | Is a    |           |          |          |             |
| 3. Eagle   | Is a    |           |          |          |             |
| 4. Wings   |         |           |          |          |             |
| 5. Feathers|         |           |          |          |             |

**Figure 14-3   Relationship matrix R$.**

The semantic net program, Listing 14-1, offers the following options that are defined in statement numbers 300 through 365:

```
ENTER A NUMBER CORRESPONDING TO ONE OF THE FOLLOWING
1-OBTAIN ALL RELATIONSHIP NODES FOR A PARTICULAR NODE
  AND A PARTICULAR RELATIONSHIP
2-OBTAIN A LIST OF ALL NAMES WITH THEIR RELATIONSHIP FOR A
  PARTICULAR NODE
3-OBTAIN ALL NODE PAIRS CORRESPONDING TO A PARTICULAR RELATIONSHIP
4-EXIT
?
```

The statements implementing these options are located in statements numbers 1000, 1100, and 1200, respectively.

**Program Listing**

Listing 14-1 is followed by a set of sample runs.

**Listing 14-1   Semantic nets.**

```
1   REM ************ SEMANTIC NETS ******************************
5 REM RELATIONSHIP ARRAY. THIS IS THE MATRIX THAT HOLDS THE ARC'S NAMES
10 DIM R$(10,10)
15 REM NAME ARRAY. THIS TELLS US THE NAME OF EACH NODE.
20 DIM N$(10)
25 REM INITIALIZE RELATIONSHIP ARRAY AND NAME ARRAY
30 FOR I=1 TO 10
35 FOR J=1 TO 10
40 R$(I,J)="":N$(I)=""
45 NEXT J
50 NEXT I
55 REM THIS SECTION SET VALUES FOR THE NAME ARRAY AND THE RELATIONSHIP ARRAY.
60 REM   THE VALUES ARE ASSIGNED BUT THE PROGRAMMER CAN REMOVE THEM AND USE
65 REM   INPUT STATEMENTS TO ASSIGN VALUES IN GENERAL.
69 REM ****************** SEMANTIC NET ***************************************
70 N$(1)="BIRD":N$(2)="FALCON":N$(3)="EAGLE":N$(4)="WINGS":N$(5)="FEATHERS"
75 R$(2,1)="IS A":R$(3,1)="IS A":R$(1,4)="HAS":R$(1,5)="HAS"
299 REM ***********************************************************************
300 PRINT"ENTER A NUMBER CORRESPONDING TO ONE OF THE FOLLOWING"
305 PRINT"1-OBTAIN ALL RELATIONSHIP NODES FOR A PARTICULAR NODE"
306 PRINT"  AND A PARTICULAR RELATIONSHIP"
310 PRINT"2-OBTAIN A LIST OF ALL NAMES WITH THEIR RELATIONSHIP FOR A"
315 PRINT"  PARTICULAR NODE"
320 PRINT"3-OBTAIN ALL NODE PAIRS CORRESPONDING TO A PARTICULAR RELATIONSHIP"
325 PRINT"4-EXIT"
360 INPUT N
365 ON N GOSUB 1000,1100,1200,1300
370 GOTO 300
1000 REM ***** OBTAIN ALL RELATIONSHIP NODES FOR A PARTICULAR NODE AND
1005 REM        A PARTICULAR RELATIONSHIP
1010 INPUT"ENTER NODE NAME YOU ARE INTERESTED IN";NN$
1015 INPUT"ENTER RELATIONSHIP NAME YOU ARE INTERESTED IN";RN$
1020 REM FIND THE NODE NUMBER CORRESPONDING TO NN$
1025 FOR I=1 TO 10
1030 IF NN$=N$(I) THEN GOTO 1040
1035 NEXT I
1040 REM FOR THIS NODE NUMBER (I) IN THE RELATIONSHIP MATRIX FIND THOSE
1045 REM NAMES (J) THAT CONTAIN THE RELATIONSHIP (RN$)
1050 FOR J=1 TO 10
1055 IF R$(I,J)=RN$ THEN PRINT N$(J)
1060 NEXT J
1065 RETURN
1100 REM ***** OBTAIN A LIST TOGETHER WITH ALL THEIR RELATIONSHIPS FOR
1105 REM        A PARTICULAR NODE
1110 INPUT"ENTER NAME OF NODE";NN$
1115 REM FIND ROW IN RELATIONSHIP MATRIX CONTAINING THE NAME
1120 FOR I=1 TO 10
1125 IF NN$=N$(I) THEN GOTO 1135
1130 NEXT I
1135 REM PRINT ALL RELATIONSHIPS AND THEIR CORRESPONDING NODES
1140 FOR J=1 TO 10
1145 IF R$(I,J)="" THEN GOTO 1155
1150 PRINT N$(J);"   ";R$(I,J)
1155 NEXT J
1160 RETURN
1200 REM ***** OBTAIN ALL NODE PAIRS CORRESPONDING TO A PARTICULAR RELATIONSHIP
1205 INPUT"ENTER THE RELATIONSHIP NAME";RN$
1210 FOR I=1 TO 10
1215 FOR J=1 TO 10
1220 IF R$(I,J)=RN$ THEN PRINT N$(I);"   ";N$(J)
1225 NEXT J
1230 NEXT I
1235 RETURN
1400 REM ***** EXIT
1405 STOP
```

## Sample Runs

```
RUN
ENTER A NUMBER CORRESPONDING TO ONE OF THE FOLLOWING
1-OBTAIN ALL RELATIONSHIP NODES FOR A PARTICULAR NODE
   AND A PARTICULAR RELATIONSHIP
2-OBTAIN A LIST OF ALL NAMES WITH THEIR RELATIONSHIP FOR A
   PARTICULAR NODE
3-OBTAIN ALL NODE PAIRS CORRESPONDING TO A PARTICULAR RELATIONSHIP
4-EXIT
?  1
ENTER NODE NAME YOU ARE INTERESTED IN? BIRD
ENTER RELATIONSHIP NAME YOU ARE INTERESTED IN? HAS
WINGS
FEATHERS

ENTER A NUMBER CORRESPONDING TO ONE OF THE FOLLOWING
1-OBTAIN ALL RELATIONSHIP NODES FOR A PARTICULAR NODE
   AND A PARTICULAR RELATIONSHIP
2-OBTAIN A LIST OF ALL NAMES WITH THEIR RELATIONSHIP FOR A
   PARTICULAR NODE
3-OBTAIN ALL NODE PAIRS CORRESPONDING TO A PARTICULAR RELATIONSHIP
4-EXIT
?  1
ENTER NODE NAME YOU ARE INTERESTED IN? EAGLE
ENTER RELATIONSHIP NAME YOU ARE INTERESTED IN? IS A
BIRD

ENTER A NUMBER CORRESPONDING TO ONE OF THE FOLLOWING
1-OBTAIN ALL RELATIONSHIP NODES FOR A PARTICULAR NODE
   AND A PARTICULAR RELATIONSHIP
2-OBTAIN A LIST OF ALL NAMES WITH THEIR RELATIONSHIP FOR A
   PARTICULAR NODE
3-OBTAIN ALL NODE PAIRS CORRESPONDING TO A PARTICULAR RELATIONSHIP
4-EXIT
?  2
ENTER NAME OF NODE? BIRD
WINGS   HAS
FEATHERS   HAS
```

In this run it is important to note that a relationship is only valid for arcs *leaving a node*. The two "is a" arcs entering the BIRD node are considered relationships of the FALCON and EAGLE, respectively.

```
ENTER A NUMBER CORRESPONDING TO ONE OF THE FOLLOWING
1-OBTAIN ALL RELATIONSHIP NODES FOR A PARTICULAR NODE
   AND A PARTICULAR RELATIONSHIP
2-OBTAIN A LIST OF ALL NAMES WITH THEIR RELATIONSHIP FOR A
   PARTICULAR NODE
3-OBTAIN ALL NODE PAIRS CORRESPONDING TO A PARTICULAR RELATIONSHIP
4-EXIT
?  3
ENTER THE RELATIONSHIP NAME? HAS
BIRD   WINGS
BIRD   FEATHERS
```

# 15

# Certainty Factors

Certainty Factors (CF) are used in the mathematical field called fuzzy logic. Since heuristics are based on expert rules that are learned from experience, we may not always be completely certain that an IF-THEN rule is correct. Nor can the user of an expert system be certain that the value he or she provides when instantiating a variable is a hundred percent correct. For example, the rule

    IF INTEREST RATES = FALL AND TAXES = DECREASED
    THEN STOCK MARKET = RISE

may not work all the time. Therefore, we may assign to the rule a CF, which is a value that approximates the degree to which we *think* the rule is correct. Values of CF range between $-1$ and $+1$. A CF of a negative number indicates a predominance of opposing evidence for the rule being correct. A positive CF indicates a predominance of confirming evidence for the rule being correct. Therefore, a CF of $+1$ indicates absolute certainty that the rule is correct, while a CF of $-1$ indicates absolute certainty that the rule is incorrect. Of course, if we had a CF that equaled $-1$, we would not even consider stating the rule.

Assume we assign a CF of 0.9 to the stock market rule. Also, assume that we are not really sure that interest rates are falling and assign a CF of 0.6 to that clause. Assume further that changes in the tax laws will include some increases as well as some reductions. But on the average we *think* the taxes will be reduced with a CF of 0.8. We can then represent the rule as

    IF INTEREST RATES = FALL (CF = 0.6) AND
    TAXES = REDUCED (CF = 0.8)
    THEN STOCK MARKET = RISE (Rule CF = 0.9)

We can calculate the CF that the stock market is rising by multiplying the minimum of the clauses connected by AND in the IF part by the CF of the rule. In our example this works out to be

(Minimum (0.6, 0.8)) * 0.9 = 0.6 * 0.9 = 0.54

We therefore have a 0.54 certainty that the stock market will rise.

If we have another rule that also tells us the stock market will rise but uses a different set of conditions to arrive at the answer, we will take the highest, or maximum, CF of the two answers. Don't worry if this sounds complicated; you will soon see an example of how this works.

We will first summarize the rules for you, then work out a general example:

1. From a rule, take the minimum CF of clauses connected by AND.
2. If there are OR connections in the rule, take the maximum CF value of all the AND clauses that are connected by ORs.
3. Multiply the final CF of the clauses by the CF of the rule.
4. If there is more than one rule leading to the same conclusion, take as the final CF the maximum CF values of all those rules.

Consider the following two rules. They both lead to the same conclusion, which is C.

    IF A (CF = 0.3) AND B (CF = 0.6)
    THEN C (CF = 0.5)
    IF D (CF = 0.4) AND E (CF = 0.7)
    THEN C (CF = 0.9)

The CF of C is the higher of the CFs of the two rules, as follows:

    Maximum ((minimum (0.3, 0.6) * 0.5),
    (minimum (0.4, 0.7) * 0.9))
    = maximum ((0.3 * 0.5), (0.4 * 0.9))
    = maximum (0.15, 0.36)
    = 0.36

Another example, this time using the logical operator OR is

    IF A (CF = 0.3) AND
      B (CF = 0.6) OR
      D (CF = 0.5)
    THEN C (CF = 0.4)

The CF for C is

Maximum (minimum (0.3, 0.6), 0.5) * 0.4
= maximum (0.3, 0.5) * 0.4
= 0.5 * 0.4 = 0.2

## Certainty Level Restrictions

In many cases certainty levels are given. What this means is that an inference is valid only if the CF exceeds this level. If the CF is below this level, a search through the knowledge base continues until an inference exceeds the level. The way the certainty level is calculated is as follows. Assume that the CF for a particular inference is 0.4. We place 0.4 for that inference into a CF accumulator. We compare the CF accumulator with the certainty level (assume it to be 0.8). The accumulated value is less than the level and therefore the knowledge base search proceeds. The next time the same inference is encountered in the knowledge base search we multiply the CF for this new inference by 1 minus the value in the CF accumulator and add the result to the CF accumulator. The 1 in the equation comes from the absolute certainty value = 1. We now compare the CF accumulator with the certainty level. If greater, we have our answer. If not, we continue the search. The equation is

Accumulated CF = old accumulated CF + (1 − old accumulated CF) * CF of the rule

For example:

Certainty level    =    0.8
Rule               =    if A then B (assume CF = 0.6)
Accumulated CF     =    0.6
New rule           =    if C then B (assume CF = 0.7)
Accumulated CF     =    0.6 + (1 − 0.6) × 0.7
                   =    0.88 (exceeds certainty level; stop)

## Programming Applications

Let's examine a program written in BASIC, Listing 15-1, which allows us to apply the certainty factor concepts we have just discussed.

### Program Explanation

The rule used to illustrate the certainty factors concepts is shown in Listing 15-1 in the REM statements 20 and 60 and executed in statements 400 and 430. Each rule has a sequence of locations assigned to it in the CF array, with one CF location for each condition variable. Since the rule has three condition variables, A, B, and C, we can assign CF(1), CF(2), and CF(3) to these variables. The user is asked to enter a value for A, B, and C along with certainty factors for each variable in statement numbers 320, 340, and 360. If the user enters a certainty factor for any of the variables, this certainty factor replaces a default certainty factor value in the CF array which is assigned to that variable as shown in statements 330, 350, and 370. Default certainty factor values are contained in the default array. Each value of the default array is initially set to a 1 as shown in statements 150 through 170. The knowledge engineer can override these values as shown in statement 190. The default values are then transferred to the CF array in statements 230 through 250. The user can replace the default values, as previously described, in statements 320 through 370. We then calculate the certainty of the result in statements 450 through 500.

## Program Listing

Listing 15-1 is followed by a set of sample runs.

**Listing 15-1 Certainty factors.**

```
10 REM ****************** CERTAINTY FACTORS ****************************
20 REM CONSIDER THE FOLLOWING RULE
30 REM   IF  A=2    (CF=.6)      AND
40 REM       B=3    (CF=.3)      AND
50 REM       C=5    (CF=1.0)
60 REM   THEN D=5 (CF=.4)
70 REM ALONGSIDE, IN PARENTHESIS, EACH CLAUSE IS THE CERTAINTY FACTOR.
80 REM THE CF NUMBERS ARE THE DEFAULT NUMBERS THAT THE WRITER OF THE RULE
90 REM HAS IN THE CLAUSE ITSELF. THESE NUMBERS ARE CONSIDERED DEFAULT VALUES.
100 REM THE USER CAN OVERRIDE THESE DEFAULT VALUES WITH HIS OR HERS OWN CF
110 REM VALUES.
120 REM THE CF DEFAULT ARRAY HOLDING THE RULE WRITERS VALUES IS
130 DIM D(100)
140 REM INITIALIZE D ARRAY
150 FOR I=1 TO 100
160 D(I)=1:REM A CF OF 1
170 NEXT I
180 REM ****************** DEFAULT VALUES ***************************
190 D(1)=.6:D(2)=.3
200 REM THE DEFAULT VALUES IS TRANSFERRED TO THE CONFIDENCE FACTOR ARRAY AT
210 REM THE START OF THE PROGRAM.
220 DIM CF(100)
230 FOR I=1 TO 100
240 CF(I)=D(I)
250 NEXT I
260 REM ************ INSTANTIATE THE VARIABLES ****************
270 PRINT"ENTER ONE VALUE FOR INSTANTIATING A VARIABLE FOLLOWED BY A COMMA"
280 PRINT"THEN OPTIONALLY FOLLOWED BY A CERTAINTY FACTOR (CF) VALUE. IF"
290 PRINT"YOU DO NOT PROVIDE A CF ENTER A "0" AND THEN THE DEFAULT VALUE"
300 PRINT"WILL BE USED"
310 REM RULE 1 WILL USE THE FIRST 3 CF ELEMENTS
320 INPUT"VARIABLE A IS ";A,C1
330 IF C1<>0 THEN CF(1)=C1
340 INPUT"VARIABLE B IS ";B,C1
350 IF C1<>0 THEN CF(2)=C1
360 INPUT"VARIABLE C IS ";C,C1
370 IF C1<>0 THEN CF(3)=C1
380 EX=0:REM EXECUTE FLAG IF EX=1 THEN EXECUTE THE THEN PART AND CF
390 IF (A=2) AND (B=3) AND (C=5) THEN EX=1
400 IF EX=0 THEN GOTO 500
410 REM EXECUTE RULE
420 D=5:PRINT"RULE EXECUTED D=";D
430 REM CALCULATE CF FOR RULE
440 REM CF=[MINIMUM C(1),C(2),C(3)] * .4
450 X=CF(1)
460 PRINT"CF(1)=";CF(1);"  CF(2)=";CF(2);"  CF(3)=";CF(3)
470 IF CF(2)<X THEN X=CF(2)
480 IF CF(3)<X THEN X=CF(3)
490 CF=X*.4:PRINT"CF IS ";CF:STOP
500 PRINT"**** RULE DID NOT FIRE":STOP
```

## Sample Runs

```
RUN
ENTER ONE VALUE FOR INSTANTIATING A VARIABLE FOLLOWED BY A COMMA
THEN OPTIONALLY FOLLOWED BY A CERTAINTY FACTOR (CF) VALUE. IF
YOU DO NOT PROVIDE A CF ENTER A 0 AND THEN THE DEFAULT VALUE
WILL BE USED
VARIABLE A IS ? 2,
VARIABLE B IS ? 3,
VARIABLE C IS ? 5,
RULE EXECUTED D= 5
CF(1)= .6  CF(2)= .3  CF(3)= 1
CF IS .12
Break in 500
Ok

ENTER ONE VALUE FOR INSTANTIATING A VARIABLE FOLLOWED BY A COMMA
THEN OPTIONALLY FOLLOWED BY A CERTAINTY FACTOR (CF) VALUE. IF
```

```
YOU DO NOT PROVIDE A CF ENTER A 0 AND THEN THE DEFAULT VALUE
WILL BE USED
VARIABLE A IS ? 2,.4
VARIABLE B IS ? 3,.6
VARIABLE C IS ? 5,
RULE EXECUTED D= 5
CF(1)= .4  CF(2)= .6  CF(3)= 1
CF IS .16
Break in 500
Ok

ENTER ONE VALUE FOR INSTANTIATING A VARIABLE FOLLOWED BY A COMMA
THEN OPTIONALLY FOLLOWED BY A CERTAINTY FACTOR (CF) VALUE. IF
YOU DO NOT PROVIDE A CF ENTER A 0 AND THEN THE DEFAULT VALUE
WILL BE USED
VARIABLE A IS ? 2,
VARIABLE B IS ? 4,
VARIABLE C IS ? 3,
**** RULE DID NOT FIRE
Break in 510
Ok
```

# 16

# Automated Learning

There are many ways a person can learn. One way is being told a fact directly, another is learning by example. If we tell a child that he may get burned by touching a hot stove, the child may not automatically infer that by touching *anything* hot he will get burned. Another way of teaching a child not to touch a hot stove is to tell him that the general rule that touching anything hot will cause a burn.

Whatever method is used to learn something, an individual may modify what was previously thought to be as a result of the newly acquired knowledge. For example, if a child didn't already infer that anything hot may burn her and then puts her hand in hot water, she may finally get the point. This modification process occurs via something known as "feedback." A diagram of this feedback structure is shown in Figure 16-1. The feedback path and an input experience both contribute to the learning process by referring to knowledge that has already been learned. A person's knowledge can thereby be modified by each learning experience.

We do the same with a "learning" computer program. We first develop an algorithm for storing a set of facts and making inferences. The conclusions are mixed in the feedback portion of the program with new inputs to modify the facts. A learning system example which we will consider will operate on the following premise:

> The learning system will only modify what it has learned if what has been learned is now thought to be wrong.

The premise is similar to what human beings do automatically. After all, isn't it true that people usually don't modify their thinking unless they know or sense that it is wrong?

Figure 16-1 **Learning mechanism.**

## Example of a Learning System

Let us consider a system that must learn to tell the difference between a car and tank. A few features that differentiate between a car and tank are shown in Figure 16-2. We can read the diagram in the figure as

The tank has a cannon and a hatch.

The car has a door and wheels.

Both the tank and car have a body.

The computer learning program that we will present can only learn to tell the difference between two objects, but the principles can be expanded to consider more than two objects.

The program has three lists: list 1 to hold the attributes of the car it will learn about; list 2 to hold the attributes of the tank it will learn

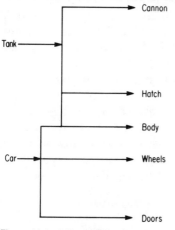

Figure 16-2 **Differentiating features.**

about; and the common list to contain those attributes that are common to both.

Note that the two objects could have been almost anything, such as rain or no rain in a weather forecasting system. The program functions in the same way no matter what objects are being compared.

The learning program will first ask the user to name the two objects. The names of the objects are entered by the following computer interaction:

```
ENTER OBJECT 1 NAME ?   CAR
ENTER OBJECT 2 NAME ?   TANK
```

The program will then assume you are observing one of the objects and are ready to enter its attributes. It will do this by the following dialogue:

```
INPUT ANY OBJECT'S ATTRIBUTES—WHEN FINISHED TYPE RETURN
ENTER ATTRIBUTE 1 ?   CANNON
ENTER ATTRIBUTE 2 ?   HATCH
ENTER ATTRIBUTE 3 ?   BODY
ENTER ATTRIBUTE 4 ?   ENTER key
```

The program will first compare the attributes entered at the computer console with the attributes in list 1, the car list. Since initially there are no attributes in that list because the program hasn't learned anything yet about a car, a score of 0 is given, indicating that no attributes match. For the same reason list 2, the tank list, produces a score of 0. Whenever there is a tie score, the computer program will guess that the attributes belong to the name assigned to list 1. In the learning system the user responds no to the question because it is really a tank that was described, not a car. Since the guess is wrong, the feedback mechanism goes into action. We have just told the system that the input attributes do not apply to a car, so no attributes can be placed on the car list, which is list 1. No attributes can be placed on the common list, either, so the three attributes are placed on list 2, the tank list. If there *had* been any attributes entered that matched attributes on list 1, they would have been removed and placed in the common list. This is done automatically because the system assumed that an attribute belonging to both objects belongs on the common list.

After all these maneuvers are complete, the three lists look like this:

| List 1 (car) | List 2 (tank) | List 3 (common) |
|---|---|---|
| | CANNON | |
| | HATCH | |
| | BODY | |

Why not design the system to place the attributes in the right list in the first place and avoid all these maneuvers? Of course that could be done, but that's the difference between being told something and learning it for oneself. This way, our system thinks like a person, not like a machine, and has to figure out where to put the attributes.

We now enter another set of attributes, for the object car:

```
INPUT ANY OBJECT'S ATTRIBUTES-WHEN FINISHED TYPE RETURN
ENTER ATTRIBUTE 1 ?  DOORS
ENTER ATTRIBUTE 2 ?  WHEELS
ENTER ATTRIBUTE 3 ?  BODY
ENTER ATTRIBUTE 4 ?  ENTER key
```

The program will first compare the attributes entered with the attributes in list 1, the car list. Since there is still nothing on the car list, it will still have a score of 0. But, when compared to list 2, the tank list, we see there is one match, namely, the attribute BODY. This gives the tank list a score of 1 and therefore leads the program to guess tank. The user will respond to the system question:

```
IS THE SYSTEM A TANK ?  NO
```

We have another wrong guess, and again the feedback mechanism is called into play. The system attempts to see if any of these attributes—DOORS, WHEELS, BODY—are on the tank list. Since there is one—the BODY attribute—the program will place it on list 3, the common list (since it is not already there). It has again assumed that any attribute belonging to both objects should be on the common list. Now the input list, less any attributes moved to the common list, is placed on list 1, the car list. The lists now look like this:

| List 1 (car) | List 2 (tank) | List 3 (common) |
|---|---|---|
| DOOR | CANNON | BODY |
| WHEELS | HATCH | |

If we now provide another set of inputs, the program will be able to guess correctly. The system has "learned," via input attributes and feedback, the difference between a car and tank. Let's summarize how this was done:

1. The system only alters itself when it makes a wrong guess. This is its feedback mechanism.

2. The system compares the input attributes with attributes for the items it is trying to identify and chooses the most likely. This is done via a score and is called its inference mechanism.

## Programming Applications

Let's examine a program, written in BASIC, which applies the LEARNING concepts of this chapter.

### Program Explanation

In Listing 16-1 the three arrays, list 1 (L1), list 2 (L2), and the common list (LC), are initialized to "empty" in statements 30 through 50. The objects are named in statements 60 and 70. The user describes the attributes of an unnamed object in statements 90 through 130. The learning program attempts to identify the object belonging to those attributes in statements 180 through 220. It does this by developing a score. The score is developed by comparing the attributes that have been input with those assigned to each object. The object with the highest score is guessed as the object with the attributes supplied by the user. This is done in statement 240. In case of tie, object 1 is guessed. If the guess is correct the attributes that are not already in the list of the object or the common list are entered into the list of the object. But first we move attributes from the other list into the common list as shown in statements 330 through 410 for object 1 and 780 through 860 for object 2. The rest of the operation occurs in statements 420 through 560 for object 1 and 920 through 990 for object 2.

### Program Listing

Listing 16-1 is followed by sample runs.

**Listing 16-1  Learning program.**

```
1 REM**********LEARNING PROGRAM******
2 REM * PROGRAM TO GUESS OBJECT FROM
3 REM * THE ATTRIBUTES
10 REM ** INITIALIZATION SECTION FOR
11 REM    LIST OF OBJECT 1 (L1$)
12 REM    LIST OF OBJECT 2 (L2$)
13 REM    LIST OF COMMON    (LC$)
14 REM    TEMPORARY ATTRIBUTE BUFER T$
20 DIM L1$(10),L2$(10),LC$(10),T$(11)
30 FOR I=1 TO 10
40 L1$ (I)="":L2$(I)="":LC$(I)=""
50 NEXT I
60 INPUT"ENTER OBJECT 1 NAME ";O1$
70 INPUT"ENTER OBJECT 2 NAME ";O2$
80 PRINT"INPUT ANY OBJECT'S ATTRIBUTES-WHEN FINISHED TYPE RETURN"
90 FOR I=1 TO 11:T$(I)="":NEXT I
95 FOR I=1 TO 11
100 PRINT "ENTER ATTRIBUTE  ";I
110 INPUT T$(I)
120 IF T$(I)="" THEN GOTO 140
130 NEXT I
140 REM NUMBER OF ATTRIBUTES IS ONE LESS SINCE A NULL WAS INCLUDED
150 L=I-1
160 REM COMPARE THE ATTRIBUTES TO OBJECT LIST 1 AND 2
170 REM INITIALLY SET SCORE FOR OBJECT 1 AND OBJECT 2 TO O
180 S1=0:S2=0
190 FOR I=1 TO L
195 FOR K=1 TO 10
200 IF O1$(K)=T$(I) THEN S1=S1+1
210 IF O2$(K)=T$(I) THEN S2=S2+1
215 NEXT K
220 NEXT I
230 REM GUESS OBJECT 2 ONLY IF SCORE 2 IS GREATER THAN SCORE 1
240 IF S1 < S2 THEN GOTO 700
250 PRINT"OBJECT IS ";O1$
260 INPUT"IS THAT CORRECT...Y OR N";I$
270 IF I$="N" THEN GOTO 780
290 REM PLACE EACH ATTRIBUTE OF THE TEMPORARY ATTRIBUTE BUFFER THAT IS NOT IN
300 REM THE COMMON LIST AND NOT IN THE OBJECT LIST 1 ... INTO LIST 1
310 REM MOVE THE ATTRIBUTES FROM LIST 2 INTO THE COMMON LIST THAT ARE
320 REM EQUAL TO BOTH I.E. COMMON
330 FOR I=1 TO L
340 FOR K=1 TO 10
350 IF T$(I)<> O2$(K) THEN GOTO 400
360 REM MOVE THE ATTRIBUTE FROM LIST 2 TO THE COMMON LIST
370 FOR L=1 TO 10
380 IF LC$(L)<>"" THEN GOTO 390
382 LC$(L)=O2$(K):O2$(K)="":T$(I)=""
390 NEXT L
400 NEXT K
410 NEXT I
420 FOR I=1 TO L:REM TEMPORARY BUFFER POINTER
430 FOR K=1 TO 10: REM COMMON LIST POINTER AND OBJECT 1 LIST POINTER
440 IF T$(I)=LC$(K) THEN GOTO 520:REM IS IT IN THE COMMON LIST
450 IF T$(I)=O1$(K) THEN GOTO 520:REM IS IT IN OBJECT 1 LIST
460 NEXT K
470 REM PLACE VARIABLE INTO LIST 1 WHICH IS NOT IN THE ABOVE LISTS
480 REM SEARCH FOR THE FIRST EMPTY SPACE AND PLACE IT THERE
490 FOR K=1 TO 10
495 IF T$(I)="" THEN GOTO 510
500 IF O1$(K)="" THEN O1$(K)=T$(I):GOTO 520
510 NEXT K
520 NEXT I: REM NEXT ATTRIBUTE
530 REM PRINT ALL LISTS
540 GOSUB 2000
550 REM ANYMORE ATTRIBUTES
560 GOTO 80
700 PRINT"OBJECT IS ";O2$
710 INPUT" IS THAT CORRECT...Y OR N ";I$
720 IF I$="N" THEN GOTO 330
740 REM PLACE EACH ATTRIBUTE OF THE TEMPORARY ATTRIBUTE BUFFER THAT IS NOT IN
750 REM THE COMMON LIST AND NOT IN THE OBJECT LIST 2... INTO LIST 2
760 MOVE THE ATTRIBUTES FROM LIST 1 INTO THE COMMON LIST THAT ARE
770 REM EQUAL TO BOTH I.E. COMMON
780 FOR I=1 TO L
790 FOR K=1 TO 10
800 IF T$(I)<> O1$(K) THEN GOTO 850
810 REM MOVE THE ATTRIBUTE FROM LIST 1 TO THE COMMON LIST
```

Listing 16-1 (*Continued*)

```
820 FOR L=1 TO 10
830 IF LC$(L)<>""THEN GOTO 840
832 LC$(L)=O1$(K):O1$(K)="":T$(I)=""
840 NEXT L
850 NEXT K
860 NEXT I
870 FOR I=1 TO L:REM TEMPORARY BUFFER POINTER
880 FOR K=1 TO 10:REM COMMON LIST POINTER AND OBJECT 2 LIST
890 IF T$(I)=LC$(K) THEN GOTO 970:REM IS IT IN THE COMMON LIST
900 IF T$(I)=O2$(K) THEN GOTO 970:REM IS IT IN OBJECT 2 LIST
910 NEXT K
920 REM PLACE VARIABLE INTO LIST 2 WHICH IS NOT IN THE ABOVE LISTS
930 REM SEARCH FOR THE FIRST EMPTY SPACE AND PLACE IT THERE
940 FOR K=1 TO 10
945 IF T$(I)="" THEN GOTO 960
950 IF O2$(K)="" THEN O2$(K)=T$(I):GOTO 970
960 NEXT K
970 NEXT I:REM NET ATTRIBUTE
980 REM PRINT ALL THIS
990 GOSUB 2000
1000 REM ANYMORE ATTRIBUTES
1010 GOTO 80
2000 REM ROUTINE TO PRINT ALL LISTS
2010 PRINT O1$,O2$,"COMMON LIST"
2020 FOR I=1 TO 10
2030 PRINT O1$(I),O2$(I),LC$(I)
2040 NEXT I
2050 RETURN
```

## Sample Run

```
RUN
ENTER OBJECT 1 NAME ? CAR
ENTER OBJECT 2 NAME ? TANK
INPUT ANY OBJECT'S ATTRIBUTES—WHEN FINISHED TYPE RETURN
ENTER ATTRIBUTE 1 ? CANNON
ENTER ATTRIBUTE 2 ? HATCH
ENTER ATTRIBUTE 3 ? BODY
ENTER ATTRIBUTE 4 ?
OBJECT IS A CAR
IS THAT CORRECT...Y or N ? N
CAR     TANK       COMMON LIST
        CANNON
        HATCH
        BODY

INPUT ANY OBJECT'S ATTRIBUTES—WHEN FINISHED TYPE RETURN
ENTER ATTRIBUTE 1 ? BODY
ENTER ATTRIBUTE 2 ? WHEELS
ENTER ATTRIBUTE 3 ? DOOR
ENTER ATTRIBUTE 4 ?
OBJECT IS A TANK
IS THAT CORRECT...Y or N ? N
CAR        TANK       COMMON LIST
WHEELS     CANNON     BODY
DOOR       HATCH
INPUT ANY OBJECT'S ATTRIBUTES—WHEN FINISHED TYPE RETURN
ENTER ATTRIBUTE 1 ? BODY
ENTER ATTRIBUTE 2 ? DOOR
ENTER ATTRIBUTE 3 ?
OBJECT IS A CAR
IS THAT CORRECT...Y or N ? Y
CAR        TANK       COMMON LIST
WHEELS     CANNON     BODY
DOOR       HATCH
```

# Languages Used in Artificial Intelligence

*PROLOG and LISP are two languages that are used to implement expert systems. Both are introduced in a very simple way in this section.*

# 17

# Using PROLOG to Design Expert Systems

PROLOG is short for Programming in Logic. It is a computer language that was created especially for answering questions about a knowledge base that consists of rules and facts. PROLOG has backward chaining built right in and also utilizes another technique known as "backtracking." Backward chaining, as you know, is a technique in which a conclusion or consequence is assumed to be true, and then a knowledge base of rules and facts is examined to see if it supports the assumption. If the assumption turns out *not* to be correct, backtracking is used to get rid of the original assumption and replace it with a new one.

## Conceptual Example

In order to understand PROLOG's concepts, let's first consider a suitable program that we will try to solve with a pencil and paper technique. The solution to this problem will demonstrate the concepts of backward chaining in conjunction with backtracking.

Consider the following rule:

IF a male named X with mother named M is in the room AND a female named Y with mother named M is in the room,
THEN the male X and female Y are brother and sister.

This rule presents a set of conditions for determining if a brother and a sister are in the same room. Before we can solve this problem, we need a set of supporting facts. These facts take the form of two lists: one contains all the males in the room and their mothers, and the other list contains all the females in the same room and their mothers. By comparing the two lists for a common mother's name, we can identify those males and females that have the same mother. Having satisfied this condition, we can then invoke the rule to conclude that a brother and sister are in the same room. Let's see how this is implemented.

Consider the two facts tables that we have compiled.

| Male Facts List | | | Female Facts List | |
| --- | --- | --- | --- | --- |
| Male | Mother | | Female | Mother |
| Daniel | Diane | | Ann | Lori |
| Larry | Lori | | Lauren | Shirley |
| Michael | Bonnie | | Susan | Bonnie |
| Peter | Jane | | | |

By just scanning both lists, you can select the following possible brother and sister pairs:

Larry with Ann (mother Lori)

Michael with Susan (mother Bonnie)

By using a pencil and paper, we can imitate PROLOG in arriving at these answers.

First assume that the THEN part of the rule is true, then assume there actually is male X and female Y who are brother and sister. We have started backward chaining by assuming this conclusion is true. We must now try to support this conclusion by seeing if each of the rule's conditions is true. The first condition is "a male X with mother named M is in the room." This is our first goal, to find a male named X with mother M in the male facts list. This is easily satisfied with the first name on top of the list, which is

Daniel with mother Diane

The value X would be instantiated to DANIEL and the mother M would be instantiated to DIANE, as follows

X = Daniel

M = Diane

We must now satisfy the second condition, which is "a female named Y with a mother named M in the room." Since M is instantiated to DIANE, we must find a female Y with a mother named DIANE in the female facts list:

| Male Facts List | | Female Facts List | |
| --- | --- | --- | --- |
| Male | Mother | Female | Mother |
| Daniel | Diane | Ann | Lori |
| | | Lauren | Shirley |
| | | Susan | Bonnie |

There is none. We must backtrack to the first condition again and try to find another male X and mother M that would meet the condition. This means resuming the search of the male facts list. The male after Daniel is

Larry with mother Lori

The value X would now be instantiated to LARRY and mother M to LORI:

X = LARRY

M = LORI

We must now satisfy the second condition again by finding a female Y with mother Lori in the female facts list:

| Male Facts List | | Female Facts List | |
| --- | --- | --- | --- |
| Male | Mother | Female | Mother |
| Daniel | Diane | Ann | Lori |
| Larry | Lori | Lauren | Shirley |
| | | Susan | Bonnie |

Scanning the female facts list, we see that the first entry, Ann, has the same mother, Lori. Therefore

Y = ANN

We can invoke the THEN part and arrive at the conclusion that

X = LARRY AND

Y = ANN

are brother and sister.

## Review

Let's examine what we have done so we can solidify the concepts:

1. We took the THEN part of the rule as a conclusion and tried to see if each condition clause supported this conclusion.
2. Our first goal was to see if the first condition was true.
3. Scanning the facts list, we were able to reach our goal of making the first condition true. This dictated the values of the variables in the first condition.
4. Our next goal was to see if the second condition was true.
5. Scanning the facts list, we couldn't reach our goal.
6. We now backtracked to see if we could reach a goal of making the first condition true again with a *new* set of X and Y facts. We did.
7. With the new values of X and Y we tried to reach our goal of making the second condition true and succeeded.
8. We now had instantiated the variables in the THEN part.

## Converting Rules to PROLOG

What we have done is only to imitate PROLOG. In reality PROLOG does all that searching for you using backward chaining and backtracking automatically. We are now ready to take a set of knowledge base rules and convert it to a set of PROLOG rules.

There is a one to one corespondence between the format of a PROLOG rule and the rules in the knowledge base. Consider the following knowledge base rule from the example used in Chapter 6:

```
IF DEGREE = NO
THEN POSITION = NO
```

A PROLOG rule that says exactly the same thing is:

```
position(no):-write('DEGREE'), read(DEGREE), DEGREE=no.
```

The "write" and "read" parts of the rule are methods for obtaining a value for the variable DEGREE. The phrase write('DEGREE') will cause DEGREE to be printed on the user's terminal as a prompt to the user to enter whether the applicant has a degree. The phrase read (DEGREE) will cause the value entered by the user to be assigned to DEGREE. The next phrase, DEGREE = no, is true if the user entered no. Using this rule as an example, here are some of the properties and syntax of PROLOG:

1. The entire PROLOG rule, position(no):-write('DEGREE'), read(DE-GREE), DEGREE = no, is called a "clause." In PROLOG, there are two types of clauses: rule clauses and fact clauses. (We will discuss fact clauses later.) The clause above is a rule clause.

2. The part of the PROLOG clause, which is equivalent to the THEN part of position(no), is written to the left of the :- and is called the "head" of the rule.

3. The IF part, which is write('DEGREE'), read(DEGREE), DE-GREE = no, is written to the right of the :- and is called the "body" of the clause.

4. The body contains a number of items separated by commas. Each of these items is called a goal. (The commas mean AND.) The body of our PROLOG clause can therefore be read as
    write ('DEGREE') AND
    read (DEGREE) AND
    DEGREE = no,
where write('DEGREE'), read(DEGREE), and DEGREE = no are each goals.

5. The entire clause is ended with a period.

6. The word preceding a parenthesis is called a "predicate." The predicates in this example are position, write, and read. Predicate words always begin with lowercase letters.

7. Each word appearing within the parentheses of a predicate is called an "argument." The argument for position(no) is no and position is the predicate. Arguments can be variables as well as values. Variable words begin with capital letters; values begin with lowercase letters. The argument word no is a value since it begins with a lowercase n.

8. The symbol :- is read as IF. The PROLOG clause qualify(yes):-degree(yes) is read as "qualify is yes if degree is yes."

Let's see how the IF-THEN rules that we used in the chapter on backward chaining for the problem of whether to offer a job to an applicant are converted to PROLOG rules. The IF-THEN rules are

   10  IF DEGREE = NO
       THEN POSITION = NO

20   IF DEGREE = YES
     THEN QUALIFY = YES

30   IF DEGREE = YES AND DISCOVERY = YES
     THEN POSITION = RESEARCH

40   IF QUALIFY = YES AND AVERAGE < 3.5 AND
     EXPERIENCE > 2
     THEN POSITION = SERVICE ENGINEERING

50   IF QUALIFY = YES AND AVERAGE < 3.5 AND
     EXPERIENCE < 2
     THEN POSITION = NO

60   IF QUALIFY = YES AND AVERAGE >= 3.5
     THEN POSITION = PRODUCT ENGINEERING

The equivalent PROLOG rules are

```
/*10*/  position(no):-write('DEGREE'), read(DEGREE), DEGREE=no.
/*20*/  qualify(yes):-write('DEGREE'), read(DEGREE), DEGREE=yes.
/*30*/  position(research):-write('DEGREE'), read(DEGREE), DEGREE=yes,
        write('DISCOVERY'), read(DISCOVERY), DISCOVERY=yes.
/*40*/  position(service engineering):-qualify(yes), write('AVERAGE'),
        read(AVERAGE),AVERAGE<3.5, write('EXPERIENCE'),
        read(EXPERIENCE), EXPERIENCE>2.0.
/*50*/  position(no):-qualify(yes), write('AVERAGE'),
        read(AVERAGE),AVERAGE<3.5,write('EXPERIENCE'),
        read(EXPERIENCE), EXPERIENCE<2.0.
/*60*/  position(product engineering):-qualify(yes), write('AVERAGE'),
        read (AVERAGE),AVERAGE>=3.5.
```

The numbers to the left of the PROLOG statement are direct trans-
lations of the equivalent numbered IF-THEN rules. In PROLOG they
are enclosed between slashes and asterisks (/*10*/, /*20*/ . . . etc.) but
have no operational effect; PROLOG ignores them. These are known as
"comment statements" and appear as an aid to your understanding. In
this case, they are used to indicate which IF-THEN rules correspond to
the PROLOG statements.
   Consider the "brother and sister in the same room" rule:

   IF a male named X with mother M is in the room AND a female named
   Y with mother M is in the room,
   THEN the male and female are brother and sister.

Next we construct a knowledge base using this rule and the set of
facts of males, females, and mothers, as follows. These facts are taken
from the male and female fact lists.

```
/*1*/  brother-sister(X, Y, M):-male(X, M), female(Y, M).
/*2*/  male(daniel, diane)
/*3*/  male(larry, lori)
```

```
/*4*/  male(michael, bonnie)
/*5*/  male(peter, jane)
/*6*/  female(ann, lori)
/*7*/  female(lauren, shirley)
/*8*/  female(susan, bonnie)
```

The "brother-sister" predicate arguments stand for X = brother, Y = sister, and M = mother. The male predicate translates into "X is a male with mother M," and the female predicate, into "Y is a female with the same mother M."

Now we will show you an actual PROLOG-user dialogue to illustrate how PROLOG answers questions. When PROLOG issues a prompt, which is ?-, it allows the user to enter a question. In response to the prompt, you might enter the following question based upon our example:

```
?-brother-sister(X, Y, M)
```

PROLOG would first try to instantiate X and M in the first term of the first rule it came to which contains the goal male (X,M). The first fact in the knowledge base with male as a predicate is fact /*2*/, male(daniel,diane). PROLOG would assume, that is, instantiate, X = daniel and M = diane. It would then try to prove that the second term, female(Y,M), is true. Since M is already instantiated to diane, it would search the facts list for a fact containing the same mother, namely, female(Y, diane). Since facts /*6*/ to /*8*/ contain female as a predicate but do not contain diane in the second argument, female (Y, diane) is *not* true. Therefore, PROLOG backtracks. The system "uninstantiates" X and M and uses (X, M) to find new values for X and M. Fact /*3*/, male(larry, lori), causes PROLOG to instantiate X to larry and M to lori. PROLOG now tries to prove female(Y, lori) true. Scanning the facts, it finds /*6*/, female(ann, lori), which meets the requirements. Therefore, Y is instantiated to ann and PROLOG will print

```
?-X=larry
   Y=ann
   M=lori
```

PROLOG verifies that Larry and Ann are brother and sister because they both have Lori as their mother.

## Summary

This chapter has introduced the reader to PROLOG and its two main features, backward chaining and backtracking.

# Chapter

# 18

# LISP

## Introduction to LISP

LISP is short for List Processing. It is a computer language that is used in many applications of artificial intelligence. One of its major qualities is that it can manipulate lists easily. A list could be the words in a sentence, the names of people on a job, or any sequence of words arranged in any order. The parts of a list can be removed from context one at a time so that various operations can be performed on them.

In this chapter we will acquaint you with some of the fundamentals of LISP—just enough to whet your appetite to do advanced reading.

## Function Evaluation

LISP evaluates functions. A function is written in prefix format, meaning that the function comes first, and is enclosed with a left parenthesis, (, and a right parenthesis, ). For example, + is a function that adds numbers, which are its arguments. If the user constructs the following LISP statement

```
( + 4 2)
```

the system will respond with 6. Prefix format requires us to write the + first, followed by the arguments. Another function, −, subtracts numbers, as in the example

```
( − 5 2)
```

with the result 3. The value 3 is automatically returned by the system. In this example, the user enters

```
(+  (−  5  2)  4)
```

and LISP returns

```
7
```

The LISP system first evaluates the function within the inner parentheses

```
(−  5  2)
```

and returns 3. The system replaces the inner parentheses function with 3 and next evaluates

```
(+  3  4)
```

and returns 7.

The multiplication and maximum functions are as follows. The user enters

```
(*  5  4)
```

and LISP returns

```
20
```

The user enters

```
(MAX  5  9  2)
```

and LISP returns

```
9
```

The important points to remember are

1. Functions are written in prefix notation.
2. Functions are enclosed in parentheses.

## Lists

A list is a set of items. We call the items in the list, "members" of the list. For example, we could construct a list of all people owing us money. This list would consist of names of people such as

```
'(BOB TOM MAY SUE)
```

You should note that a list is enclosed in parentheses, just as a function is. Another example of a list are the items on a desk:

```
'(PENCIL PEN PAPER CLOCK PAPER-CLIP)
```

You will note that there can be *no* embedded blanks in a member's name. Therefore, the name PAPER-CLIP has a connecting hyphen. A space is used only to separate the names of the members of the list.

We could also have lists of numbers. These could be the number of people in each department of a company, such as

```
'(20 10 30)
```

We could also have a list of lists. For example, you may want a list of all people you know in three different towns:

```
'((BOB LORI JANE) (TOM HARRY) (JOHN DAVID))
```

Notice the two left parentheses at the start. The first one designates a list of something. Since that something is also a list, this inner list must also start with a parenthesis. In other words, the members of this list are lists.

We hope you noticed the single quotation mark at the start of each list. Let's examine why this single quotation mark must precede each list. Suppose we had the following list:

```
'(GOTO YOUR HOME)
```

If there was no quotation mark in front of the parenthesis, it would have all the characteristics of a function, whose concepts we just discussed. Remember, functions are written in prefix form in which the first symbol at the left parenthesis is the function name. Without the quotation mark, LISP would then interpret GOTO as a function. What the quotation mark does is tell LISP to accept whatever follows as is and not evaluate it in any way. GOTO would then be correctly interpreted as the first member of a list.

## List Functions

List functions perform "operations" on lists. Some important functions are CAR, CDR, CONS, and APPEND.

CAR removes the first member of a list. The user enters

```
(CAR '(A B C))
```

and LISP returns the first member

```
A
```

In the next example, (1 2) is the first member and also happens to be a list. The user enters

```
(CAR '((1 2) A B))
```

and LISP returns

```
(1 2)
```

CDR returns the remainder of a list *after* the first member is removed. The user enters

```
(CDR '(A B C))
```

and LISP returns

```
(B C)
```

This is a list comprising every member of the original after the first member is removed. The user enters

```
(CDR '((A B) (C D)))
```

and LISP returns

```
((C D))
```

where the first member (A B) is removed, leaving the list (C D) as the only member.

CONS adds a member to the beginning of a list. The user enters

```
(CONS 'K '(J K L))
```

and LISP returns

(K J K L)

The user enters

(CONS '(A B) '(J K L))

and LISP returns

((A B) J K L)

APPEND joins two lists together, that is, makes them one list. The user enters

(APPEND '(A B) '(J K L))

and LISP returns

(A B J K L)

LISP provides many more functions that we won't discuss here; our objective is to lay the groundwork for your understanding of how LISP operates.

## Predicates or Testing Functions

Remember that a conditional clause contained in the IF part of an IF-THEN rule can be either true or false. If it is true, the THEN part is invoked. If FALSE, it is not. LISP has a set of functions that perform tests and then tell us if the results of the tests are true or false. In LISP, true is designated by T and false by NIL. Functions that perform a test and return T or NIL are called "predicates."

Let's examine some predicate functions. The EQUAL predicate returns a T if its arguments are the same. For example, the user enters

(EQUAL 8 8)

and LISP returns

T

The user enters

(EQUAL 3 2)

and LISP returns

```
NIL
```

The user enters

```
(EQUAL '(1 2 A) '(1 2 A))
```

and LISP returns

```
T
```

The > symbol checks arguments to see if each succeeding argument is greater than the next one. For example, the user enters

```
(> 5 2 1)
```

and LISP returns

```
T
```

The user enters

```
(> 1 3 2)
```

and LISP returns

```
NIL
```

Now here's one

```
(> 5 4 (+ 1 2))
```

which LISP first evaluates to

```
(> 5 4 3)
```

and then returns

```
T
```

## Variable Assignments

The next concept we should understand is how LISP instantiates variables. The value of a variable can be assigned by the following LISP function:

```
(SETQ X Y)
```

where X is instantiated to the value of Y. For example, the user enters

```
(SETQ X 25)
```

and LISP returns

```
25
```

The variable X will be instantiated to the value 25. Here is another example:

```
(SETQ X '(A B C))
```

will instantiate X to the list (A B C).

## IF-THEN Rules through the Condition Function

The condition (COND) function allows us to test a set of conditions and then do something if a condition is T. This sounds like an IF-THEN statement because it is very close to one. As an example, consider the following:

```
(COND ((EQUAL 5 2) (SETQ X 5)))
```

The condition, or IF part, of the COND statement is (EQUAL 5 2). The THEN part is (SETQ X 5). Since (EQUAL 5 2) is a NIL because 5 does not equal 2, we cannot invoke the THEN part, which is (SETQ X 5). But consider

```
(COND ((EQUAL 3 3) (SETQ X 5)))
```

We see that (EQUAL 3 3) returns a T and therefore will cause (SETQ X 5) to be invoked, resulting in X being instantiated to 5. Let's examine two more COND statements:

```
(COND((EQUAL Y 3) (SETQ X 5)))
(COND((GREATERP 4 Z) (SETQ P 3)))
```

The first statement is translated as follows: IF Y has a value 3, THEN instantiate X to 5. The second statement says IF 4 is greater than Z, THEN instantiate P to 3.

For our examples, the COND statement consists of an IF part and a THEN part, that is

```
(COND((< IF part >)(< THEN part >)))
```

In general, the COND function can be expanded to include many IF-THEN parts.

## New Functions

New functions are defined in LISP with the DEFUN function. An example of how this works is

```
(DEFUN ADD-DIF (X Y Z)
  (+ Z (- X Y)))
```

The first symbol after the DEFUN is the name of the function. In our example, the name of the function is ADD-DIF. The items in parentheses after the function name are the variables that will be used in the function evaluation part. In this case the variables are X, Y, and Z. The evaluation part is

```
(+ Z (- X Y))
```

This should look somewhat familiar because we discussed this type of example earlier in the chapter. What we do to evaluate the function is subtract Y from X and then add the result to Z. Let's see how this works. If we typed the procedure ADD-DIF with

```
(ADD-DIF 5 4 6)
```

we would get 7. The function first instantiates X to 5, Y to 4, and Z to 6 and then subtracts 4 from 5, leaving 1. We would then add 1 to 6 giving us 7.

Before we continue, let us give an example of the PRINT function. If we entered

```
(PRINT'EXAMPLE)
```

we would get the following lines from LISP

```
EXAMPLE
EXAMPLE
```

It is not necessary here to understand why EXAMPLE prints twice. The following new function

```
(DEFUN IF-THEN (X)
  (COND((EQUAL X 3)(PRINT'EXAMPLE))))
```

will cause the PRINT to take place if X equals 3. That is, the user enters

```
(IF-THEN 3)
```

and LISP returns

```
EXAMPLE
EXAMPLE
```

But if the user enters

```
(IF-THEN 4)
```

LISP returns

```
NIL
```

The reason for this is that the condition part of the COND statement is (EQUAL X 3). If this is T, the THEN part, (PRINT'EXAMPLE) is invoked. In the first example, (IF-THEN 3) results in the first part of the COND to be (EQUAL 3 3) returning a T. Therefore COND invokes the PRINT function. But the next example (IF-THEN 4) results in the first part of the COND to be (EQUAL 4 3) which returns a NIL.

## Summary

Let us now summarize the important concepts.

1. We have shown you the concepts of functions and the role of parentheses in defining them.
2. We have discussed the concepts of a list.

We recommend that you try these concepts on one of the many LISP programs for your computer.

# Bibliography and Recommended Readings

The following is a list and description of books and articles related to the subject matter of this book. The description discusses each book and article with regard to individual subject matter.

## Books

Barr, A., and E. A. Feigenbaum: *The Handbook of Artificial Intelligence Volumes I and II*. HeurisTech Press and William Kaufmann, Inc., Los Altos, CA, 1981.

Cohn, P. R. and E. A. Feigenbaum: *The Handbook of Artificial Intelligence Volume III*, HeurisTech Press and William Kaufmann, Inc., Los Altos, CA, 1982.

All topics discussed in our book are also discussed in a more mathematically rigorous way in one of the volumes of *The Handbook*.

Clocksin, W. F. and C. S. Mellish: *Programming in PROLOG*, Springer-Verlag New York, Inc., 1984.

PROLOG is discussed throughout the book. Many well-illustrated examples are used to explain the concepts. Backward chaining and backtracking are discussed in Chapter 1, "Tutorial Introduction," and Chapter 4, "Backtracking and Cuts." Natural language processing and other areas related to artificial intelligence have working examples in the later chapters.

Graham, Neil: Artificial Intelligence—Making Machines "Think," TAB Books Inc., Blue Ridge Summit, PA, 1979.

Semantic nets are discussed on pages 203–205. Examples are included. Object-oriented programming is discussed under the topics "Property Lists" (pages 201–203), and "Frames" (pages 205–207). Examples are included. Natural language processing is discussed on pages 209–219.

Hayes-Roth, F., D. A. Waterman, and D. B. Lenat: *Building Expert Systems*, Addison-Wesley Publishing Co. Inc., Reading, MA, 1983.

Blackboard concept is discussed in the way it's used in two expert systems, Age and Hearsay. Fuzzy applications and certainty factors are discussed under the topic "Unreliable Data or Knowledge" (pages 93–96).

Lipschutz, S.: *Finite Mathematics*, McGraw-Hill Book Company, New York, 1966.

Use of probability and fuzzy conditions in expert systems is discussed in terms of conditional probability and Bayes theorems in Chapter 18. In addition, it covers interesting concepts such as Markov chains (Chapter 20) and game theory (Chapter 25) which can be applied to expert systems engaged in winning strategies.

Naylor, Chris: *Build Your Own Expert System,* Halsted Press, a Division of John Wiley and Sons Inc., New York, 1983.
Use of probability and fuzzy conditions in expert systems is discussed in terms of probability theory in the design of expert systems. Many programming examples are included. Automated learning concepts are initially provided via a simple learning program (page 37) which is enhanced as you continue reading.

Negoita, C. N.: *Expert Systems and Fuzzy Systems,* The Benjamin/Cummings Publishing Co., Menlo Park, CA, 1985.
Certainty factors are discussed under the topic "Degrees of Belief" (pages 27–30). Use of probability and fuzzy conditions in expert systems is discussed in terms of fuzzy conditions. Linguistic variables and hedges are discussed throughout the book. Under the topic "Production Rules Can Be Derived from Verbal Models" (pages 74–77) two tables are presented which show the affects of hedges. The book contains an extensive bibliography on the subject matter.

Winston, P. H. and B. K. P. Horn: *LISP,* Addison-Wesley Publishing Co. Inc., Reading, MA, 1981.
LISP is discussed throughout the book. There is a section of the book which produces answers to all the problems. Object-oriented programming is also discussed. Chapter 5, "Properties, A-Lists, Arrays, and Access Functions," provides some basics. Chapter 22, "Frames," discusses objects, slots, inheritance, demons, and active values. Backward and forward chaining is discussed in Chapter 8, "Expert Problem Solving Using IF-THEN Rules."

## Articles

The articles are listed by subject matter.

### Fuzzy Logic

Zadeh, L. A.: "Making Computers Think Like People" *IEEE SPECTRUM,* vol. 21, no. 8, August 1984, pp. 26–32.

### General Overview of Artifical Intelligence

Hayes-Roth, F.: "The Knowledge-Based Expert Systems: A Tutorial," *IEEE COMPUTER,* vol. 17, no. 9, September 1984, pp. 11–28.

### Knowledge Representation
### (Semantic Nets, PROLOG, etc.)

*IEEE COMPUTER* vol. 16, no. 10 October, 1983.

### Object-Oriented Programming

Cox, B. J.: "Message/Object Programming: An Evolutionary Change in Programming Technology," *IEEE SOFTWARE,* vol. 1, no. 1, Jauary, 1984, pp. 51–61.
Mudge, T. N.: "Object Based Computing and the Ada Language," *IEEE COMPUTER,* vol. 18, no. 3, March 1985, pp 11–19.

# References for Chapters on Expert Systems

## Financial Planning

Casey, Douglas: *Crisis Investing,* Pocket Books, Simon & Schuster Publishing Co., New York, 1979.

Huang, Stanley: *Investment Analysis and Management,* Little, Brown & Co., Boston, 1981.

Weinstein, Grace W.: *The Lifetime Book of Money Management,* The New American Library, Inc., New York, 1983.

## Sales

Buzzotte, V. R., R. E. Lefton, and M. Sherberg: *Effective Selling through Psychology,* Psychological Associates, 1981.

Haas, Kenneth and J. W. Ernest: *Creative Salesmanship, Understanding Essentials,* Glencoe Publishing Co., Inc. Encino, CA, 1974.

## Learning Evaluation System

Brutten, Milton, Sylvia Richardson, and Charles Mangel: *Something's Wrong with My Child,* Harcourt Brace Jovanovich, New York, 1973.

DeHirsch, Katrina: "Learning Disabilities: An Overview," *Bulletin,* N.Y. Academy of Medicine, vol. 50 no. 4, April 1974.

Green, L. J.: *Kids Who Hate School; A Survival Handbook on Learning Disabilities,* Humanics Press, Atlanta, GA, 1984.

Machalaba, Danielle, "Hidden Handicap; For Americans Unable to Read Well, Life Is a Series of Small Crises," *Wall Street Journal,* Tuesday, January 17, 1984.

Sanders, Marion: *Clinical Assessment of Learning Problems,* Allyn & Bacon, Inc., Newton, MA, 1978.

# Index